Marx Machiavelli Chesterton Cooper Emerson Joyce
Abbott Hardy Montaigne Austen
Defoe Melville Haggard Hugo
Carroll Christie Eliot Grimm
Stoker Molière
Wilde Maupassant Byron
Engels Schiller
Garnett Einstein Fitzgerald Smith
Goethe Hawthorne Kafka
Cotton Dostoyevsky Hall
Baum Kipling Doyle Willis
Leslie Dumas Henry Nietzsche
Flaubert Turgenev Balzac
Stockton Vatsyayana Crane
Burroughs Whitman Verne
Curtis Tocqueville Gogol Vinci
Homer Widger Tolstoy Busch
Darwin Thoreau
Potter Freud Zola Twain Plato Scott
Lawrence
Kant Jowett Stevenson Dickens
Andersen Burton Hesse Harte
London Descartes Cervantes
Poe Aristotle Wells Voltaire
Hale James Hastings
Bunner Shakespeare Cooke
Richter Chambers Irving
Doré Swift Dante Chekhov da Shaw Wodehouse Benedict Alcott
Pushkin
Newton

tredition®

tredition was established in 2006 by Sandra Latusseck and Soenke Schulz. Based in Hamburg, Germany, tredition offers publishing solutions to authors and publishing houses, combined with worldwide distribution of printed and digital book content. tredition is uniquely positioned to enable authors and publishing houses to create books on their own terms and without conventional manufacturing risks.

For more information please visit: www.tredition.com

TREDITION CLASSICS

This book is part of the TREDITION CLASSICS series. The creators of this series are united by passion for literature and driven by the intention of making all public domain books available in printed format again - worldwide. Most TREDITION CLASSICS titles have been out of print and off the bookstore shelves for decades. At tredition we believe that a great book never goes out of style and that its value is eternal. Several mostly non-profit literature projects provide content to tredition. To support their good work, tredition donates a portion of the proceeds from each sold copy. As a reader of a TREDITION CLASSICS book, you support our mission to save many of the amazing works of world literature from oblivion. See all available books at www.tredition.com.

Project Gutenberg

The content for this book has been graciously provided by Project Gutenberg. Project Gutenberg is a non-profit organization founded by Michael Hart in 1971 at the University of Illinois. The mission of Project Gutenberg is simple: To encourage the creation and distribution of eBooks. Project Gutenberg is the first and largest collection of public domain eBooks.

A Narrative of Some of the Lord's Dealings with George Müller Written by Himself, First Part

George Müller

Imprint

This book is part of TREDITION CLASSICS

Author: George Müller
Cover design: Buchgut, Berlin – Germany

Publisher: tredition GmbH, Hamburg - Germany
ISBN: 978-3-8472-3000-7

www.tredition.com
www.tredition.de

The intention of the TREDITION CLASSICS series is to make world literature in the public domain available in printed format. Literary enthusiasts and organizations, such as Project Gutenberg, worldwide have scanned and digitally edited the original texts. tredition has subsequently formatted and redesigned the content into a modern reading layout. Therefore, we cannot guarantee the exact reproduction of the original format of a particular historic edition. Please also note that no modifications have been made to the spelling, therefore it may differ from the orthography used today.

PREFACE

TO THE

FIRST EDITION OF THE FIRST PART.

It was only after the consideration of many months, and after much self-examination as to my motives, and after much earnest prayer, that I came to the conclusion to write this little work. I have not taken one single step in the Lord's service, concerning which I have prayed so much. My great dislike to increasing the number of religious books would, in itself, have been sufficient to have kept me for ever from it, had I not cherished the hope of being instrumental in this way to lead some of my brethren to value the Holy Scriptures more, and to judge by the standard of the word of God the principles on which they act. But that which weighed more with me than any thing was, that I have reason to believe from what I have seen among the children of God, that many of their trials arise, either from want of confidence in the Lord as it regards temporal things, or from carrying on their business in an unscriptural way. On account, therefore, of the remarkable way in which the Lord has dealt with me in temporal things, within the last ten years, I feel that I am a debtor to the Church of Christ, and that I ought, for the benefit of my poorer brethren especially, to make known, as much as I can, the way in which I have been led. In addition to this, I know it to be a fact, that to many souls the Lord has blessed what I have told them about the way in which He has led me, and therefore it seemed to me a duty to use such means, whereby others also, with whom I could not possibly converse, might be benefited. That which at last, on May 6, 1836, induced me finally to determine to write this Narrative was, that, if the Lord should permit the book to sell, I might, by the profits arising from the sale, be enabled in a greater degree to help the poor brethren and sisters among whom I labour, a matter which just at that time weighed much on my mind. I therefore at last began to write. But after three days I was obliged to lay the work again aside, on account of my other pressing engagements. On May 15th I was laid aside on account of an abscess and now being unable, for many weeks, to walk about as usual, though able to work at home, I had time for writing. When the manuscript was nearly completed, I gave it to a brother to look it over, that I might have his judgment; and the Lord so refreshed his spirit through it, that he offered to advance the means for having it printed, with the understanding that if the book should not sell, he would never consider me his debtor. By this offer not a small obstacle was removed, as I have no means of my own to defray the expense of printing. These two last circumstances, connected with many other points, confirmed me that I had not been mistaken, when I came to the conclusion that it was the will of God, that I should serve His church in this way.

The fact of my being a foreigner, and therefore but very imperfectly acquainted with the English language, I judged to be no sufficient reason for keeping me from writing. The Christian reader being acquainted with this fact, will candidly excuse any inaccuracy of expression.

For the poor among the brethren this Narrative is especially intended, and to their prayers I commend it in particular.

GEORGE MÜLLER.

Bristol, July 5, 1837.

EXTRACT FROM THE PREFACE TO THE SECOND EDITION OF THE FIRST PART

As to this second edition I would mention, that, while in substance it is the same as the first, yet, on account of my increased acquaintance with the English language, many verbal alterations have been made; also several alterations have been made on account of the increased light which the Lord has been pleased to grant me since July, 1937; a few paragraphs have been entirely left out, and a few new paragraphs have been added.

GEORGE MÜLLER.

Bristol, October 28, 1840.

EXTRACT FROM THE PREFACE TO THE THIRD EDITION OF THE FIRST PART

As the second edition of four thousand copies is exhausted, and as the Lord condescends to bless this Narrative more and more, both to believers and unbelievers, it has appeared to me a debt which I owe to the church of God to publish this third edition. Several new paragraphs of considerable length have been introduced.

GEORGE MÜLLER.

Bristol, June 17, 1845.

PREFACE TO THE EIGHTH EDITION OF THE FIRST PART

The Seventh edition of eight thousand copies is also exhausted, and the Lord condescends to bless yet more and more this Narrative, both to the the conversion of unbelievers, and to the edification of His own children. On this account I feel it my duty, as well as my privilege, to send forth this new edition, in which scarcely any alterations have been made.

GEORGE MÜLLER.

Bristol, December, 1881.

PREFACE TO THE NINTH EDITION

The reason which led me to the publication of the Eighth edition of this Narrative, has influenced me also to publish this Ninth edition.

GEORGE MÜLLER.

Bristol, March, 1895.

A

NARRATIVE,

&c. &c.

I was born at Kroppenstaedt, near Halberstadt, in the kingdom of Prussia, on September 27th, 1805. In January 1810 my parents removed to Heimersleben, about four miles from Kroppenstaedt, where my father was appointed collector in the excise. As a warning to parents I mention, that my father preferred me to my brother, which was very injurious to both of us. To me, as tending to produce in my mind a feeling of self-elevation; and to my brother, by creating in him a dislike both towards my father and me.

My father, who educated his children on worldly principles, gave us much money, considering our age; not in order that we might spend it, but, as he said, to accustom us to possess money without spending it. The result was, that it led me and my brother into many sins. For I repeatedly spent a part of the money in a childish way, and afterwards, when my father looked over my little treasure, I sought to deceive him in making up the accounts, either by not putting down all the money which he had given me, or by professing to have more money in hand than was the case, and counting it out accordingly before him. Now, though this deceit was found out at last, and I was punished, yet I remained the same. For before I was ten years old I repeatedly took of the government money which was intrusted to my father, and which he had to make up; till one day, as he had repeatedly missed money, he detected my theft, by depositing a counted sum in the room where I was, and leaving me to myself for a while. Being thus left alone, I took some of the money, and hid it under my foot in my shoe. When my father, after his return, had counted and missed the money, I was searched and my theft detected.

Though I was punished on this and other occasions, yet I do not remember that at any time, when my sins were found out, it made any other impression upon me than to make me think how I might do the thing the next time more cleverly, so as not to be detected.

Hence it came, that this was not the last time that I was guilty of stealing.

When I was between ten and eleven years of age, I was sent to Halberstadt, to the cathedral classical school, there to be prepared for the university; for my father's desire was, that I should become a clergyman: not, indeed, that thus I might serve God, but that I might have a comfortable living. My time was now spent in studying, reading novels, and indulging, though so young, in sinful practices. Thus it continued till I was fourteen years old, when my mother was suddenly removed. The night she was dying, I, not knowing of her illness, was playing at cards till two in the morning, and on the next day, being the Lord's day, I went with some of my companions in sin to a tavern, and then we went about the streets, half intoxicated.

The following day I attended, for the first time, the religious instruction, which I was to receive previous to my confirmation. This likewise was attended to in a careless manner; and when I returned to my lodgings, my father had arrived to fetch my brother and me home to our mother's funeral. This bereavement made no lasting impression on my mind. I grew worse and worse. Three or four days before I was confirmed, (and thus admitted to partake of the Lord's supper,) I was guilty of gross immorality; and the very day before my confirmation, when I was in the vestry with the clergyman to confess my sins, (according to the usual practice,) after a formal manner, I defrauded him; for I handed over to him only the twelfth part of the fee which my father had given me for him.

In this state of heart, without prayer, without true repentance, without faith, without knowledge of the plan of salvation, I was confirmed, and took the Lord's supper, on the Sunday after Easter 1820. Yet I was not without some feeling about the solemnity of the thing, and I stayed at home in the afternoon and evening, whilst the other boys and girls, who had been confirmed with me, walked about in the fields I also made resolutions to turn from those vices in which I was living, and to study more. But as I had no regard to God, and attempted the thing in my own strength, all soon came to nothing, and I still grew worse.

Six weeks after my confirmation I went for a fortnight to Brunswick, to a sister of my father, where I became attached to a young female, who was a Roman catholic. My time till Midsummer 1821 was spent partly in study, but in a great degree in playing the piano-forte and guitar, reading novels, frequenting taverns, forming resolutions to become different, yet breaking them almost as fast as they were made. My money was often spent on my sinful pleasures, through which I was now and then brought into trouble, so that once, to satisfy my hunger, I stole a piece of coarse bread, the allowance of a soldier who was quartered in the house where I lodged. What a bitter, bitter thing is the service of Satan, even in this world!!

At Midsummer 1821 my father obtained an appointment at Schoenebeck, near Magdeburg, and I embraced the opportunity of entreating him to remove me to the cathedral classical school of Magdeburg; for I thought, that, if I could but leave my companions in sin, and get out, of certain snares, and be placed under other tutors, I should then live a different life. But as my dependence in this matter also was not upon God, I fell into a still worse state. My father consented, and I was allowed to leave Halberstadt, and to stay at Heimersleben till Michaelmas. During that time I superintended, according to my father's wish, certain alterations, which were to be made in his house there, for the sake of letting it profitably. Being thus quite my own master, I grew still more idle, and lived as much as before in all sorts of sin.

When Michaelmas came, I persuaded my father to leave me at Heimersleben till Easter, and to let me read the classics with a clergyman living in the same place. As Dr. Nagel was a very learned man, and also in the habit of having pupils under his care, and a friend of my father, my request was granted. I was now living on the premises belonging to my father, under little real control, and intrusted with a considerable sum of money, which I had to collect for my father, from persons who owed it to him. My habits soon led me to spend a considerable part of this money, giving receipts for different sums, yet leaving my father to suppose I had not received them.

In November I went on a pleasure excursion to Magdeburg, where I spent six days in much sin; and though my absence from home had been found out by my father, before I returned from thence; yet I took all the money I could obtain, and went to Brunswick, after I had, through a number of lies, obtained permission from my tutor. The reason of my going to Brunswick was, the attachment I had formed eighteen months previously to the young female residing there. I spent a week at Brunswick, in an expensive hotel. At the end of the week my money was expended. This, as well as the want of a passport, prevented my staying any longer in the hotel; but as I still wished to remain at Brunswick, I went to my uncle, the husband of my father's sister, and made some excuse for not having gone to him in the first instance. My uncle, seeing I suppose my unsteady life, intimated after a week, that he did not wish me to remain with him any longer.

I then went, without money, to another hotel, in a village near Brunswick, where I spent another week in an expensive way of living. At last, the owner of the hotel suspecting that I had no money, asked for payment, and I was obliged to leave my best clothes as a security, and could scarcely thus escape from being arrested. I then walked about six miles, to Wolfenbuttel, went to an inn, and began again to live as if I had plenty of money. Here I stayed two days, looking out for an opportunity to run away; for I had now nothing remaining to leave as a pledge. But the window of my room was too high to allow of my escaping, by getting down at night. On the second or third morning I went quietly out of the yard, and then ran off; but being suspected and observed, and therefore seen to go off, I was immediately called after, and so had to return.

I now confessed my case, but found no mercy. I was arrested, and taken between two soldiers to a police officer. Being suspected by him to be a vagabond or thief, I was examined for about three hours, and then sent to gaol. I now found myself at the age of sixteen, an inmate of the same dwelling with thieves and murderers, and treated accordingly. My superior manners profited nothing. For though, as a particular favour, I received the first evening some meat with my bread, I had the next day the common allowance of the prisoners,—very coarse bread and water, and for dinner vegetables, but no meat. My situation was most wretched. I was locked up in this place day and night, without permission to leave my cell. The dinner was such that on the first day I completely loathed it; and left it untouched. The second day I took a little, the third day all, and the fourth and following days I would fain have had more. On the second day I asked the keeper for a Bible, not to consider its blessed contents, but to pass away the time. However, I received none. Here then I was; no creature with me; no book, no work in my hands, and large iron rails before my narrow window.

During the second night I was awakened out of my sleep by the rattling of the bolts and keys. Three men came into my room. When I asked them in my fright what it meant, they laughed at me, continuing quietly to try the iron rails, to see whether I could escape.—After a few days I found out, that a thief was imprisoned next to me, and, as far as a thick wooden partition would allow of it, I conversed with him; and shortly after the governor of the prison allowed him, as a favour to me, to share my cell. We now passed away our time in relating our adventures, and I was by this time so wicked, that I was not satisfied with relating things of which I had been really guilty, but I even invented stories, to show him what a famous fellow I was.

I waited in vain day after day to be liberated.—After about ten or twelve days my fellow prisoner and I disagreed, and thus we two wretched beings, to increase our wretchedness, spent day after day without conversing together.—I was in prison from December 18th, 1821, till January 12th, 1822, when the keeper came and told me to go with him to the police office. Here I found, that the Commissioner, before whom I had been tried, had first written to my uncle at Brunswick, and when he had written in reply, that it was better to acquaint my father with my conduct, the Commissioner had done so; and thus I was kept in prison till my father sent the money which was needed for my traveling expenses, to pay my debt in the inn, and for my maintenance in the prison. So ungrateful was I now, for certain little kindnesses shown to me by my fellow-prisoner, that, although I had promised to call on his sister, to deliver a message from him, I omitted to do so; and so little had I been benefited by this my chastisement, that, though I was going home to meet an angry father, only two hours after I had left the town where I had been imprisoned, I chose an avowedly wicked person as my traveling companion for a great part of my journey.

My father, who arrived two days after I had reached Heimersleben, after having severely beaten me, took me home to Schoenebeck, intending to keep me there till Easter, and then to send me to a classical school at Halle, that I might be under strict discipline and the continual inspection of a tutor. In the meantime I took pupils, whom I instructed in Latin, French, arithmetic, and German Grammar. I now endeavoured, by diligence in study, to regain the favour of my father. My habits were, as to outward appearance, exemplary. I made progress in my own studies, benefited my pupils, and was soon liked by every body around me, and in a short time my father had forgotten all. But all this time I was in heart as bad as ever; for I was still in secret habitually guilty of great sins.

Easter came, and on account of my good behaviour, my diligence in study, and also because I was no expense to my father, but earned much more than I cost him, I easily persuaded him to let me stay at home till Michaelmas. But after that period he would not consent to my remaining any longer with him, and therefore I left home, pretending to go to Halle to be examined. But having a hearty dislike to the strict discipline of which I had heard, and knowing also that I should meet there young men attending the university with whom I was acquainted, enjoying all the liberty of German students, whilst I myself was still at school: for these and other reasons I went to Nordhausen, and had myself examined by the director of the gymnasium, to be received into that school. I then went home, but never told my father a word of all this deception, till the day before my departure, which obliged me to invent a whole chain of lies. He was then very angry; but at last, through my entreaties and persuasion, he gave way and allowed me to go. This was in the beginning of October, 1822.

I continued at Nordhausen two years and six months, till Easter, 1825. During this time I studied with considerable diligence the Latin classics, French, history, my own language, &c.; but did little in Hebrew, Greek, and the Mathematics. I lived in the house of the director, and got, through my conduct, highly into his favour, so much so, that I was held up by him in the first class as an example to the rest, and he used to take me regularly with him in his walks, to converse with me in Latin. I used now to rise regularly at four, winter and summer, and generally studied all the day, with little exception, till ten at night.

But whilst I was thus outwardly gaining the esteem of my fellow-creatures, I did not care in the least about God, but lived secretly in much sin, in consequence of which I was taken ill, and for thirteen weeks confined to my room. During my illness I had no real sorrow of heart, yet being under certain natural impressions of religion, I read through Klopstock's works without weariness. I cared nothing about the word of God. I had about three hundred books of my own, but no Bible. I practically set a far higher value upon the writings of Horace and Cicero, Voltaire and Moliere, than upon the volume of inspiration. Now and then I felt that I ought to become a different person, and I tried to amend my conduct, particularly when I went to the Lord's supper, as I used to do twice every year, with the other young men. The day previous to attending that ordinance, I used to refrain from certain things; and on the day itself I was serious, and also swore once or twice to God, with the emblem of the broken body in my mouth, to become better, thinking that for the oath's sake I should be induced to reform. But after one or two days were over, all was forgotten, and I was as bad as before.

I had now grown so wicked, that I could habitually tell lies without blushing. And further, to show how fearfully wicked I was, I will mention, out of many others, only one great sin, of which I was guilty, before I left this place. Through my dissipated life I had contracted debts, which I had no means of discharging; for my father could allow me only about as much as I needed for my regular maintenance. One day, after having received a sum of money from him, and having purposely shown it to some of my companions, I afterwards feigned that it was stolen, having myself by force injured the lock of my trunk, and having also designedly forced open my guitar case. I also feigned myself greatly frightened at what had happened, ran into the director's room with my coat off, and told him that my money was stolen. I was greatly pitied. Some friends also gave me now as much money as I pretended to have lost, and the circumstance afforded me a ground upon which to ask my creditors to wait longer. But this matter turned out bitterly; for the director, having ground to suspect me, though he could not prove anything, never fully restored me to his confidence.

As it regards my own feeling, though I was very wicked, yet this desperate act of depravity was too much, even for my hardened conscience; for it never afterwards allowed me to feel easy in the presence of the director's wife, who, like a kind mother, had waited on me in my illness, and on whom I had now so willfully brought trouble. How long-suffering was God at this time, not to destroy me at once! And how merciful that he did not suffer me to be tried before the police, who easily would have detected that the whole was a fabrication! I was heartily glad for many reasons, but particularly on account of this latter circumstance, to be able soon after to exchange the school for the university.

I had now obtained what I had fondly looked forward to. I became a member of the university, and that with very honourable testimonials. I had thus obtained permission to preach in the Lutheran Establishment, but I was as truly unhappy, and as far from God as ever. I had made strong resolutions, now at last, to change my course of life, for two reasons: first, because, without it, I thought no parish would choose me as their pastor; and secondly, that without a considerable knowledge of divinity I should never get a good living, as the obtaining of a valuable cure, in Prussia, generally depends upon the degree which the candidates of the ministry obtain in passing the examination. But the moment I entered Halle, the university town, all my resolutions came to nothing.—Being now more than ever my own master, and without any control as long as I did not fight a duel, molest the people in the streets, &c., I renewed my profligate life afresh, though now a student of divinity. When my money was spent, I pawned my watch and a part of my linen and clothes, or borrowed in other ways. Yet in the midst of it all I had a desire to renounce this wretched life, for I had no enjoyment in it, and had sense enough left to see, that the end one day or other would be miserable; for I should never get a living. But I had no sorrow of heart on account of offending God.

One day when I was in a tavern with some of my wild fellow-students, I saw among them one of my former school-fellows, named Beta, whom I had known four years before at Halberstadt, but whom at that time had despised, because he was so quiet and serious. It now appeared well to me to choose him as my friend, thinking that if I could but have better companions, I should by that means improve my own conduct. I entered into familiar discourse with him, and we were soon much knit to one another. "Cursed be the man that trusteth in man, and maketh flesh his arm." Jeremiah xvii. 5.

This Beta was a backslider. When formerly he was so quiet at school, I have reason to believe it was because the Spirit of God was working on his heart; but now, having departed from the Lord, he tried to put off the ways of God more and more, and to enjoy the world of which he had known but little before. I sought his friendship because I thought it would lead me to a steady life; and he gladly formed an acquaintance with me, as he told me afterwards, because he thought it would bring him into gay society. Thus my poor foolish heart was again deceived. And yet, God, in His abundant mercy, made him, after all, in a way which was never thought of by me, the instrument of doing me good, not merely for time, but for eternity.

About this period, June 1825, I was again taken ill in consequence of my profligate and vicious life. My state of health would therefore no longer allow me to go on in the same course, but my desires were still unchanged. About the end of July I recovered. After this, my conduct was outwardly rather better; but this arose only from want of money. At the commencement of August, Beta and I with two other students, drove about the country, for four days. All the money for this expensive pleasure had been obtained by pledging some of our remaining articles. When we returned, instead of being truly sorry on account of this sin, we thought of fresh pleasures, and, as my love for traveling was stronger than ever, through what I had seen on this last journey, I proposed to my friends to set off for Switzerland. The obstacles in the way, the want of money, and the want of the passports, were removed by me. For, through forged letters from our parents, we procured passports; and through pledging all we could, particularly our books, we obtained as much money as we thought would be enough. Beta was one of the party.

On August 18th we left Halle. It will be enough to say that we went as far as Mount Rigi in Switzerland, by the way of Erfurt, Frankfort, Heidelberg, Stuttgart, Zurich, and returned by the way of Constance, Ulm, and Nuremberg. Forty-three days we were, day after day, traveling, almost always on foot. I had now obtained the desire of my heart. I had seen Switzerland. But still I was far from being happy. The Lord most graciously preserved us from many calamitous circumstances, which, but for His gracious providence, might have overtaken us. But I did not see His hand at that time, as I have seen it since. Sickness of one or more of us, or separation from one another, which might have so easily befallen us, would have brought us, being so far from home, and having but just as much money as was absolutely needed, into a most miserable condition. I was on this journey like Judas; for, having the common purse, I was a thief. I managed so, that the journey cost me but two-thirds of what it cost my friends. Oh! how wicked was I now. At last all of us became tired of seeing even the most beautiful views; and whilst at first, after having seen certain scenes, I had been saying with Horace, at the end of the day, in my pagan heart, "Vixi," (I have lived), I was now glad to get home again.

September 29th we reached Halle, from whence each of us, for the remainder of the vacation, went to his father's house. I had now, by many lies, to satisfy my father concerning the traveling expenses, and succeeded in deceiving him. During the three weeks I stayed at home I determined to live differently for the future. Once more the Lord showed me what resolutions come to, when made in man's strength. I was different for a few days; but when the vacation was over, and fresh students came, and, with them, fresh money, all was soon forgotten.

At that time Halle was frequented by 1260 students, about 900 of whom studied divinity, all of which 900 were allowed to preach, although, I have reason to believe, not nine of them feared the Lord.

The time was now come when God would have mercy upon me. His love had been set upon such a wretch as I was before the world was made. His love had sent His Son to bear the punishment due to me on account of my sins, and to fulfill the law which I had broken times without number. And now at a time when I was as careless about Him as ever, He sent His Spirit into my heart. I had no Bible, and had not read in it for years. I went to church but seldom; but, from custom, I took the Lord's supper twice a year. I had never heard the gospel preached, up to the beginning of November 1825. I had never met with a person who told me that he meant, by the help of God, to live according to the Holy Scriptures. In short, I had not the least idea, that there were any persons really different from myself, except in degree.

One Saturday afternoon, about the middle of November 1825, I had taken a walk with my friend Beta. On our return he said to me, that he was in the habit of going on Saturday evenings to the house of a Christian, where there was a meeting. On further enquiry he told me that they read the Bible, sang, prayed, and read a printed sermon. No sooner had I heard this, than it was to me as if I had found something after which I had been seeking all my life long. I immediately wished to go with my friend, who was not at once willing to take me; for knowing me as a gay young man, he thought I should not like this meeting. At last, however, he said he would call for me.—I would here mention, that Beta seems to have had conviction of sin, and probably also a degree of acquaintance with the Lord, when about fifteen years old. Afterwards, being in a cold and worldly state, he joined me in this sinful Journey to Switzerland. On his return, however, being extremely miserable, and convinced of his guilt, he made a full confession of his sin to his father; and whilst with him, sought the acquaintance of a Christian brother, named Richter. This Dr. Richter, who himself had studied a few years before at Halle, gave him, on his return to the university, a letter of introduction to a believing tradesman, of the name of Wagner. It was this brother, concerning whom Beta spoke to me, and in whose house the meeting was held.

We went together in the evening. As I did not know the manners of believers, and the joy they have in seeing poor sinners, even in any measure caring about the things of God, I made an apology for coming. The kind answer of this dear brother I shall never forget. He said: "Come as often as you please; house and heart are open to you." We sat down and sang a hymn. Then brother Kayser, now a missionary in Africa, in connection with the London Missionary Society, who was then living at Halle, fell on his knees, and asked a blessing on our meeting. This kneeling down made a deep impression upon me; for I had never either seen any one on his knees, nor had I ever myself prayed on my knees. He then read a chapter and a printed sermon; for no regular meetings for expounding the Scriptures were allowed in Prussia, except an ordained clergyman was present. At the close we sang another hymn, and then the master of the house prayed. Whilst he prayed, my feeling was something like this: "I could not pray as well, though I am much more learned than this illiterate man." The whole made a deep impression on me. I was happy; though, if I had been asked, why I was happy, I could not have clearly explained it.

When we walked home, I said to Beta, "All we have seen on our journey to Switzerland, and all our former pleasures, are as nothing in comparison with this evening." Whether I fell on my knees when I returned home, I do not remember; but this I know, that I lay peaceful and happy in my bed. This shows that the Lord may begin His work in different ways. For I have not the least doubt, that on that evening, He began a work of grace in me, though I obtained joy without any deep sorrow of heart, and with scarcely any knowledge. That evening was the turning point in my life.—The next day, and Monday, and once or twice besides, I went again to the house of this brother, where I read the Scriptures with him and another brother; for it was too long for me to wait till Saturday came again.

Now my life became very different, though not so, that all sins were given up at once. My wicked companions were given up; the going to taverns was entirely discontinued; the habitual practice of telling falsehoods was no longer indulged in, but still a few times after this I spoke an untruth.—At the time when this change took place, I was engaged in translating a novel out of French into German, for the press, in order to obtain the means of gratifying my desire to see Paris, &c. This plan about the journey was now given up, though I had not light enough to give up the work in which I was engaged, but finished it. The Lord, however, most remarkably put various obstacles in the way and did not allow me to sell the manuscript. At last, seeing that the whole was wrong, I determined never to sell it, and was enabled to abide by this determination. The manuscript was burnt.

I now no longer lived habitually in sin, though I was still often overcome, and sometimes even by open sins, though far less frequently than before, and not without sorrow of heart. I read the

Scriptures, prayed often, loved the brethren, went to church from right motives, and stood on the side of Christ; though laughed at by my fellow-students.

It had pleased God to teach me something of the meaning of that precious truth: "God so loved the world, that He gave His only begotten Son, that whosoever believeth in Him should not perish, but have everlasting life." I understood something of the reason why the Lord Jesus died on the cross, and suffered such agonies in the Garden of Gethsemane: even that thus, bearing the punishment due to us, we might not have to bear it ourselves. And, therefore, apprehending in some measure the love of Jesus for my soul, I was constrained to love Him in return. What all the exhortations and precepts of my father and others could not effect; what all my own resolutions could not bring about, even to renounce a life of sin and profligacy: I was enabled to do, constrained by the love of Jesus. The individual who desires to have his sins forgiven, must seek for it through the blood of Jesus. The individual who desires to get power over sin, must likewise seek it through the blood of Jesus.

In January 1826, I began to read missionary papers, and was greatly stirred up to become a missionary myself. I prayed frequently concerning this matter, and thus made more decided progress for a few weeks. But soon, alas! I was drawn aside. I used frequently to meet a young female, who also came to the meetings on Saturday evenings; and being the only pious female of my own age, whom I knew, I soon felt myself greatly attached to her. This led away my heart from missionary work, for I had reason to believe that her parents would not allow her to go with me. My prayers now became cold and formal, and at length were almost entirely given up. My joy in the Lord left me. In this state I continued for about six weeks. At the end of that time, about Easter 1826, I saw a devoted young brother, named Hermann Ball, a learned man, and of wealthy parents, who, constrained by the love of Christ, preferred labouring in Poland among the Jews as a missionary, to having a comfortable living near his relations. His example made a deep impression on me. I was led to apply his case to my own, and to compare myself with him; for I had given up the work of the Lord, and, I may say, the Lord Himself, for the sake of a girl. The result of this comparison was, that I was enabled to give up this connexion, which I had entered into without prayer, and which thus had led me away from the Lord. When I was enabled to be decided, the Lord smiled on me, and I was, for the first time in my life, able fully and unreservedly to give up myself to Him.

It was at this time that I began truly to enjoy the peace of God, which passeth all understanding. In this my joy I wrote to my father and brother, entreating them to seek the Lord, and telling them how happy I was; thinking, that if the way to happiness were but set before them, they would gladly embrace it. To my great surprise an angry answer was returned.—About this period the Lord sent a believer, Dr. Tholuck, as professor of divinity to Halle, in consequence of which a few believing students came from other universities. Thus also, through becoming acquainted with other brethren, the Lord led me on.

With the revival of the work of grace in my heart, after the snare above referred to had been broken, my former desire, to give myself to missionary service, returned, and I went at last to my father to obtain his permission, without which I could not be received into any of the German missionary institutions. My father was greatly displeased, and particularly reproached me, saying that he had expended so much money on my education, in hope that he might comfortably spend his last days with me in a parsonage, and that he now saw all these prospects come to nothing. He was angry, and told me he would no longer consider me as his son. But the Lord gave me grace to remain steadfast. He then entreated me, and wept before me; yet even this by far harder trial the Lord enabled me to bear. Before I went away I took an opportunity of reminding my brother of my former wicked life, and told him that now, having been thus blessed by God, I could not but live for Him. After I had left my father, though I wanted more money than at any previous period of my life, as I had to remain two years longer in the university, I determined, never to take any more from him; for it seemed to me wrong, so far as I remember, to suffer myself to be supported by him, when he had no prospect that I should become, what he would wish me to be, namely, a clergyman with a good living. This resolution I was enabled to keep.

By the way I would here observe, that the Lord afterwards, in a most remarkable way, supplied my temporal wants. For shortly after this had occurred, several American gentlemen, three of whom were professors in American colleges, came to Halle for literary purposes; and as they did not understand German, I was recommended by Dr. Tholuck to teach them. These gentlemen, some of whom were believers, paid so handsomely for the instruction which I gave them, and for the lectures of certain professors which I wrote out for them, that I had enough and to spare. Thus did the Lord richly make up to me the little which I had relinquished for His sake. "0 fear the Lord, ye His saints; for there is no want to them that fear Him." Psalm xxxiv. 9.

On my return from my father to Halle, I found that the more experienced brethren thought that I ought for the present to take no further steps respecting my desire to go out as a missionary. But still it was more or less in my mind.—Whitsuntide and the two days following I spent in the house of a pious clergyman in the country: for all the ministers at Halle, a town of more than 30,000 inhabitants, were unenlightened men, God greatly refreshed me through this visit. Dear Beta was with me. On our return we related to two of our former friends, whose society we had not quite given up, though we did not any longer live with them in sin, how happy we had been on our visit. I then told them how I wished they were as happy as ourselves. They answered, we do not feel that we are sinners. After this I fell on my knees, and asked God to show them that they were sinners. Having done so, I left them, and went into my bed-room, where I continued to pray for them. After a little while I returned to my sitting-room, and found them both in tears, and both told me that they now felt themselves to be sinners. From that time a work of grace commenced in their hearts.

Shortly after this, being still greatly exercised about going out as a missionary, and wishing much (according to my natural mind, as I now see,) to have the matter settled, in one way or the other, without being willing quietly, patiently, and prayerfully to wait on the Lord, I came to the conclusion to ascertain the Lord's mind by the lot. To this end I not merely drew a lot in private, but I bought a ticket in the royal lottery; and I left it thus with the Lord, that if I gained any thing, I should take it to be His will that I should become a missionary, if not, that I should remain at home. My ticket came out with a small sum, on account of which it appeared to me that I should be a missionary. I therefore applied to the Berlin Missionary Society, but was not accepted, because my father had not given his consent.

Very soon afterwards I was led to see in some degree, and since then much more fully, the error into which I had fallen respecting the lot. In the first place it was altogether wrong, that I, a child of God, should have any thing to do with so worldly a system as that of the lottery. But it was also unscriptural to go to the lot at all for the sake of ascertaining the Lord's mind, and this I ground on the following reasons. We have neither a commandment of God for it, nor the example of our Lord, nor that of the apostles, after the Holy Spirit had been given on the day of Pentecost. 1. We have many exhortations in the word of God to seek to know His mind by prayer and searching the Holy Scriptures, but no passage which exhorts us to use the lot. 2. The example of the apostles (Acts i.) in using the lot, in the choice of an apostle, in the room of Judas Iscariot, is the only passage, which can be brought in favour of the lot, from the New Testament, (and to the Old we have not to go under this dispensation, for the sake of ascertaining how we ought to live as disciples of Christ). Now concerning this circumstance we have to remember, that the Spirit was not yet given (John vii. 39; ch. xiv. 16, 17; ch. xvi. 7, 13), by whose teaching especially it is that we may know the mind of the Lord; and hence we find, that, after the day of Pentecost, the lot was no more used, but the apostles gave themselves to prayer and fasting to ascertain how they ought to act.

In addition to this I would give my own experience concerning the lot, but only by way of illustrating the view just given; for the word of God is quite sufficient on the subject. And first as it regards my using the lot in the above case. How did it turn out? I had repeatedly asked the Lord to show me His mind, whether He would have me to be a missionary or not. But not coming to a satisfactory assurance, and being very anxious to have the matter settled, I found out in my own judgment a much shorter way, namely, the lot. I ought to have said to myself, how can an individual, so ignorant as you are, think about being a teacher to others? For though I was truly begotten again, and rested upon Christ alone for salvation, still I should not have been able to give a clear explanation of even the most elementary truths of the Gospel. How then could I be fit to teach others? The first thing therefore I ought to have done, was, to seek through much prayer, and searching the Scriptures, and a holy life, to obtain more knowledge of divine things. Further, as to my impatience in wishing the matter settled, how could I have been fit to endure in that state the hardships and trials of a missionary life, in which my patience, no doubt, would have been much more severely tried? I therefore ought to have said to myself, if I cannot wait quietly, though it be many months longer, before the Lord shows me clearly His will concerning the matter, how then can I be fit for missionary work? Instead of thus comparing my state of heart and knowledge, with what is required in the Scriptures from him who is to be a teacher, I ran hastily to the lot, and thought I had done it prayerfully. And how did it end? According to my prayers the lot decided I should be a missionary among the heathen (and my mind, at that time, especially inclined to the East Indies). But the way in which the Lord has led me since has been very different. And it ought not to be said in defense of the practice of deciding by lot—Perhaps the Lord meant you to be a missionary among the heathen, but you did not give yourself to the work? for I actually offered myself to a society, but was not accepted. Moreover, since 1826 I have repeatedly offered myself most solemnly to the Lord for this work, and am as sure that it is not His will that I should go out a missionary for the present, as I am sure of any thing. Nor could it be said, that perhaps the Lord yet may call me for this work. For if He should be pleased to do so tomorrow, yet that would prove nothing concerning the above point. For I did not use the lot to ascertain whether at any period of my life I should be engaged in missionary work, but whether I should then set about it. And to put such an explanation on the matter, would be acting as false prophets, who, when their prophecies fail, try to find out some way or other, whereby they may show that their prophecies were true.

About two years after I used the lot in another instance. I went one day to a village about fifteen miles from Halle, to see the few believers there. When I was about three miles from the place, it began to get dark; and finding myself in a spot where the road divided, and not knowing which way I should choose, I was greatly perplexed. I stood a moment, and then prayed to God to show me by the lot, which was the right way. Now, truly one may say, if the use of the lot in our day is according to the will of God, this was particularly a case for the Lord to direct me through this means. For here was one of His children in need, looking up to his Father to help him, through the lot, out of his difficulty, and this His child also on a journey in His service. I drew the lot and went the way to the left. After some time I found I was on the wrong road. Now, at last, as I did not know how to get into the right one, I did what I ought to have done before, and what I believe to be a scriptural way of acting; I prayed that the Lord graciously would send some one to put me into the right way; and almost immediately a carriage came up, and I was directed on my journey.

In one other instance I used the lot some years after. It concerned a most important matter, important for my whole life. I had then a degree of conviction, that I ought prayerfully and patiently to wait for the Lord's decision. But my natural mind would have the decision at once, and thus after prayer I drew the lot, to have the matter in one way or other settled. But facts turned out completely different from what the lot decided.

To ascertain the Lord's will we ought to use scriptural means. Prayer, the word of God, and His Spirit should be united together. We should go to the Lord repeatedly in prayer, and ask Him to teach us by His Spirit through His word. I say, by His Spirit through His word. For if we should think that His Spirit led us to do so and so, because certain facts are so and so, and yet His word is opposed to the step which we are going to take, we should be deceiving ourselves.

For instance: A brother in business thinks he ought to leave the house in which he lives, because it is not in a good situation. He wishes to know the Lord's mind, as he says, and prays about the matter. After a few days, unexpectedly, a house is offered to him without seeking after it, in a much better situation. The house is very suitable, as he thinks; the rent very moderate; and moreover the person who offers him the house tells him, that, because he is a believer he will let him have it at this cheap rent. There is, however, this scriptural objection in the way. If he goes into this house, he must carry on so large a business, to cover his expenses, that his time will be so occupied as to encroach upon those hours, which ought to be devoted to his spiritual interests. Now the scriptural way of deciding would be this: No situation, no business will be given to me by God, in which I have not time enough to care about my soul (Matthew vi. 33). Therefore, however outward circumstances may appear, it can only be considered as permitted of God, to prove the genuineness of my love, faith, and obedience, but by no means as the leading of His providence to induce me to act contrary to His revealed will.

In connexion with this I would mention, that the Lord very graciously gave me, from the very commencement of my divine life, a measure of simplicity and of childlike disposition in spiritual things, so that whilst I was exceedingly ignorant of the Scriptures, and was still from time to time overcome even by outward sins, yet I was enabled to carry most minute matters to the Lord in prayer. And I have found "godliness profitable unto all things, having promise of the life that now is, and of that which is to come." Though very weak and ignorant, yet I had now, by the grace of God, some desire to benefit others, and he who so faithfully had once served Satan, sought now to win souls for Christ.

I may mention a few instances. I circulated every month, in different parts of the country, about 300 missionary papers. I also sold and distributed a considerable number of tracts, and often took my pockets full in my walks, and distributed them, and spoke to poor people whom I met. I also wrote letters to some of my former companions in sin. I visited for thirteen weeks a sick man, who, when I first began to speak to him about the things of God, was completely ignorant of his state as a sinner, trusting for salvation in his upright and moral life. After some weeks, however, the Lord allowed me to see a decided change in him, and he afterwards repeatedly expressed his gratitude, that I had been sent to him by God, to be the means of opening his blind eyes. May this encourage the believing reader to sow the seed, though he does not see it spring up at once.

Thus the Lord condescended to begin to use me soon after my conversion, though but little; for I could bear but very little, as I did not see at that time, as I do now, that God alone can give spiritual life at the first, and keep it up in the soul afterwards. How imperfectly, however, on account of my ignorance, some of these things were done, I will show by the following instance. Once I met a beggar in the fields, and spoke to him about his soul. But when I perceived it made no impression upon him, I spoke more loudly; and when he still remained unmoved, I quite bawled in talking to him; till at last I went away, seeing it was of no use. Though none had sought the Lord less than myself, when He was pleased to begin His work in me; yet so ignorant was I of the work of the Spirit, that I thought my speaking very loudly would force him into repentance towards God, and faith in the Lord Jesus.

Having heard that there was a schoolmaster living in a village, about six miles from Halls, who was in the habit of holding a prayer meeting at four o'clock every morning, with the miners, before they went into the pit, giving them also an address, I thought he was a believer; and as I knew so very few brethren, I went to see him, in order, if it might be, to strengthen his hands. About two years afterwards he told me, that when I came to him first, he knew not the Lord, but that he had held these prayer-meetings merely out of kindness to a relative, whose office it was, but who bad gone on a journey; and that those addresses which lie had read were not his own, but copied out of a book. He also told me, that he was much impressed with my kindness, and, what he considered condescension on my part in coming to see him, and this, together with my conversation, had been instrumental in leading him to care about the things of God; and I knew him ever afterwards as a true believer.

This schoolmaster asked me, whether I would not preach in his parish, as the aged and infirm clergyman would be very glad of my assistance. Up to this time I had never preached, though for fifteen months past I might have done so as a student of divinity; for before Christmas 1825 I had been mercifully kept from attempting to preach, (though I wrote to my father about July that I had preached, because I knew it would please him), and after Christmas, when I knew the Lord, I refrained from doing so, because I felt that I was yet too little instructed in the things of God. The same reason ought to have still kept me from preaching; yet I thought, that, by taking a sermon, or the greater part of one, written by a spiritual man, and committing it to memory, I might benefit the people. Had I reasoned scripturally, I should have said, surely it cannot be the will of God, that I should preach in this way, if I have not enough knowledge of the Scriptures to write a sermon. Moreover, I had not enough light nor tenderness of conscience to see, that I was a deceiver in the pulpit; for every body supposes, that the sermon a man preaches is, if not entirely, at least as to the most part, his own composition.

I now set about putting a printed sermon into a suitable form, and committing it to memory. It was hard work. There is no joy in man's own doings and choosings. It took me nearly a whole week to commit to memory such a sermon as would take up nearly an hour in repeating. I got through it, but had no enjoyment in the work. It was on August 27, 1826, at eight in the morning, in a chapel of ease, in connexion with which my friend was schoolmaster.5 At eleven I repeated the same sermon verbatim in the parish church. There was one service more, in the afternoon, at which I needed not to have done any thing; for the schoolmaster might have read a printed sermon, as he used to do. But having a desire to serve the Lord, though I often knew not how to do it scripturally; and knowing that this aged and unenlightened clergyman had had this living for forty-eight years, and having therefore reason to believe, that the gospel scarcely ever had been preached in that place; I had it in my heart to preach again in the afternoon. But I had no second sermon committed to memory. It came, however, to my mind to read the 5th chapter of Matthew, and to make such remarks as I was able. I did so. Immediately upon beginning to expound "Blessed are the poor in spirit, &c." I felt myself greatly assisted; and whereas in the morning my sermon had not been simple enough for the people to understand it, I now was listened to with the greatest attention, and I think was also understood. My own peace and joy were great. I felt this a blessed work. After the service I left the aged clergyman as soon as possible, lest I should lose my enjoyment.

On my way to Halle I thought, this is the way I should like always to preach. But then it came immediately to my mind, that such sort of preaching might do for illiterate country people, but that it never would do before a well educated assembly in town. I thought, the truth ought to be preached at all hazards, but it ought to be given in a different form, suited to the hearers. Thus I remained unsettled in my mind as it regards the mode of preaching; and it is not surprising that I did not then see the truth concerning this matter, for I did not understand the work of the Spirit, and therefore saw not the powerlessness of human eloquence. Further, I did not keep in mind, that if the most illiterate persons in the congregation can comprehend the discourse, the most educated will understand it too; but that the reverse does not hold true.

It was not till three years afterwards that I was led, through grace, to see what I now consider the right mode of preparation for the public preaching of the Word. But about this, if God permit, I will say more when I come to that period of my life.

I now preached frequently, both in the churches of villages and towns, but never had any enjoyment in doing so, except when speaking in a simple way; though the repetition of sermons, which had been committed to memory, brought more praise from my fellow-creatures. But from neither way of preaching did I see any fruit. It may be, that the last day may show the benefit even of these feeble endeavours. One reason why the Lord did not permit me to see fruit, seems to me, that I should have been most probably lifted up by success. It may be also, because I prayed exceedingly little respecting the ministry of the Word, and because I walked so little with God, and was so rarely a vessel unto honour, sanctified, and meet for the Master's use.

About the time that I first began to preach I lived for about two months in free lodgings, provided for poor students of divinity in the Orphan-House, built in dependence upon God, by that devoted and eminent servant of Christ, A. H. Franke, Professor of Divinity at Halle, who died 1727. I mention this, as some years afterwards I was benefited myself through the faith of this dear man of God.—About that time I was still so weak that I fell repeatedly into open sins, yet could not continue in them, nay, not even for a few days, without sorrow of heart, confession before God, and fleeing to the blood of the Lamb. And so ignorant was I still, that I bought a crucifix in a frame, and hung it up in my room, hoping that being thus frequently reminded of the sufferings of my Saviour, I should not fall so frequently into sin. But in a few days the looking to the crucifix was as nothing, and I fell about that very time more than once deeply.

About this time I formed an intimate acquaintance with a brother, who was also a divinity student: and as we loved one another so much, and were so happy in one another's society, we thought that it would greatly add to our joy, and to one another's benefit, to live together, and that thus we might mutually help one another. Accordingly in September 1826, I left the free lodgings in the Orphan-House, and lived with him. But alas! we were not aware, that because God is greatly glorified by the love and union of His people, for this very reason Satan particularly hates it, and will, therefore, in every possible way, seek to divide them. We ought to have especially prayed, and that frequently, that the Lord would keep us together in love; instead of which, I do not think that we at all feared disunion, as we loved one another so much. For this reason our great adversary soon got an advantage by our neglecting prayer concerning this point, and we were disunited, and love and union were not fully restored between us till after we had been for some time separated.

Having heard that a very rich lady of title, residing at Frankfort-on-the-Maine, about two hundred miles from Halle, was a very pious person, and,in visiting a charitable institution at Dusselthal, had given very liberally; and wishing much about the commencement of the year 1827 to help a poor relative with a small sum of money, and also to pay the remainder of the debt which I had contracted for my traveling expenses to Switzerland: I wrote to this lady, asking her to lend me a small sum of money, in actual amount only little above £5., but, as money in the North of Germany has much more value than in England, it was as much as £ 12. or £ 15. in this country. Whilst I was writing, however, the thought occurred to me, Suppose this lady should not be a believer? I, therefore, pointed out to her the way of salvation, and related to her how I had been brought to the knowledge of the truth. But I received no answer by the time I might have had one.—I would just notice, that since 1829 my practice, on account of what I found in the Scriptures, Rom. xiii. 8, as it regards borrowing money, has been different. And, moreover, I have considered that there is no ground to go away from the door of the Lord to that of a believer, so long as He is so willing to supply our need.

About January 20th I was one day very wretched. Satan obtained an advantage over me through over-much work; for I was in the habit of writing about fourteen hours a day. One morning I was in so wretched a state, that I said in my heart, what have I now gained by becoming a Christian? Afterwards I walked about in the streets in this wretched state of heart, and at last I went into a confectioner's shop, where wine and ardent spirits were sold, to eat and to drink. But as soon as I had taken a piece of cake I left the shop, having no rest, as I felt that it was unbecoming a believer, either to go to such places, or to spend his money in such a way. In the afternoon of the very day on which, in the ingratitude of my heart, I had had such unkind thoughts about the Lord, (who was at that very time in so remarkable a manner supplying my temporal wants, by my being employed in writing for an AMERICAN Professor), He graciously showed me my sin, not by a severe chastisement, as I most righteously deserved, but by adding another mercy to the many He had already shown me. Oh! how long-suffering is our Lord. How does He bear with us! May I at least now seek, for the few days whilst I may stay in this world, to be more grateful for all His mercies!

At two o'clock I received a parcel from Frankfort, containing the exact sum of money of which I had requested the loan. There was no letter to be found. I was overwhelmed with the Lord's mercy, but very much regretted that there was no letter. At last, on carefully examining the paper in which the silver had been packed, I found one, which I have kept, and which I translate from the German.

"A peculiar providence has brought me acquainted with the letter which you have written to Lady B. But you are under a mistake concerning her, both as it regards her character, and her stay at D., where she never was. She has been taken for another individual. But that I may lessen in some measure the difficulties in which you seem to be, I send you the enclosed small sum, for which you may thank, not the unknown giver, but the Lord, who turneth the hearts like rivers of water. Hold fast the faith which God has given you by His Holy Spirit; it is the most precious treasure in this life, and it contains in itself true happiness. Only seek by watching and prayer more and more to be delivered from all vanity and self-complacency, by which even the true believer may be ensnared when he least expects it. Let it be your chief aim to be more and more humble, faithful, and quiet. May we not belong to those who say and write continually,' Lord,' 'Lord,' but who have Him not deeply in their hearts. Christianity consists not in words, but in power. There must be life in us. For, therefore, God loved us first that we might love Him in return; and that loving we might receive power, to be faithful to Him, and to conquer ourselves, the world, distress, and death. May His Spirit strengthen you for this, that you may be an able messenger of His Gospel! Amen.

"AN ADORING WORSHIPPER OF THE

SAVIOUR, JESUS CHRIST."

Frankfort-on-the-Maine, January 14th, 1827.

I saw, in some measure, at the time when I received t letter, how much I needed such a faithful, and, at the same time, loving word of admonition; but I have seen it more fully since. Self-complacency, and a want of quietness and saying and writing more frequently "Lord," "Lord," than acknowledging Him by my life as such; these were the evils against which at that time I particularly needed to be cautioned; and up to this day I am still much, very much, lacking in these points: though the Lord, to His praise I would say it, has done much for me in these particulars since that time.

After having read this letter, my heart was full of joy, shame and gratitude. Truly it was the goodness of God which brought my heart into this state, and not the money for that was gone in a few hours after for the two purposes above referred to. With my heart full of peculiar feelings, and ashamed of my conduct in the morning, I left the town towards the evening, to walk alone in a solitary place. And now, being particularly conscious of my ingratitude to the Lord for all His mercies, and of my want of steadfastness in His ways, I could not forbear falling down on my knees behind a hedge, though the snow was a foot deep, anew to surrender myself wholly to Him, and to pray for strength that I might for the future live more to His glory, and also to thank Him for His late mercy. It was a blessed time, I continued about half an hour in prayer.

After such an experience, it may be difficult for one, who does not know the plague of his own heart, to think that I was at that time a true believer, when I tell hint that so base was I, so altogether like a beast before my God, and unmindful of His mercies to me in Christ, that only a few weeks after I fell into a wretched backsliding state, in which I continued for many days, during which time prayer was almost entirely given up. It was on one of these days that I rang my bell, and ordered the servant to fetch me wine. And now I began to drink. But how good was the Lord! Though I desired to drink, that I might be able more easily to go on in sin, yet He would not allow me to give up myself to the wickedness of my heart. For whilst in my ungodly days I had drunk once about five quarts of strong beer in one afternoon, in the way of bravado, and once also much wine at one time, without remorse of conscience, I could now take only two or three glasses before the wickedness of my conduct was brought before me; and my conscience told me that I drank merely for the sake of drinking, and thus I gave it up.

It was about this time that I formed the plan of exchanging the University of Halle for that of Berlin, on account of there being a greater number of believing professors and students in the latter place. But the whole plan was formed without prayer, or at least without earnest prayer. When, however, the morning came on which I had to take decided steps concerning it, and to apply for the university-testimonials, the Lord graciously stirred me up, prayer-fully to consider the matter; and finding that I bad no sufficient reason for leaving Halle, I gave up the plan, and have never had reason to regret having done so.

In the vacations, Michaelmas, 1826, and Easter, 1827, and at other times, I visited a Moravian settlement, called Gnadau, which was only about three miles distant from the place where my father then resided. Through the instrumentality of the brethren, whom I met there, my spirit was often refreshed.

The public means of grace by which I could be benefited were very few. Though I went regularly to church when I did not preach myself, yet I scarcely ever heard the truth; for there was no enlightened clergyman in the town. And when it so happened that I could bear Dr. Tholuck, or any other godly minister, the prospect of it beforehand, and the looking back upon it afterwards, served to fill me with joy. Now and then I walked ten or fifteen miles to enjoy this privilege. May those who enjoy the faithful ministry of the Word feel exceedingly thankful for it. There are few blessings on earth greater for a believer; and yet the Lord is frequently obliged to teach us the value of this blessing by depriving us of it for a season.

Another means of grace which I attended, besides the Saturday evening meetings in brother Wagner's house, was a meeting every Lord's day evening with the believing students, which consisted of six or more in number, and increased, before I left Halle, to about 20; and which, after the Easter vacation of 1827, was held in my room till I left Halle. In these meetings one, or two, or more of the brethren prayed, and we read the Scriptures, sang hymns, and sometimes also one or another of the brethren spoke a little in the way of exhortation, and we read also such writings of godly men as were calculated for edification. I was often greatly stirred up and refreshed in these meetings; and twice, being in a backsliding state, and therefore cold and miserable, I opened my heart to the brethren, and was brought out of that state through the means of their exhortations and prayers. "Forsake not the assembling of yourselves together," is a most important exhortation. Even if we should not derive any especial benefit, at the time, so far as we are conscious, yet we may be kept from much harm. And very frequently the beginning of coldness of heart is nourished by keeping away from the meetings of the saints. I know, when I was cold, and had no real desire to be brought out of that state, I went a few times into the villages, where I was sure not to meet with brethren, that I might not be spoken to about the things of God. Yet so gracious was the Lord, that my very wretchedness brought me back after a few hours. The Lord had begun a good work in me; and being faithful, though I was faithless, He would not give me up, but carried on His gracious work in me; though it would have progressed much more rapidly, had not my rebellious heart resisted. As to the other means of grace I would say: I fell into the snare, into which so many young believers fall, the reading of religious books in preference to the Scriptures. I could no longer read French and German novels, as I had formerly done, to feed my carnal mind; but still I did not put into the room of those books the best of all books. I read tracts, missionary papers, sermons, and biographies of godly persons. The last kind of books I found more profitable than others, and had they been well selected, or had I not read too much of such writings, or had any of them tended particularly to endear the Scriptures to me, they might have done me much good.—I never had been at any time in my life in the habit of reading the Holy Scriptures. When under fifteen years of age, I occasionally read a little of them at school; afterwards God's precious book was entirely laid aside, so that I never read one single chapter of it, as far as I remember, till it pleased God to begin a work of grace in my heart. Now the scriptural way of reasoning would have been: God Himself has condescended to become an author, and I am ignorant about that precious book, which His Holy Spirit has caused to be written through the instrumentality of His servants, and it contains that which I ought to know, and the knowledge of which will lead me to true happiness; therefore I ought to read again and again this most precious book, this book of books, most earnestly, most prayerfully, and with much meditation; and in this practice I ought to continue all the days of my life. For I was aware, though I read it but little, that I knew scarcely anything of it. But instead of acting thus, and being led by my ignorance of the word of God to study it more, my difficulty in understanding it, and the little enjoyment I had in it, made me careless of reading it (for much prayerful reading of the Word, gives not merely more knowledge, but increases the delight we have in reading it); and thus, like many believers, I practically preferred, for the first four years of my divine life, the works of uninspired men to the oracles of the living God. The consequence was, that I remained a babe, both in knowledge and grace. In knowledge I say; for all true knowledge must be derived, by the Spirit, from the Word. And as I neglected the Word, I was for nearly four years so ignorant, that I did not clearly know even the fundamental points of our holy faith. And this lack of knowledge most sadly kept me back from walking steadily in the ways of God. For it is the truth that makes us free, (John viii. 31, 32,) by delivering us from the slavery of the lusts of the flesh, the lusts of the eyes, and the pride of life. The Word proves it. The experience of the saints proves it; and also my own experience most decidedly proves it. For when it pleased the Lord in Aug. 1829, to bring me really to the Scriptures, my life and walk became very different. And though even since that I have very much fallen short of what I might and ought to be, yet, by the grace of God, I have been enabled to live much nearer to Him than before.

If any believers read this, who practically prefer other books to the Holy Scriptures, and who enjoy the writings of men much more than the word of God, may they be warned by my loss. I shall consider this book to have been the means of doing much good, should it please the Lord, through its instrumentality, to lead some of His people no longer to neglect the Holy Scriptures, but to give them that preference, which they have hitherto bestowed on the writings of men. My dislike to increase the number of books would have been sufficient to deter me from writing these pages, had I not been convinced, that this is the only way in which the brethren at large may be benefited through my mistakes and errors, and been influenced by the hope, that in answer to my prayers, the reading of my experience may be the means of leading them to value the Scriptures more highly, and to make them the rule of all their actions.

Before I leave this subject I would only add: If the reader understands very little of the word of God, he ought to read it very much; for the Spirit explains the Word by the Word. And if he enjoys the reading of the Word little, that is just the reason why he should read it much; for the frequent reading of the Scriptures creates a delight in them, so that the more we read them, the more we desire to do so. And if the reader should be an unbeliever, I would likewise entreat him to read the Scriptures earnestly, but to ask God previously to give him a blessing. For in doing so, God may make him wise unto salvation, 2 Tim. iii. 16.

If any one should ask me, how he may read the Scriptures most profitably,
I would advise him, that

I. Above all he should seek to have it settled in his own mind, that God alone, by His Spirit, can teach him, and that therefore, as God will be inquired of for blessings, it becomes him to seek God's blessing previous to reading, and also whilst reading.

II. He should have it, moreover, settled in his mind, that although the Holy Spirit is the best and sufficient teacher, yet that this teacher does not always teach immediately when we desire it, and that, therefore, we may have to entreat Him again and again for the explanation of certain passages; but that He will surely teach us at last, if indeed we are seeking for light prayerfully, patiently, and with a view to the glory of God.

III. It is of immense importance for the understanding of the word of God, to read it in course, so that we may read every day a portion of the Old and a portion of the New Testament, going on where we previously left off. This is important—1, because it throws light upon the connexion, and a different course, according to which one habitually selects particular chapters, will make it utterly impossible ever to understand much of the Scriptures. 2, Whilst we are in the body, we need a change even in spiritual things, and this change the Lord has graciously provided in the great variety which is to be found in His word. 3, It tends to the glory of God; for the leaving out some chapters here and there, is practically saying, that certain portions are better than others; or, that there are certain parts of revealed truth unprofitable or unnecessary. 4, It may keep us, by the blessing of God, from erroneous views, as in reading thus regularly through the Scriptures, we are led to see the meaning of the whole, and also kept from laying too much stress upon certain favourite views. 5, The Scriptures contain the whole revealed will of God, and therefore we ought to seek to read from time to time through the whole of that revealed will. There are many believers, I fear, in our day, who have not read even once through the whole of the Scriptures; and yet in a few months, by reading only a few chapters every day, they might accomplish it.

IV. It is also of the greatest importance to meditate on what we read, so that perhaps a small portion of that which we have read, or, if we have time, the whole may be meditated upon in the course of the day. Or a small portion of a book, or an epistle, or a gospel, through which we go regularly for meditation, may be considered every day, without, however, suffering oneself to be brought into bondage by this plan.

Learned commentaries I have found to store the head with many notions, and often also with the truth of God; but when the Spirit teaches, through the instrumentality of prayer and meditation, the heart is affected. The former kind of knowledge generally puffs up, and is often renounced, when another commentary gives a different opinion, and often also is found good for nothing, when it is to be carried out into practice. The latter kind of knowledge generally humbles, gives joy, leads us nearer to God, and is not easily reasoned away; and having been obtained from God, and thus having entered into the heart, and become our own, is also generally carried out. If the inquirer after truth does not understand the Hebrew and Greek languages, so as to be able to compare the common translation with the original, he may, concerning several passages, get light by an improved rendering, provided he can be sure that the translator was a truly spiritual person.

The last and most important means of, grace, namely, prayer, was comparatively but little improved by me. I prayed, and I prayed often. I also prayed, in general, by the grace of God, with sincerity; but had I been more earnestly praying, or even only as much, as I have prayed of late years, I should have made much more rapid progress.

In August, 1827, I heard that the Continental Society in England intended to send a minister to Bucharest, the residence of many nominal German Christians, to help an aged brother in the work of the Lord; the two other German Protestant ministers in that place being, the one a Socinian, and the other an unenlightened orthodox preacher. After consideration and prayer I offered myself for this work to professor Tholuck, who was requested to look out for a suitable individual; for with all my weakness I had a great desire to live wholly for God. Most unexpectedly my father gave his consent, though Bucharest was above a thousand miles from my home, and as completely a missionary station as any other. I considered this a remarkable providence; though I see now, that a servant of Christ has to act for his Master, whether it be according to the will of his earthly father or not. I then went home to, spend a short time with my father. In the town where he lived, containing about 3000 inhabitants, I could not hear of a single believer, though I made many inquiries. The time I stayed with my father was more profitably spent than it had formerly been. I was enabled more than ever before to realize my high calling. I had by the grace of God power over sin; at least much more than at any former period of my life.

I returned to Halle, and now prepared with earnestness for the work of the Lord. I set before me the sufferings which might await me. I counted the cost. And he, who once so fully-served Satan, was now willing, constrained by the love of Christ, rather to suffer affliction for the sake of Jesus, than to enjoy the pleasures of sin for a season. I also prayed with, a degree of earnestness concerning my future work.

One day, at the end of October, the above-mentioned brother, Hermann Ball, missionary to the Jews, attended the Lord's day evening meeting in my room, on his way through Halle, and stated that he feared, on account of his health, his should be obliged to give up labouring among the Jews. When I heard this, I felt a peculiar desire to fill up his place. About this very time also I became exceedingly fond of the Hebrew language, which I had cared about very little up to that time, and which I had merely studied now and then, from a sense of duty. But now I studied it, for many weeks, with the greatest eagerness and delight. Whilst I thus from time to time felt a desire to fill up Brother Ball's place as a missionary to the Jews, (about which, however, I did not seriously think, because Dr. Tholuck daily expected a letter from London, finally to settle the particulars respecting my going to Bucharest); and whilst I thus greatly delighted in the study of Hebrew: I called in the evening of Nov. 17th on Dr. Tholuck. In the course of conversation he asked me, whether I had ever had a desire to be a missionary to the Jews, as I might be connected with the London Missionary Society, for promoting Christianity among them, for which he was an agent. I was struck with the question, and told him what had passed in my mind, but added that it was not proper to think anything about that, as I was going to Bucharest: to which he agreed.

When I came home, however, these few words were like fire within me. The next morning I felt all desire for going to Bucharest gone, which appeared to me very wrong and fleshly, and I therefore entreated the Lord, to restore to me the former desire for labouring on that missionary station. He graciously did so almost immediately. My earnestness in studying Hebrew, and my peculiar love for it, however, continued. About this time I had an offer of becoming tutor to the sons of a pious Gentleman of title, which I did not accept on account of my purpose of going to Bucharest, and if that should come to nothing, on account of my desire of being a missionary to the Jews.

About ten days after, Dr. Tholuck received a letter from the Continental Society, stating, that, on account of the war between the Turks and Russians, it appeared well to the committee, for the time being to give up the thought of sending a minister to Bucharest, as it was the seat of war between the two armies. Dr. Tholuck then asked me again, what I now thought about being a missionary to the Jews. My reply was, that I could not then give an answer, but that I would let him know, after I had prayerfully considered the matter. After prayer and consideration, and consulting with experienced brethren, in order that they might probe my heart as to my motives, I came to this conclusion, that, though I could not say with certainty it was the will of God that I should be a missionary to the Jews, yet, that I ought to offer myself to the committee, leaving it with the Lord to do with me afterwards, as it might seem good in His sight. Accordingly Dr. Tholuck wrote, about the beginning of December, 1827, to the committee in London.

At Christmas I spent a few days at Belleben, a village about fifteen miles from Halle, where I had been once or twice before, both for the sake of refreshing the few brethren living there, and also of having my own spirit refreshed by their love. One evening, when I was expounding the Scriptures to them, an unconverted young man happened to be present, and it pleased the Lord to touch his heart, so that he was brought to the knowledge of the truth.

In the beginning of the year 1828 there was a new workhouse established at Halle, into which persons of bad character were put for a time, and made to work. Being disposed to benefit unbelievers, I heartily desired to have permission statedly to preach the word of truth to them while I stayed at Halle, particularly as I understood that one of the lecturers of divinity in the university, who was a Socinian, had applied for this living. I wrote to the magistrates of the city, and offered to preach to those criminals gratuitously, hoping that in this way there would be less objection to my doing so. The reply was, that Dr.—had applied for this living, and that it had been laid before the provincial government for consideration, but that they would be glad if I would preach in the workhouse till the matter was decided. The decision did not come for some time, and I had thus an opportunity of preaching twice every Lord's day, and once or twice on the week evenings; and besides this I took the criminals one by one into a room, to converse with them about their souls. Thus the Lord condescended to give to one so unworthy, so ignorant, so weak in grace, and so young in the faith and in years, a most important field of labour. However, it was well, that even under these circumstances I should have laboured there; for humanly speaking, had I not been there, they would have had either no instruction at all, or a Socinian, or an unenlightened preacher would have preached to them. And besides this, I had at least some qualification for ministering there; for I knew the state of those poor sinners, having been myself formerly, in all probability, a great deal worse than most of them, and my simplicity and plainness of speech they would not have found in every minister. After some months the matter was decided, the Socinian lecturer of divinity, Dr. —, was appointed to the living, and I had to discontinue my labours.

It was not before March 1828, that Professor Tholuck received an answer from London respecting me, in which the committee put a number of questions to me, on the satisfactory answers to which my being received by them would depend. After replying to this first communication, I waited daily for an answer, and was so much the more desirous of having it, as my course in the university was completed. But no answer came. Had my desire, to serve the Lord among the Jews, been of the flesh, it would in all likelihood not have continued; but I still thought about it, and continued to make it a subject of prayer. At last, on June 13th, I received a letter from London, stating that the committee had determined, to take me as a missionary student for six months on probation, provided that I would come to London.

I had now had the matter before me about seven months, having supposed, not only that it would have been settled in a few weeks, but also, that, if I were accepted, I should be sent out immediately, as I had passed the university. Instead of this, not only seven months passed over before the decision came, but I was also expected to come to London, and not only so, but, though I had from my infancy been more or less studying, and now at last wished actively to be engaged, it was required that I should again become a student. For a few moments, therefore, I was greatly disappointed and tried. But, on calmly considering the matter, it appeared to me but right that the committee should know me personally, and that it was also well for me to know them more intimately than merely by correspondence, as this afterwards would make our connexion much more comfortable. I determined therefore, after I had seen my father, and found no difficulty on his part, to go to London.

There was, however, an obstacle in the way of my leaving the country. Every Prussian male subject is under the necessity of being for three years a soldier, provided his state of body allows it; but those who have had a classical education up to a certain degree, and especially those who have passed the university, need to be only one year in the army, but have to equip and maintain themselves during that year. Now, as I had been considered fit for service, when I was examined in my twentieth year, and had only been put back, at my own request, till my twenty-third year, and as I was now nearly twenty-three, I could not obtain a passport out of the country, till I had either served, my time, or had been exempted by the King himself. The latter I hoped would be the case; for it was a well known fact that those who had given themselves to missionary service, had been always exempted. Certain brethren of influence, living in the capital, to whom I wrote on the subject, advised me, however, to write first to the president of the government of the province to which I belonged. This was done, but I was not exempted. Then those brethren wrote to the King himself; but he replied, that the matter must be referred to the ministry and to the law, and no exception was made in my favour.

I now knew not what to do. In the meantime, at the beginning of August, I was taken ill. It was a common cold at first, but I could not get rid of it, as formerly. At last a skillful physician was consulted, and powerful means were used. After some time, he prescribed tonics and wine. For a day or two I seemed to get better, but after that it appeared, by the return of giddiness in my head, that the tonics had been too soon resorted to. At last, having used still other means, I seemed in a fit state for tonics, and began again to take them. At the same time one of my friends, an American Professor, took me as a companion with him to Berlin and other places, so that we rode about the country for about ten days together. As long as I was day after day in the open air, going from place to place, drinking wine and taking tonics, I felt well; but as soon as I returned to Hale, the old symptoms returned. A second time the tonics were given up, and the former means used.

About ten weeks had by this time passed away, since I was first taken ill. This illness, in which a particular care for the body seemed to be so right, and in which therefore frequent walks were taken, and in which I thought myself justified in laying aside the study of Hebrew, &c., had not at all a beneficial effect on my soul. In connexion with this one of my chief companions at this time, the last-mentioned American Professor, was a backslider. If the believing reader does not know much of his own heart and of man's weakness, he will scarcely think it possible that, after I had been borne with by the Lord so long, and had received so many mercies at His hands, and had been so fully and freely pardoned through the blood of Jesus, which I both knew from His word, and had also enjoyed; and after that I had been in such various ways engaged in the work of the Lord; I should have been once more guilty of great backsliding, and that at the very time when the hand of God was lying heavily upon me. Oh! how desperately wicked is the human heart.

It was in this cold state of heart, that I rode with my friend to Leipsic, at the time of the famous Michaelmas fair. He wished me to go with him to the Opera. I went, but had not the least enjoyment. After the first act I took a glass of ice for refreshment. After the second act I was taken faint in consequence of this, my stomach being in a very weak state; but I was well enough; after a while, to go to the hotel, where I passed a tolerable night. On the next morning my friend ordered the carriage for our return to Halle. This circumstance the Lord graciously used as a means of arousing me; and on our way home, I freely opened my mind to my friend about the way in which we had been going on; and he then told me that he was in a different state of heart, when he left America. He also told me, when I was taken faint, that he thought it was an awful place to die in. This was the second and last time, since I have believed in the Lord Jesus, that I was in a theatre; and but once, in the year 1827, I went to a concert, when I likewise felt, that it was unbecoming for me, as a child of God, to be in such a place. On my return to Halle I broke a blood-vessel in my stomach, in consequence of the glass of ice. I was now exceedingly weak, in which state I continued far several weeks, and then went for change of air into the country, to the house of a beloved brother in the Lord, who, up to this day, has continued a kind and faithful friend to me. My heart was now again in a better state than it had been before the rupture of the blood-vessel, Thus the Lord, in the faithful love of His heart, seeing that I was in a backsliding state, chastised me for my profit; and the chastisement yielded, in a measure at least, the peaceable fruit of righteousness. Heb. xii. 10, 11.

Whilst I was staying in the country, I received a letter from the American Professor, who had in the meantime changed Halle for Berlin, and who wished me to come to Berlin, where, being near the Court, I should be more likely to obtain an exemption from my military duty; and he mentioned, at the same time, that all the expenses, connected with my staying in Berlin, would be fully covered by the remuneration I should receive for teaching German to himself and two of his friends, for a few hours every week. As I had no more connexion with the university at Halle, my course having been finished for more than six months past, and as I had the prospect of being spiritually benefited through my stay in Berlin, and there was no probability, if I remained at Halle, of obtaining the above-mentioned exemption, I came to the conclusion to go to Berlin.

Two ladies of title traveled with me to Berlin in a hired carriage. As I knew that we should be for two days together, I thought, in my fleshly wisdom, that though I ought to speak to them about the things of God, I should first show them kindness and attention, and that, after having thus opened a way to their hearts, I might fully set before them their state by nature, and point them to the Lamb of God. We went on together most amicably, I making only a few general remarks about divine things. On the second evening, however, when we were near the end of our journey, I felt that it was high time to speak. And no sooner had I begun plainly to do so, than one of them replied, "Oh! Sir, I wish you had spoken sooner about these things, for we have, for a long time, wished to have some one to whom we might open our hearts; but seeing that the ministers whom we know do not live consistently, we have been kept from speaking to them." I now found that they had been under conviction of sin for some time, but did not know the way to obtain peace, even by faith in the Lord Jesus. After this I spoke freely to them during the hour that yet remained. They parted from me under feelings of gratitude and regret that they could hear no more, for they only passed through Berlin. I felt myself greatly reproved, and all I could do was, by a long letter, to seek to make up for my deficiency in ministering to them on the journey. May this circumstance never be forgotten by me, and may it prove a blessing to the believing reader.

My chief concern now was how I might obtain a passport for England, through exemption from military duty. But the more certain brethren tried, though they knew how to set about the matter, and were also persons of rank, the greater difficulty there appeared to be in obtaining my object; so that in the middle of January 1829 it seemed as if I must immediately become a soldier. There was now but one more way untried, and it was at last resorted to. A believing major, who was on good terms with one of the chief generals, proposed that I should actually offer myself for entering the army, and that then I should be examined as to my bodily qualifications, in the hope, that, as I was still in a very weak state of body, I should be found unfit for military service. In that case it would belong to the chief general finally to settle the matter; who, being a godly man himself, on the major's recommendation would, no doubt, hasten the decision, on account of my desire to be a missionary to the Jews. At the same time it stood so, that, if I should be found fit for service, I should have to enter the army immediately.

Thus far the Lord had allowed things to go, to show me, it appears, that all my friends could not procure me a passport till His time was come. But now it was come. The King of kings had intended that I should go to England, because He would bless me there, and make me a blessing, though I was at that time, and am still most unworthy of it; and, therefore, though the King of Prussia had not been pleased to make an exemption in my favour, yet now all was made plain, and that at a time when hope had almost been given up, and when the last means had been resorted to. I was examined, and was declared to be unfit for military service. With a medical certificate to this effect, and a letter of recommendation from the major I went to this chief general, who received me very kindly and who himself wrote instantaneously to a second military physician, likewise to examine me at once. This was done, and it was by him confirmed that I was unfit. Now the chief general himself, as his adjutants happened to be absent, in order to hasten the matter, wrote with his own hands the papers which were needed, and I got a complete dismissal, and that for life, from all military engagements. This was much more than I could have expected. This military gentleman spoke to me in a very kind way, and pointed out certain parts of the Scriptures, which he in particular advised me to bring before the Jews, especially Romans xi.

On considering why the Lord delayed my obtaining this permission, I find that one of the reasons may have been, that I might both be profited myself by my stay in Berlin, and that I also might be instrumental in benefiting others. As to the first, I would mention, that I learned a lesson in Berlin which I did not know before. Whilst I was at Halle, I thought I should much enjoy being among so many christians as there are in Berlin. But when I was there I found, that enjoyment in the Lord does not depend upon the multitude of believers, by whom we are surrounded. As to the second point, perhaps the last day may show, that the Lord had some work for me in Berlin: for, from the time of my coming until I left, I preached three, four, or five times every week in the wards of a poorhouse, which was inhabited by about three hundred aged and infirm people. I also preached once in a church, and likewise visited one of the prisons several times on Lord's days to converse with the prisoners about their souls, where I was locked in by the keeper with the criminals in their cells.

On the whole my time in Berlin was not lost; and I was in a better state of heart than I had been for any length of time before, I was not once overcome by my former outward besetting sins, though I have nothing to boast of even as it regards that period; and were only the sins of those days brought against me, had I not the blood of Jesus to plead, I should be most miserable. But I think it right to mention, for the glory of God, as I have so freely spoken about my falls, that whilst I was more than ever unobserved by others; and whilst I was living in the midst of more gaiety and temptations than ever; and had far more money than at any previous time of my life; I was kept from things of which I had been habitually guilty in my unconverted days!—My health was in a very weak state, almost the whole time whilst I was staying in Berlin, and was in no degree better, till, on the advice of, a believing medical professor, I gave up all medicine.

Having now without any further difficulty obtained my passport, I left Berlin on February 3rd, 1829, for London. The Lord gave me more grace on my way from Berlin than on my way to it; for my mouth was almost immediately opened to my fellow-travelers, and the message of the Gospel seemed to be listened to with interest, particularly by one. On February 5th I arrived at my father's house; it was the place where I had lived as a boy, and the scene of many of my sins, my father having now returned to it after his retirement from office. I came to it with peculiar feelings. These feelings were not excited merely by the fact of my having been seven years absent from it, but arose from the spiritual change I had undergone since I last saw the place; for I had never been at Heimersleben since my father fetched me from thence, which was a few days after my imprisonment at Wolfenbüttel had come to an end. There were but three persons in the whole town with whom my soul had any fellowship. One of them had spent all his money in coal mines, and was then earning his daily bread by thrashing corn. As a boy I had in my heart laughed at him, for he seemed so different from all other people. Now I sought him out, having previously been informed that he was a believer, to acknowledge him as such, by having fellowship with him, and attending, a meeting in his house on the Lord's day evening. My soul was refreshed, and his also. Such a spiritual feast, as meeting with a brother, was a rare thing to him. May we believers who live in Great Britain, and especially those of us who are surrounded by many children of God, seek for grace, more highly to prize the blessings which, we enjoy through fellowship with brethren! This dear brother, who had then been a believer for more than twenty years, had only a few times heard the gospel preached during all that period. What a wonderful thing that I, one of the vilest of those brought up in that small town, should have been so abundantly favoured, as to have been brought to the knowledge of the truth, whilst none of all my relations, and scarcely one of those who grew up with me, so far as it has come to my knowledge, know the Lord!

I left my father's house on February 10th, with the prospect of seeing him again in about a twelvemonth, as a missionary among the Jews. But how has the Lord graciously altered matters!—I was kindly lodged for a night at Halberstadt by an aged brother, and then proceeded towards Rotterdam, by the way of Munster. At Munster I rested a few days, and was very kindly received by several brethren. They were officers in the army, and two of them had been, but a little while before this, Roman Catholics. I lodged in the house of a beloved brother, a tailor, who likewise had been a Roman Catholic.

About February 22nd I arrived at Rotterdam. I took lodgings in the house of a believer, where two German brethren lodged, whom I had known at Halle, and who intended to go out as missionaries in connexion with the Dutch Missionary Society. It was a peculiar feeling to me, for the first time in my life to find myself among Christians of another nation, to attend their family prayer, hear them sing, &c. In spirit I had fellowship with them, though our communication was but broken, as I understood but little of the Dutch language. Here also I heard for the first time the preaching of the Gospel in English, of which I knew enough to understand a part of what was said.—My going to England by the way of Rotterdam was not the usual way; but consulting with a brother in Berlin, who had been twice in England, I was told that this was the cheapest route. My asking this brother, to be profited by his experience, would have been quite right, had I, besides this, like Ezra, sought of the Lord the right way. Ezra viii. 21. But I sought unto men only, and not at all unto the Lord, in this matter. When I came to Rotterdam, I found that no vessels went at that time from that port to London, on account of the ice having just broken up in the river, and that it would be several weeks before the steamers would again begin to ply. Thus I had to wait nearly a month at Rotterdam, and, therefore, not only needed much more time than I should have required to go by way of Hamburgh, but also much more money.

On March 19th, 1829, I landed in London. I now found myself, in a great measure, as it regards liberty, brought back to the years when I was at school; yea, almost all the time I had been at school, and certainly for the last four years, previous to my coming to England, I was not so much bound to time and order as I was in this seminary; and had not there been a degree of grace in me, yea, so much as not to regard the liberty of the flesh, I should now probably have given up all idea of being a missionary to the Jews. But as I did not see that anything was expected from me which I could not conscientiously accede to, I thought it right to submit myself, for the Lord's sake, to all the regulations of the institution.

My brethren in the seminary, most of them Germans, had instruction in Hebrew, Latin, Greek, French, German, &c., scarcely any of them having had a classical education; I read only Hebrew, and was exempted from all the rest. I remember how I longed to be able to expound the Scriptures in English, when I heard a German brother do so, a few days after my arrival. And I also remember what joy it gave me, when a few weeks after, for the first time, I spoke in English to a little boy, whom I met alone in the fields, about his soul, thinking that he would bear with my broken English.—I now studied much, about twelve hours a day, chiefly Hebrew; commenced Chaldee; perfected myself in reading the German-Jewish in Rabbinic characters, committed portions of the Hebrew Old Testament to memory, &c.; and this I did with prayer, often falling on my knees, leaving my books for a little, that I might seek the Lord's blessing, and also, that I might be kept from that spiritual deadness, which is so frequently the result of much study. I looked up to the Lord even whilst turning over the leaves of my Hebrew dictionary, asking His help, that I might quickly find the words. I made comparatively little progress in English; for living with some of my countrymen, I was continually led to converse in German.

My experience in this particular leads me to remark, that, should this fall into the hands of any who are desirous to labour as missionaries among a people whose language is not their own, they should seek not merely to live among them, for the sake of soon learning their language, but also, as much as possible, to be separated from those who speak their own language; for, when, some months after, I was in Devonshire, completely separated from those who spoke German, I daily made much progress, whilst I made comparatively little in London.

Soon after my arrival in England, I heard one of the brethren in the seminary speak about a Mr. Groves, a dentist in Exeter, who, for the Lord's sake, had given up his profession, which brought him in about fifteen hundred pounds a year, and who intended to go as a missionary to Persia, with his wife and children, simply trusting in the Lord for temporal supplies. This made such an impression on me, and delighted me so, that I not only marked it down in my journal, but also wrote about it to my German friends.

I came to England weak in body, and in consequence of much study, as I suppose, I was taken ill on May 15, and was soon, at least in my own estimation, apparently, beyond recovery. The weaker I became in body, the happier I was in spirit. Never in my whole life had I seen myself so vile, so guilty, so altogether what I ought not to have been, as at this time. It was as if every sin, of which I had been guilty, was brought to my remembrance; but, at the same time, I could realize that all my sins were completely forgiven that I was washed and made clean, completely clean, in the blood of Jesus. The result of this was, great peace. I longed exceedingly to depart and to be with Christ. When my medical attendant came to see me, my prayer was something like this: "Lord, Thou knowest that he does not know what is for my real welfare, therefore do Thou direct him." When I took my medicine, my hearty prayer each time was something like this: "Lord, Thou knowest that this medicine is in itself nothing, no more than as if I were to take a little water. Now please, 0 Lord, to let it produce the effect which is for my real welfare, and for Thy glory. Let me either be taken soon to Thyself or let me be soon restored; let me be ill for a longer time, and then taken to Thyself, or let me be ill for a longer time, and then restored. 0 Lord, do with me as seemeth Thee best!" One sin in particular was brought to my mind, which I never had seen before, viz., that whilst all my life, even in former sicknesses, I had been blessed with uninterrupted refreshing sleep, which now, for some nights, had almost entirely fled from my eyes, I had never heartily thanked God for it.

After I had been ill about a fortnight, my medical attendant unexpectedly pronounced me better. This, instead of giving me joy, bowed me down, so great was my desire to be with the Lord; though almost immediately afterwards grace was given me to submit myself to the will of God. After some days I was able to leave my room. Whilst recovering I still continued in a spiritual state of heart, desiring to depart and to be with Christ. As I recovered but slowly, my friends entreated me to go into the country for change of air; but my heart was in such a happy and spiritual frame, that I did not like the thought of traveling and seeing places. So far was I changed, who once had been so passionately fond of traveling. But as my friends continued to advise me to go into the country, I thought at last that it might be the will of God that I should do so, and I prayed therefore thus to the Lord: "Lord, I will gladly submit myself to Thy will, and go if Thou wilt have me to go. And now let me know Thy will by the answer of my medical attendant. If, in reply to my question, he says it would be very good for me, I will go; but if he says it is of no great importance, then I will stay." When I asked him, he said that it was the best thing I could do. I was then enabled willingly to submit, and accordingly went to Teignmouth. It was there that I became acquainted with my beloved brother, friend, and fellow-labourer, Henry Craik.

A few days after my arrival at Teignmouth, the chapel, called Ebenezer, was reopened, and I attended the opening. I was much impressed by one of those who preached on the occasion. For though I did not like all he said, yet I saw a gravity and solemnity in him different from the rest. After he had preached, I had a great desire to know more of him; and being invited by two brethren of Exmouth, in whose house he was staying, to spend some time with them, I had an opportunity of living ten days with him under the same roof. Through the instrumentality of this brother the Lord bestowed a great blessing upon me, for which I shall have cause to thank Him throughout eternity.

I will mention some points which God then began to show me.

1. That the word of God alone is our standard of judgment in spiritual things; that it can be explained only by the Holy Spirit; and that in our day, as well as in former times, He is the teacher of His people. The office of the Holy Spirit I had not experimentally understood before that time. Indeed, of the office of each of the blessed persons, in what is commonly called the Trinity, I had no experimental apprehension. I had not before seen from the Scriptures that the Father chose us before the foundation of the world; that in Him that wonderful plan of our redemption originated, and that He also appointed all the means by which it was to be brought about. Further, that the Son, to save us, had fulfilled the law, to satisfy its demands, and with it also the holiness of God; that He had borne the punishment due to our sins, and had thus satisfied the justice of God. And further, that the Holy Spirit alone can teach us about our state by nature, show us the need of a Saviour, enable us to believe in Christ, explain to us the Scriptures, help us in preaching, &c. It was my beginning to understand this latter point in particular, which had a great effect on me; for the Lord enabled me to put it to the test of experience, by laying aside commentaries, and almost every other book, and simply reading the word of God and studying it. The result of this was, that the first evening that I shut myself into my room, to give myself to prayer and meditation over the Scriptures, I learned more in a few hours than I had done during a period of several months previously. But the particular difference was, that I received real strength for my soul in doing so. I now began to try by the test of the Scriptures the things which I had learned and seen, and found that only those principles, which stood the test, were really of value.

2. Before this period I had been much opposed to the doctrines of election, particular redemption, and final persevering grace; so much so that, a few days after my arrival at Teignmouth, I called election a devilish doctrine. I did not believe that I had brought myself to the Lord, for that was too manifestly false; but yet I held, that I might have resisted finally. And further, I knew nothing about the choice of God's people, and did not believe that the child of God, when once made so, was safe for ever. In my fleshly mind I had repeatedly said, If once I could prove that I am a child of God for ever, I might go back into the world for a year or two, and then

return to the Lord, and at last be saved. But now I was brought to examine these precious truths by the word of God. Being made willing to have no glory of my own in the conversion of sinners, but to consider myself merely as an instrument; and being made willing to receive what the Scriptures said; I went to the Word, reading the New Testament from the beginning, with a particular reference to these truths. To my great astonishment I found that the passages which speak decidedly for election and persevering grace, were about four times as many as those which speak apparently against these truths; and even those few, shortly after, when I had examined and understood them, served to confirm me in the above doctrines. As to the effect which my belief in these doctrines had on me, I am constrained to state, for God's glory, that though I am still exceedingly weak, and by no means so dead to the lusts of the flesh, and the lust of the eyes, and the pride of life, as I might and as I ought to be, yet, by the grace of God, I have walked more closely with Him since that period. My life has not been so variable, and I may say that I have lived much more for God than before. And for this have I been strengthened by the Lord, in a great measure, through the instrumentality of these truths. For in the time of temptation, I have been repeatedly led to say: Should I thus sin? I should only bring misery into my soul for a time, and dishonour God; for, being a son of God for ever, I should have to be brought back again, though it might be in the way of severe chastisement. Thus, I say, the electing love of God in Christ (when I have been able to realize it) has often been the means of producing holiness, instead of leading me into sin. It is only the notional apprehension of such truths, the want of having them in the heart, whilst they are in the head, which is dangerous.

3. Another truth, into which, in a measure, I was led during my stay in Devonshire, respected the Lord's coming. My views concerning this point, up to that time, had been completely vague and unscriptural. I had believed what others told me, without trying it by the Word. I thought that things were getting better and better, and that soon the whole world would be converted. But now I found in the Word, that we have not the least Scriptural warrant to look for the conversion of the world before the return of our Lord. I found in the Scriptures, that that which will usher in the glory of the church,

and uninterrupted joy to the saints, is the return of the Lord Jesus, and that, till then, things will be more or less in confusion. I found in the Word, that the return of Jesus, and not death, was the hope of the apostolic Christians; and that it became me, therefore, to look for His appearing. And this truth entered so into my heart, that, though I went into Devonshire exceedingly weak, scarcely expecting that I should return again to London, yet I was immediately, on seeing the truth, brought off from looking for death, and was made to look for the return of the Lord. Having seen this truth, the Lord also graciously enabled me to apply it, in some measure at least, to my own heart, and to put the solemn question to myself—What may I do for the Lord, before He returns, as He may soon come?

4. In addition to these truths, it pleased the Lord to lead me to see a higher standard of devotedness than I had seen before. He led me, in a measure, to see what is my true glory in this world, even to be despised, and to be poor and mean with Christ. I saw then, in a measure, though I have seen it more fully since, that it ill becomes the servant to seek to be rich, and great, and honoured in that world, where his Lord was poor, and mean, and despised.

I do not mean to say that all that which I believe at present concerning these truths, and those which, in connexion with them, the Lord has shown me since August 1829, were apprehended all at once; and much less did I see them all at once with the same clearness, as, by the grace of God, I do now; yet my stay in Devonshire was a most profitable time to my soul. My prayer had been, before I left London, that the Lord would be pleased to bless my journey to the benefit of my body and soul. This prayer was answered in both respects; for in the beginning of September I returned to London much better in body; and, as to my soul, the change was so great, that it was like a second conversion.

After my return to London, I sought to benefit my brethren in the seminary, and the means which I used were these. I proposed to them to meet together every morning from six to eight for prayer and reading the Scriptures, and that then each of us should give out what he might consider the Lord had shown him to be the meaning of the portion read. One brother in particular was brought into the same state as myself; and others, I trust, were more or less benefited. Several times, when I went to my room after family prayer in the evening, I found communion with God so sweet, that I continued in prayer till after twelve, and then, being full of joy, went into the room of the brother just referred to; and, finding him also in a similar frame of heart, we continued praying until one or two and even then I was a few times so full, of joy, that I could scarcely sleep, and at six in the morning again called the brethren together for prayer.

All this moreover did not leave me idle, as it regards actual engagements in the Lord's work, as I will now show. After I had been for about ten days in London, and had been confined to the house on account of my studies, my health began again to decline; and I saw that it would not be well, my poor body being only like a wreck or brand brought out of the devil's service, to spend my little remaining strength in study, but that I now ought to set about actual engagements in the Lord's work, particularly as He had now given me more light about His truth, and also a heart to serve Him. I consequently wrote to the committee of the Society, requesting them to send me out at once, as they had now had an opportunity of knowing me; and, that they might do so with more confidence, to send me as a fellow-labourer to an experienced brother. However I received no answer.

After having waited about five or six weeks, in the meantime seeking in one way or other to labour for the Lord, it struck me that I was wrong and acting unscripturally, in waiting for the appointment to missionary work from my fellow-men; but that, considering myself called by the Lord to preach the gospel, I ought to begin at once to labour among the Jews in London, whether I had the title of missionary or not. In consequence of this I distributed tracts among the Jews, with my name and residence written on them, thus inviting them to conversation about the things of God; preached to them in those places where they most numerously collect together; read the Scriptures regularly with about fifty Jewish boys; and became a teacher in a Sunday school. In this work I had much enjoyment and the honour of being reproached and ill-treated for the name of Jesus. But the Lord gave me grace, never to be kept from the work by any danger, or the prospect of any suffering.

My light increased more and more during the months of September, October, and November. At the end of November it became a point of solemn consideration with me, whether I could remain connected with the Society in the usual way. My chief objections were these: 1. If I were sent out by the Society, it was more than probable, yea, almost needful, if I were to leave England, that I should labour on the Continent, as I was unfit to be sent to eastern countries on account of my health, which would probably have suffered, both on account of the climate, and of my having to learn other languages. Now, if I did go to the Continent, it was evident, that without ordination I could not have any extensive field of usefulness, as unordained ministers are generally prevented from labouring freely there; but I could not conscientiously submit to be ordained by unconverted men, professing to have power to set me apart for the ministry, or to communicate something to me for this work which they do not possess themselves. Besides this, I had other objections to being connected with any state church or national religious establishment, which arose from the increased light which I had obtained through the reception of this truth, that the word of God is our only standard, and the Holy Spirit our only teacher. For as I now began to compare what I knew of the establishment in England and those on the Continent, with this only true standard, the word of God, I found that all establishments, even because they are establishments, i.e. the world and the church mixed up together, not only contain in them the principles which necessarily must lead to departure from the word of God; but also, as long as they remain establishments, entirely preclude the acting throughout according to the Holy Scriptures. – Then again, if I were to stay in England, the Society would not allow me to preach in any place indiscriminately, where the Lord might open a door for me; and to the ordination of English bishops I had still greater objections, than to the ordination of a Prussian Consistory. 2. I further had a conscientious objection against being led and directed by men in my missionary labours. As a servant of Christ it appeared to me, I ought to be guided by the Spirit, and not by men, as to time and place; and this I would say, with all deference to others, who may be much more taught and much more spiritually minded than myself. A servant of Christ has but one Master. 3. I had love for the Jews, and I had been enabled to give proofs of it; yet I could not conscientiously say, as the committee would expect from me, that I would spend the greater part of my time only among them. For the scriptural plan seemed to me, that, in coming to a place, I should seek out the Jews, and commence my labour particularly among them; but that, if they rejected the gospel, I should go to the nominal Christians—The more I weighed these points, the more it appeared to me that I should be acting hypocritically, were I to suffer them to remain in my mind, without making them known to the committee.

The question that next occurred to me was, how I ought to act if not sent out by the Society. With my views I could not return to Prussia; for I must either refrain from preaching, or imprisonment would be the result. The only plan that presented itself to me was, that I should go from place to place throughout England, as the Lord might direct me, and give me opportunity, preaching wherever I went, both among Jews and nominal Christians. To this mode of service I was especially stirred up through the recently received truth of the Lord's second coming, having it impressed upon my heart to seek to warn sinners, and to stir up the saints; as He might soon come. At the same time it appeared to me well, that I should do this in connexion with the Society for promoting Christianity among the Jews, serving them without any salary, provided they would accept me on these conditions. An objection which came to my mind against taking any step which might lead to the dissolution of my connexion with the Society, namely, that I had been some expense to it, and that thus I should appear ungrateful, and the money would seem to have been thrown away, was easily removed in this way:

1. When I engaged with the Society, I did it according to the light I then had. 2. I have but one Master; His is the money, and to Him I have to give an account. 3. Though I have nothing to boast of, but much reason to be ashamed before God on account of my lack of service; yet, speaking after the manner of men, in some measure I did work, not only in the Lord's service, but even in that particular line for which the money had been put into the hands of the committee.

There remained now only one point more to be settled:

How I should do for the future as it regarded the supply of my temporal wants, which naturally would have been a great obstacle, especially as I was not merely a foreigner, but spoke so little English, that whilst I was greatly assisted in expounding the Scriptures, it was with difficulty I could converse about common things. On this point, however, I had no anxiety; for I considered, that, as long as I really sought to serve the Lord, that is, as long as I sought the kingdom of God and His righteousness, these my temporal supplies would be added to me. The Lord most mercifully enabled me to take the promises of His word, and rest upon them, and such as Matthew vii. 7, 8, John xiv. 13, 14, Matthew vi. 25-34, were the stay of my soul concerning this point. In addition to this, the example of brother Groves, the dentist before alluded to, who gave up his profession, and went out as a missionary, was a great encouragement to me. For the news, which by this time had arrived, of how the Lord had aided him on his way to Petersburg, and at Petersburg, strengthened my faith.

At last, on December 12, 1829, I came to the conclusion to dissolve my connexion with the Society, if they would not accept my services under the above conditions, and to go throughout the country preaching, (being particularly constrained to do so from a desire to serve the Lord as much as in me lay, BEFORE HIS RETURN), and to trust in Him for the supply of my temporal wants. Yet at the same time it appeared well to me to wait a month longer, and to consider the matter still further, before I wrote to the committee, that I might be sure I had weighed it fully.

On December 24th I went to the Church Missionary Institution at Islington, in the hope of benefiting the students there, if it were the Lord's will. I returned very happy, as I almost invariably was at that time, and went to bed full of joy. Next morning, (being that of Christmas day), I awoke in a very different state of heart from what I had experienced for many weeks past. I had no enjoyment, and felt cold and lifeless in prayer. At our usual morning meeting, however, one of the brethren exhorted me to continue to pray, saying that the Lord surely would again smile on me, though now for a season, for wise purposes, He seemed to have withdrawn Himself. I did so. At the Lord's table, in the morning, a measure of enjoyment returned. Afterwards I dined in a family, in company with the brother just referred to. My former enjoyment gradually returned. Towards evening the Lord gave me an opportunity of speaking about His return, and I had great enjoyment in doing so. At eight o'clock I was asked to expound at family prayer, and was much assisted by the Lord. About half an hour after the exposition was over, I was requested to come out of the room to see one of the servants, and the mother of another of the servants, who had been present at family prayer. I found them in tears, and both deeply impressed and under concern about their souls. I then went home, at least as happy as on the previous evening. I have related this circumstance, because I am aware that it is a common temptation of Satan to make us give up the reading of the Word and prayer when our enjoyment is gone; as if it were of no use to read the Scriptures when we do not enjoy them, and as if it were of no use to pray when we have no spirit of prayer; whilst the truth is, in order to enjoy the Word, we ought to continue to read it, and the way to obtain a spirit of prayer, is, to continue praying; for the less we read the word of God, the less we desire to read it, and the less we pray, the less we desire to pray.

About the beginning of the next year my fellow students had a fortnight's vacation, and as with them I had conformed myself to the order of the Institution, I felt that I might also partake of their privileges; not indeed to please the flesh, but to serve the Lord. On December 30th, I therefore left London for Exmouth, where I intended to spend my vacation in the house of my Christian friends, who had kindly lodged me the summer before, that I might preach there during this fortnight, and still more fully weigh the matter respecting my proposal to time Society. I arrived at Exmouth on December 31st, at six in the evening, an hour before the commencement of a prayer-meeting at Ebenezer Chapel. My heart was burning with a desire to tell of the Lord's goodness to my soul, and to speak forth what I considered might not be known to most with whom I met. Being, however, not called on, either to speak or pray, I was silent. The next morning I spoke on the difference between being a Christian and a happy Christian, and showed, whence it generally comes, that we rejoice so little in the Lord. This my first testimony was blessed to many believers, that God, as it appears, might show me that He was with me. Among others it proved a blessing to a Christian female, who had been for ten years in bondage, and who, in the providence of God, had been brought from Exeter to be present that morning. This she told me many months after, when I met her on a journey.

At the request of several believers I spoke again in the afternoon, and also proposed a meeting in the chapel every morning at ten, to expound the epistle to the Romans. I had also most days a meeting in a room with several ladies, for reading the Scriptures with them. This I did that I might make the best of my fortnight. The second day after my arrival, a brother said to me: "I have been praying for this month past that the Lord would do something for Lympstone, a large parish where there is little spiritual light. There is a Wesleyan chapel, and I doubt not you would be allowed to preach there." Being ready to speak of Jesus wherever the Lord might open a door, yet so, that I could be faithful to the truths which he had been pleased to teach me, I went, and easily obtained liberty to preach twice on the next day, being the Lord's day. Besides this I preached in another village near Exmouth; so that I spoke once, twice, or three times in public or private meetings every day for the first ten or twelve days, and that with great enjoyment to my own soul.

During the first days of January, 1830, whilst at Exmouth, it became more and more clear to me, that I could not be connected with the Society under the usual conditions; and as I had an abundance of work where I was, and little money to spend in traveling (for all I possessed was about five pounds), it appeared best to me to write at once to the committee, that, whilst they were coming to a decision respecting me, I might continue to preach. I therefore wrote to them, stating what had been my views before I became acquainted with them, and what they were now. I also stated my difficulty in remaining, connected with them on the usual terms, as stated in substance above; and then concluded, that as, however, I owed them much, as having been instrumental in bringing me to England, where the Lord had blessed me so abundantly: and as I, also, should like to obtain from them the Hebrew Scriptures and tracts for the Jews: I would gladly serve them without any salary, if they would allow me to labour in regard to time and place as the Lord might direct me. Some time after I received a very kind private letter from one of the secretaries, who always had been very kind to me, together with the following official communication from the committee.

"London Society for promoting Christianity amongst the Jews."

At a Meeting of the Missionary Sub-Committee, held January 27, 1830, Society House, 10, Wardrobe Place, Doctors' Commons, a Letter was read from Mr. G. F. Müller.

"Resolved, That Mr. Müller be informed, that while the committee cordially rejoice in any real progress in knowledge and grace which he may have made under the teaching of the Holy Spirit, they, nevertheless, consider it inexpedient for any society to employ those who are unwilling to submit themselves to their guidance with respect to missionary operations; and that while, therefore, Mr. Müller holds his present opinions on that point, the committee cannot consider him as a missionary student; but should more mature reflection cause him to alter that opinion, they will readily enter into further communication with him."

Thus my connexion with the Society was entirely dissolved. Fifty-two years have passed away since, and I never have, even for one single moment, regretted the step I took, but have to be sorry that I have been so little grateful for the Lord's goodness to me in that matter. The following part of the Narrative also will prove to the enlightened reader, how God blessed my acting out the light He had been pleased to give me. But I cannot leave this subject, without adding, that it is far from my intention to throw any blame upon the Society. I have no wish to do so: nay, I confess, were the last-mentioned circumstances not so intimately connected with my being in England, I would rather have left out the matter altogether. But being under the necessity of saying something about my connexion with it, it appeared best to me to relate the circumstances just as they were. Yet I do testify that I have not done it in the least for the sake of injuring the Society; for I have received much kindness from some of those connected with it, particularly from two worthy men, then taking a prominent part in managing its affairs. If I be judged differently, I can only say, "Judge nothing before the time, until the Lord come."

After I had preached about three weeks at Exmouth and its neighbourhood, I went to Teignmouth, with the intention of staying there ten days, to preach the Word among the brethren with whom I had become acquainted during the previous summer, and thus to tell them of the Lord's goodness to me. One of the brethren said almost immediately on my arrival at Teignmouth, I wish you would become our minister, as the present one is going to leave us. My answer was, I do not intend to be stationary in any place, but to go through the country, preaching the Word as the Lord may direct me. In the evening, Monday, I preached for brother Craik, at Shaldon, in the presence of three ministers, none of whom liked the sermon; yet it pleased God, through it, to bring to the knowledge of His dear Son, a young woman who had been servant to one of these ministers, and who had heard her master preach many times. How differently does the Lord judge from man! Here was a particular opportunity for the Lord to get glory to Himself. A foreigner was the preacher, with great natural obstacles in the way, for he was not able to speak English with fluency; but he had a desire to serve God, and was by this time also brought into such a state of heart as to desire that God alone should have the glory, if any good were done through his instrumentality. How often has it struck me, both at that time and since, that His strength was made perfect in my weakness.

On Tuesday evening I preached at Ebenezer Chapel, Teignmouth, the same chapel at the opening of which I became acquainted with the brother, whom the Lord had afterwards used as an instrument of benefiting me so much. My preaching was also disliked there by many of the hearers; but the Lord opened the hearts of a few to receive the truth, and another young woman was brought to the Lord through the instrumentality of the word then preached. On Wednesday I preached again in the same chapel, and the word was disliked still, perhaps more, though the few, who received the truth in the love of it, increased in number. On Thursday I preached again at Shaldon, and on Friday at Teignmouth. The effect was the same; dislike on the one side, and joy and delight in the truth on the other. By this time I began to reflect about the cause of this opposition; for the same brethren who had treated me with much kindness the summer previous, when I was less spiritually minded, and understood much less of the truth, now seemed to oppose me, and I could not explain it in any other way than this, that the Lord intended to work through my instrumentality at Teignmouth, and that therefore Satan, fearing this, sought to raise opposition against me.

On the Lord's day I dined with a brother, whose heart the Lord had opened to receive me as a servant of Christ. After dinner I talked to a young woman, his servant, at the request of her sister, who on the Tuesday previous had been convinced of sin, and on the Friday brought to enjoy peace in the Lord. This young woman also was, through the instrumentality of this conversation, brought to see her sinful state, though she could not rejoice in the Lord until about seven months after. How differently the Lord dealt with her sister, and yet the work of grace was as real in the one as in the other, as I had full opportunity of seeing afterwards! On this same Lord's day I preached twice at Teignmouth, and once at Shaldon; for so precious did every opportunity seem to me, and so powerfully did I feel the importancc of those precious truths, which I had so recently been led to see, that I longed to be instrumental in communicating them to others.

By this time the request, that I might stay at Teignmouth, and be the minister of the above chapel, had been repeatedly expressed by an increasing number of the brethren; but others were decidedly against my remaining there. This opposition was instrumental in settling it in my mind that I should stay for awhile, at least until I was formally rejected. In consequence of this conclusion I took the following step, which, it may be, I should not repeat under similar circumstances, but which was certainly taken in love to those who were concerned in the matter, and for the glory of God, as far as I then had light.

On the Tuesday following, after preaching, I told the brethren how, in the providence of God, I had been brought to them without the least intention of staying among them, but that, on finding them without a minister, I had been led to see it to be the will of God to remain with them. I also told them, as far as I remember, that I was aware of the opposition of some, but that I nevertheless intended to preach to them till they rejected me; and if they should say, I might preach, but they would give me no salary, that would make no difference on my part, as I did not preach for the sake of money; but I told them, at the same time, that it was an honour, to be allowed to supply the temporal wants of any of the servants of Christ. The latter point I added, as it seemed right to me, to give out the whole counsel of God, as far as I knew it. On the next day, Wednesday, I left, and having preached in two or three places near Exmouth, and taken leave of my friends there, I returned to Teignmouth.

Here I preached again three times on the Lord's day, none saying we wish you not to preach, though many of the hearers did not hear with enjoyment. Some of them left, and never returned; some left, but returned after awhile. Others came to the chapel, who had not been in the habit of attending there previous to my coming. There was sufficient proof that the work of God was going on, for there were those who were glad to hear what I preached, overlooking the infirmities of the foreigner, delighting in the food for their souls, without caring much about the form in which the truth was set before them; and these were not less spiritual than the rest: and there were those who objected decidedly; some, however, manifesting merely the weakness of brethren, and others the bitterness of the opposers of the cross. There was, in addition to this, a great stir, a spirit of inquiry, and a searching of the Scriptures, whether these things were so. And what is more than all, God set His seal upon the work, in converting sinners. Twelve weeks I stood in this same position, whilst the Lord graciously supplied my temporal wants, through two brethren, unasked for. After this time, the whole little church, eighteen in number, unanimously gave me an invitation to become their pastor. My answer to them was, that their invitation did not show me more than I had seen before, that it was the will of God that I should remain with them, yet that for their sakes I could not but rejoice in this invitation, as it was a proof to me that God had blessed them through my instrumentality, in making them thus of one mind. I also expressly stated to the brethren, that I should only stay so long with them, as I saw it clearly to be the will of the Lord; for I had not given up my intention of going from place to place, if the Lord would allow me to do so. The brethren, at the same time, now offered to supply my temporal wants, by giving me £55. a year, which sum was afterwards somewhat increased, on account of the increase of the church.

I now had Teignmouth for my residence, but I did not confine my labours to this place; for I preached regularly once a week in Exeter, once a fortnight at Topsham, sometimes at Shaldon, often at Exmouth, sometimes in the above-mentioned villages near Exmouth, regularly once a week at Bishopsteignton, where a part of the church lived, and afterwards repeatedly at Chudleigh, Collumpton, Newton Bushel, and elsewhere.

That which I now considered the best mode of preparation for the public ministry of the Word, no longer adopted from necessity, on account of want of time, but from deep conviction, and from the experience of God's blessing upon it, both as it regards my own enjoyment, the benefit of the saints, and the conversion of sinners, is as follows:—1. I do not presume to know myself what is best for the hearers, and I therefore ask the Lord in the first place, that He would graciously be pleased to teach me on what subject I shall speak, or what portion of His word I shall expound. Now sometimes it happens, that previous to my asking Him, a subject or passage has been in my mind, on which it has appeared well for me to speak. In that case I ask the Lord, whether I should speak on this subject or passage. If, after prayer, I feel persuaded that I should I fix upon it, yet so, that I would desire to leave myself open to the Lord to change it, if He please. Frequently, however, it occurs, that I have no text or subject in my mind, before I give myself to prayer for the sake of ascertaining the Lord's will concerning it. In this case I wait some time on my knees for an answer, trying to listen to the voice of the Spirit to direct me. If then a passage or subject, whilst I am on my knees, or after I have finished praying for a text, is brought to my mind, I again ask the Lord, and that sometimes repeatedly, especially if, humanly speaking, the subject or text should be a peculiar one, whether it be His will that I should speak on such a subject or passage. If after prayer my mind is peaceful about it, I take this to be the text, but still desire to leave myself open to the Lord for direction, should He please to alter it, or should I have been mistaken. Frequently also, in the third place, it happens, that I not only have no text nor subject on my mind previous to my praying for guidance in this matter, but also I do not obtain one after once, or twice, or more times praying about it. I used formerly at times to be much perplexed, when this was the case, but for more than forty-five years it has pleased the Lord, in general at least, to keep me in peace about it. What I do is, to go on with my regular reading of the Scriptures, where I left off the last time, praying (whilst I read) for a text, now and then also laying aside my bible for prayer, till I get one. Thus it has happened, that I have had to read five, ten; yea twenty chapters, before it has pleased the Lord to give me a text: yea, many times I have even had to go to the place of meeting without one, and obtained it perhaps only a few minutes before I was going to speak; but I have never lacked the Lord's assistance at the time of preaching, provided I had earnestly sought it in private. The preacher cannot know the particular state of the various individuals who compose the congregation, nor what they require, but the Lord knows it; and if the preacher renounces his own wisdom, he will be assisted by the Lord; but if he will choose in his own wisdom, then let him not be surprised if he should see little benefit result from his labours.

Before I leave this part of the subject, I would just observe one temptation concerning the choice of a text. We may see a subject to be so very full, that it may strike us it would do for some other occasion. For instance, sometimes a text, brought to one's mind for a week-evening meeting, may appear more suitable for the Lord's day, because then there would be a greater number of hearers present. Now, in the first place, we do not know whether the Lord ever will allow us to preach on another Lord's day; and, in the second place, we know not whether that very subject may not be especially suitable for some or many individuals present just that week-evening. Thus I was once tempted, after I had been a short time at Teignmouth, to reserve a subject, which had been just opened to me, for the next Lord's day. But being able, by the grace of God, to overcome the temptation by the above reasons, and preaching about it at once, it pleased the Lord to bless it to the conversion of a sinner, and that too an individual who meant to come but that once more to the chapel, and to whose case the subject was most remarkably suited.

2. Now when the text has been obtained in the above way, whether it be one or two or more verses, or a whole chapter or more, I ask the Lord that He would graciously be pleased to teach me by His Holy Spirit, whilst meditating over it. Within the last fifty years, I have found it the most profitable plan to meditate with my pen in my hand, writing down the outlines, as the Word is opened

to me. This I do, not for the sake of committing them to memory, nor as if I meant to say nothing else, but for the sake of clearness, as being a help to see how far I understand the passage. I also find it useful afterwards to refer to what I have thus written. I very seldom use any other help besides the little I understand of the original of the Scriptures, and some good translations in other languages. My chief help is prayer. I have NEVER in my life begun to study one single part of divine truth, without gaining some light about it, when I have been able really to give myself to prayer and meditation over it. But that I have often found a difficult matter, partly on account of the weakness of the flesh, and partly also on account of bodily infirmities and multiplicity of engagements. This I most firmly believe, that no one ought to expect to see much good resulting from his labours in word and doctrine, if he is not much given to prayer and meditation.

3. Having prayed and meditated on the subject or text, I desire to leave myself entirely in the hands of the Lord. I ask Him to bring to my mind what I have seen in my room, concerning the subject I am going to speak on, which He generally most kindly does, and often teaches me much additionally, whilst I am preaching.

In connection with the above, I must, however, state, that it appears to me there is a preparation for the public ministry of the Word, which is even more excellent than the one spoken of. It is this: to live in such constant and real communion with the Lord, and to be so habitually and frequently in meditation over the truth, that without the above effort, so to speak, we have obtained food for others, and know the mind of the Lord as to the subject or the portion of the Word on which we should speak. But this I have only in a small measure experienced, though I desire to be brought into such a state, that habitually "out of my belly may flow rivers of living water."

That which I have found most beneficial in my experience for the last fifty-one years in the public ministry of the Word, is, expounding the Scriptures, and especially the going now and then through a whole gospel or epistle. This may be done in a two-fold way, either by entering minutely into the bearing of every point occurring in the portion, or by giving the general outlines, and thus leading the hearers to see the meaning and connexion of the whole. The benefits which I have seen resulting from expounding the Scriptures are these: 1. The hearers are thus, with God's blessing, led to the Scriptures. They find, as it were, a practical use of them in the public meetings. This induces them to bring their bibles, and I have observed that those who at first did not bring them, have afterwards been induced to do so: so that in a short time few, of the believers at least, were in the habit of coming without them. This is no small matter; for every thing, which in our day will lead believers to value the Scriptures, is of importance. 2. The expounding of the Scriptures is in general more beneficial to the hearers than if, on a single verse, or half a verse, or two or three words of a verse some remarks are made, so that the portion of Scripture is scarcely anything but a motto for the subject; for few have grace to meditate much over the Word, and thus exposition may not merely be the means of opening up to them the Scriptures, but may also create in them a desire to meditate for themselves. 3. The expounding of the Scriptures leaves to the hearers a connecting link, so that the reading over again the portion of the Word, which has been expounded, brings to their remembrance what has been said; and thus, with God's blessing, leaves a more lasting impression on their minds. This is particularly of importance as it regards the illiterate, who sometimes have neither much strength of memory nor capacity of comprehension. 4. The expounding of large portions of the Word, as the whole of a gospel or an epistle, besides leading the hearer to see the connexion of the whole, has also this particular benefit for the teacher, that it leads him, with God's blessing, to the consideration of portions of the Word, which otherwise he might not have considered, and keeps him from speaking too much on favourite subjects, and leaning too much to particular parts of truth, which tendency must surely sooner or later injure both himself and his hearers.—Expounding the word of God brings little honour to the preacher from the unenlightened or careless hearer, but it tends much to the benefit of the hearers in general.

Simplicity in expression, whilst the truth is set forth, is, in connexion with what has been said, of the utmost importance. It should be the aim of the teacher to speak so, that children, servants, and people who cannot read, may be able to understand him, so far as the natural mind can comprehend the things of God. It ought also to be remembered, that there is, perhaps, not a single congregation in which there are not persons of the above classes present, and that if they can understand, the well-educated or literary persons will understand likewise; but the reverse does not hold good. It ought further to be remembered that the expounder of the truth of God speaks for God, for eternity, and that it is not in the least likely that he will benefit the hearers, except he uses plainness of speech, which nevertheless needs not to be vulgar or rude. It should also be considered, that if the preacher strive to speak according to the rules of this world, he may please many, Particularly those who have a literary taste; but, in the same proportion, he is less likely to become an instrument in the hands of God for the conversion of sinners, or for the building up of the saints. For neither eloquence nor depth of thought make the truly great preacher, but such a life of prayer and meditation and spirituality, as may render him a vessel meet for the Master's use, and fit to be employed both in the conversion of sinners and in the edification of the saints.

About the beginning of April I went to preach at Sidmouth. While I was staying there, three sisters in the Lord had, in my presence, a conversation about baptism, one of whom had been baptized after she had believed. When they had conversed a little on the subject, I was asked to give my opinion concerning it. My reply was, "I do not think, that I need to be baptized again." I was then asked by the sister who bad been baptized, "But have you been baptized?" I answered, "Yes, when I was a child." She then replied, "Have you ever read the Scriptures, and prayed with reference to this subject?" I answered, "No." "Then," she said, "I entreat you, never to speak any more about it till you have done so." It pleased the Lord to show me the importance of this remark; for whilst at that very time I was exhorting every one to receive nothing which could not be proved by the word of God, I had repeatedly spoken against believers' baptism, without having ever earnestly examined the Scriptures, or prayed concerning it; and now I determined, if God would help me, to examine that subject also, and if infant baptism were found to be scriptural, I would earnestly defend it; and if believers' baptism were right, I would as strenuously defend that, and be baptized.

As soon as I had time, I set about examining the subject. The mode I adopted was as follows: I repeatedly asked God to teach me concerning it, and I read the New Testament from the beginning, with a particular reference to this point. But now, when I earnestly set about the matter, a number of objections presented themselves to my mind.

1. Since many holy and enlightened men have been divided in opinion concerning this point, does this not prove, that it is not to be expected we should come to a satisfactory conclusion about this question in the present imperfect state of the church?—This question was thus removed: If this ordinance is revealed in the Bible, why may I not know it, as the Holy Spirit is the teacher in the church of Christ now as well as formerly? 2. There have been but few of my friends baptized, and the greater part of them are opposed to believers' baptism, and they will turn their backs on me. Answer: Though all men should forsake me, if the Lord Jesus takes me up, I shall be happy. 3. You will be sure to lose one half of your income if you are baptized. Answer: As long as I desire to be faithful to the Lord, He will not suffer me to want. 4. People will call you a baptist, and you will be reckoned among that body, and you cannot approve of all that is going on among them. Answer: It does not follow that I must in all points go along with all those who hold believers' baptism, although I should be baptized. 5. You have been preaching for some years, and you will have thus publicly to confess, that you have been in an error, should you be led to see that believers' baptism is right. Answer: It is much better to confess that I have been in error concerning that point than to continue in it. 6. Even if believers' baptism should be right, yet it is now too late to attend to it, as you ought to have been baptized immediately on believing. Answer: It is better to fulfill a commandment of the Lord Jesus ever so late, than to continue in the neglect of it.

It had pleased God, in his abundant mercy, to bring my mind into such a state, that I was willing to carry out into my life whatever I should find in the Scriptures concerning this ordinance, either the one way or the other. I could say, "I will do His will," and it was on that account, I believe, that I soon saw which "doctrine is of God," whether infant baptism or believers' baptism. And I would observe here, by the way, that the passage to which I have just now alluded,

John vii. 17, has been a most remarkable comment to me on many doctrines and precepts of our most holy faith. For instance: "Resist not evil: but whosoever shall smite thee on thy right cheek, turn to him the other also. And if any man will sue thee at the law, and take away thy coat, let him have thy cloak also. And whosoever shall compel thee to go a mile, go with him twain. Give to him that asketh thee, and from him that would borrow of thee turn not thou away. Love your enemies, bless them that curse you, do good to them that hate you, and pray for them which despitefully use you, and persecute you." Matthew v. 39-44. "Sell that ye have, and give alms." Luke xii. 33. "Owe no man any thing, but to love one another." Rom. xiii. 8. It may be said, surely these passages cannot be taken literally, for how then would the people of God be able to pass through the world. The state of mind enjoined in John vii. 17, will cause such objections to vanish. Whosoever is WILLING To ACT OUT these commandments of the Lord LITERALLY, will, I believe, be led with me to see that, to take them LITERALLY, is the will of God.—Those who do so take them will doubtless often be brought into difficulties, hard to the flesh to bear, but these will have a tendency to make them constantly feel that they are strangers and pilgrims here, that this world is not their home, and thus to throw them more upon God, who will assuredly help us through any difficulty into which we may be brought by seeking to act in obedience to His word.

As soon as I was brought into this state of heart, I saw from the Scriptures that believers ONLY are the proper subjects for baptism, and that immersion is the only true Scriptural mode, in which it ought to be attended to. The passage which particularly convinced me of the former, is Acts viii. 36-38, and of the latter, Rom. vi. 3-5. Some time after, I was baptized. I had much peace in doing so, and never have I for one single moment regretted it.—Before I leave this point, I would just say a few words concerning the result of this matter, so far as it regards some of the objections which occurred to my mind when I was about to examine the Scriptures concerning baptism.

1. Concerning the first objection, my conviction now is, that of all revealed truths not on is more clearly revealed in the Scriptures, not even the doctrine of justification by faith, and that the subject has

only become obscured by men not having been willing to take the Scriptures alone to decide the point.

2. Not one of my true friends in the Lord has turned his back on me, as I supposed, and almost all of them have been themselves baptized since.

3. Though in one way I lost money in consequence of being baptized, yet the Lord did not suffer me to be really a loser, even as it regards temporal things; for He made up the loss most bountifully. In conclusion, my example has been the means of leading many to examine the question of baptism, and to submit, from conviction, to this ordinance and seeing this truth I have been led to speak on it as well as on other truths; and during the forty-five years that I have now resided in Bristol, more than three thousand believers have been baptized among us.

In June of this year (1830) I went to preach at the opening of a chapel in a village near Barnstaple, built by that blessed man of God, Thomas Pugsley, now with the Lord. It pleased God to bring two souls to Himself through this my visit, and one more was converted on another visit. So graciously did the Lord condescend to use me, that almost everywhere He blessed the Word which I preached, thereby testifying that He had sent me, and thereby also getting glory to Himself in using such an instrument. It was so usual for me to preach with particular assistance, especially during the first months of this year, that once, when it was otherwise, it was much noticed by myself and others. The circumstance was this. One day, before preaching at Teignmouth, I had more time than usual, and therefore prayed and meditated about six hours, in preparation for the evening meeting, and I thought I saw many precious truths in the passage on which I had meditated. It was the first part of the first chapter of the epistle to the Ephesians. After I had spoken a little time, I felt that I spoke in my own strength, and I, being a foreigner, felt particularly the want of words, which had not been the case before. I told the brethren, that I felt I was left to myself, and asked their prayers. But after having continued a little longer, and feeling the same as before, I closed, and proposed that we should have a meeting for prayer, that the Lord still might be pleased to help me. We did so, and I was particularly assisted the next time.

During this summer also it appeared to me scriptural, according to the example of the Apostles, Acts xx. 7, to break bread every Lord's day, though there is no commandment given to do so, either by the Lord, or by the Holy Ghost through the Apostles. And at the same time it appeared to me scriptural, according to Eph. iv., Rom. xii., &c., that there should be given room for the Holy Ghost to work through any of the brethren whom He pleased to use; that thus one member might benefit the other with the gift which the Lord has bestowed upon him. Accordingly at certain meetings any of the brethren had an opportunity to exhort or teach the rest, if they considered that they had any thing to say which might be beneficial to the hearers.—I observe here, that, as the Lord gave me grace to endeavour at once to carry out the light which He had been pleased to give me on this point, and as the truth was but in part apprehended, there was much infirmity mixed with the manner of carrying it out. Nor was it until several years after that the Lord was pleased to teach me about this point more perfectly. That the disciples of Jesus should meet together, on the first day of the week, for the breaking of bread, and that that should be their principal meeting, and that those, whether one or several, who are truly gifted by the Holy Spirit for service, be it for exhortation, or teaching, or rule, &c., are responsible to the Lord for the exercise of their gifts: these are to me no matters of uncertainty, but points on which my soul, by grace, is established, through the revealed will of God.

On October 7th, 1830, I was united by marriage to Miss Mary Groves, sister of the brother whose name has already been mentioned. This step was taken after prayer and deliberation, from a full conviction that it was better for me to be married: and I have never regretted since, either the step itself or the choice, but desire to be truly grateful to God for having given me such a wife.

About this time I began to have conscientious objections against any longer receiving a stated salary. My reasons against it were these:—

1. The salary was made up by pew-rents; but pew-rents are, according to James ii. 1-6, against the mind of the Lord, as, in general, the poor brother cannot have so good a seat as the rich. (All pew-rents were therefore given up, and all the seats made free, which

was stated at the entrance of the chapel). 2. A brother may gladly do something towards my support if left to his own time; but when the quarter is up, he has perhaps other expenses, and I do not know, whether he pays his money grudgingly, and of necessity, or cheerfully; but God loveth a cheerful giver. Nay, I knew it to be a fact, that sometimes it had not been convenient to individuals to pay the money, when it had been asked for by the brethren who collected it. 3. Though the Lord had been pleased to give me grace to be faithful, so that I had been enabled not to keep back the truth, when He had shown it to me; still I felt that the pew-rents were a snare to the servant of Christ. It was a temptation to me, at least for a few minutes, at the time when the Lord had stirred me up to pray and search the Word respecting the ordinance of baptism, because £30. of my salary was at stake, if I should be baptized.

For these reasons I stated to the brethren, at the end of October, 1830, that I should for the future give up having any regular salary. After I had given my reasons for doing so, I read Philippians iv., and told the saints, that if they still had a desire to do something towards my support, by voluntary gifts, I had no objection to receive them, though ever so small, either in money or provisions. A few days after it appeared to me, that there was a better way still; for if I received personally every single gift, offered in money, both my own time and that of the donors would be much taken up; and in this way also the poor might, through temptation, be kept from offering their pence, a privilege of which they ought not to be deprived; and some also might in this way give more than if it were not known who was the giver; so that it would still be doubtful whether the gifts were given grudgingly or cheerfully. For these reasons especially, there was a box put up in the chapel, over which was written, that whoever had a desire to do something towards my support, might put his offering into the box.

At the same time it appeared to me right, that henceforth I should ask no man, not even my beloved brethren and sisters, to help me, as I had done a few times according to their own request, as my expenses, on account of traveling much in the Lord's service, were too great to be met by my usual income. For unconsciously I had thus again been led, in some measure, to trust in an arm of flesh; going to man, instead of going to the Lord at once. To come to this conclusion before God, required more grace than to give up my salary.

About the same time also my wife and I had grace given to us to take the Lord's commandment, "Sell that ye have, and give alms," Luke xii. 33, literally, and to carry it out. Our staff and support in this matter were Matthew vi. 19-34, John xiv. 13, 14. We leaned on the arm of the Lord Jesus. It is now fifty-one years, since we set out in this way, and we do not in the least regret the step we then took. Our God also has, in His tender mercy, given us grace to abide in the same mind concerning the above points, both as it regards principle and practice; and this has been the means of letting us see the tender love and care of our God over His children, even in the most minute things, in a way in which we never experimentally knew them before; and it has, in particular, made the Lord known to us more fully than we knew Him before, as a prayer hearing God. As I have written down how the Lord has been pleased to deal with us since, I shall be able to relate some facts concerning this matter, as far as they may tend to edification.

Extracts from my Journal.

Nov. 18th, 1830.—Our money was reduced to about eight shillings. When I was praying with my wife in the morning, the Lord brought to my mind the state of our purse, and I was led to ask Him for some money. About four hours after, we were with a sister at Bishopsteignton, and she said to me, "Do you want any money?" "I told the brethren," said I, "dear sister, when I gave up my salary, that I would for the future tell the Lord only about my wants." She replied, "But He has told me to give you some money. About a fortnight ago I asked Him, what I should do for Him, and He told me to give you some money; and last Saturday it came again powerfully to my mind, and has not left me since, and I felt it so forcibly last night, that I could not help speaking of it to Brother P." My heart rejoiced, seeing the Lord's faithfulness, but I thought it better not to tell her about our circumstances, lest she should be influenced to give accordingly; and I also was assured, that, if it were of the Lord, she could not but give. I therefore turned the conversation to other subjects, but when I left she gave me two guineas. We were full of joy on account of the goodness of the Lord.—I would call upon the reader to admire the gentleness of the Lord, that He did not try our faith much at the commencement, but gave us first encouragement, and allowed us to see His willingness to help us, before He was pleased to try it more fully.

The next Wednesday I went to Exmouth, our money having then again been reduced to about nine shillings. I asked the Lord on Thursday, when at Exmouth, to be pleased to give me some money. On Friday morning, about eight o'clock, whilst in prayer, I was particularly led to ask again for money; and before I rose from my knees I had the fullest assurance, that we should have the answer that very day. About nine o'clock I left the brother with whom I was staying, and he gave me half a sovereign, saying, "Take this for the expenses connected with your coming to us." I did not expect to have my expenses paid, but I saw the Lord's fatherly hand in sending me this money within one hour after my asking Him for some. But even then I was so fully assured that the Lord would send more that very day, or had done so already, that, when I came home about twelve o'clock, I asked my wife whether she had received any letters. She told me she had received one the day before from a brother in Exeter, with three sovereigns. Thus even my prayer on the preceding day had been answered. The next day one of the brethren came and brought me £4., which was due to me of my former salary, but which I could never have expected, as I did not even know that this sum was due to me. Thus I received, within thirty hours, in answer to prayer, £7. 10s.

In the commencement of December I went to Collumpton, where I preached several times, and likewise in a neighbouring village. In driving home from the village late at night, our driver lost his way. As soon as we found out our mistake, being then near a house, it struck me that the hand of God was in this matter; and having awakened the people of the house, I offered a man something if he would be kind enough to bring us into the right road. I now walked with the man before the gig, and conversed with him about the things of God, and soon found out that he was an awful backslider. May God, in mercy, bless the word spoken to him, and may we learn from this circumstance, that we have to ask on such occasions, why the Lord has allowed such and such things to happen to us.— Since the publication of the first edition, one day, about eight years after this circumstance had happened, the individual who drove me that night introduced himself to me as a believer, and told me that on that evening he received his first impressions under the preaching of the Word. The missing of the right road may have been connected with his state of mind. May I and my fellow-labourers in the Gospel be encouraged by this, patiently to continue to sow the seed, though only after eight years or more we should see the fruit of it. I only add, that up to that time, the individual had been a very dissipated young man, who caused his believing parents very much grief. Their love led them to convey me and my wife to this village and back again, and truly the Lord gave them a reward in doing so.

Between Christmas and the new year, when our money was reduced to a few shillings, I asked the Lord for more; when a few hours after there was given to us a sovereign by a brother from Axminster. This brother had heard much against me, and was at last determined to hear for himself, and thus came to Teignmouth, a distance of forty miles; and having heard about our manner of living, gave us this money.

With this closes the year 1830. Throughout it the Lord richly supplied all my temporal wants, though at the commencement of it I had no certain human prospect for one single shilling; so that, even as it regards temporal things, I had not been in the smallest degree a loser in acting according to the dictates of my conscience; and, as it regards spiritual things, the Lord had indeed dealt bountifully with me, and led me on in many respects, and, moreover, had condescended to use me as an instrument in doing His work.

On January 6th, 7th, and 8th, 1831, I had repeatedly asked the Lord for money, but received none. On the evening of January 8th I left my room for a few minutes, and was then tempted to distrust the Lord, though He had been so gracious to us, in that He not only up to that day had supplied all our wants, but had given us also those answers of prayer, which have been in part just mentioned. I was so sinful, for about five minutes, as to think it would be of no use to trust in the Lord in this way. I also began to say to myself, that I had perhaps gone too far in living in this way. But, thanks to the Lord! this trial lasted but a few minutes. He enabled me again to trust in Him, and Satan was immediately confounded; for when I returned to my room (out of which I had not been absent ten minutes), the Lord had sent deliverance. A sister in the Lord, who resided at Exeter, had come to Teignmouth, and brought us £2. 4s.; so the Lord triumphed, and our faith was strengthened.

Jan. 10. Today, when we had again but a few shillings, £5. was given to us, which had been taken out of the box. I had, once for all, told the brethren, who had the care of these temporal things, to have the kindness to let me have the money every week; but as these beloved brethren either forgot to take it out weekly, or were ashamed to bring it in such small sums, it was generally taken out every three, four, or five weeks. As I had stated to them, however, from the commencement, that I desired to look neither to man nor the box, but to the living God, I thought it not right on my part, to remind them of my request to have the money weekly, lest it should hinder the testimony which I wished to give, of trusting in the living God alone. It was on this account that on January 28th, when we had again but little money, though I had seen the brethren on January the 24th open the box and take out the money, I would not ask the brother, in whose hands it was, to let me have it; but, standing in need of it, as our coals were almost gone, I asked the Lord to incline his heart to bring it, and but a little time afterwards it was given to us, even £1. 8s. 6d.

I would here mention, that since the time I began living in this way, I have been kept from speaking, either directly or indirectly, about my wants, at the time I was in need. But whilst I have refrained, and do still habitually refrain, from speaking to my fellow creatures about my wants at the time, I desire to speak well of the Lord's goodness, after He has delivered me; not only in order that He thus may get glory, but also that the children of God may be encouraged to trust in Him.

On February 14th we had again very little money, and, whilst praying, I was led to ask the Lord, graciously to supply our wants; and the instant that I rose from my knees, a brother gave me £1., which had been taken out of the box.

On March 7th I was again tempted to disbelieve the faithfulness of the Lord, and though I was not miserable, still I was not so fully resting upon the Lord, that I could triumph with joy. It was but one hour after, when the Lord gave me another proof of His faithful love. A Christian lady at Teignmouth had been from home for some time, and on her return she brought from the sisters in the Lord, with whom she had been staying, five sovereigns for us, with these words written in the paper;—"I was an hungered, and ye gave me meat; I was thirsty, and ye gave me drink. Lord, when saw we Thee an hungered, and fed Thee? or thirsty, and gave Thee drink? The King shall answer and say unto them, "Verily, verily, I say unto you, inasmuch as ye have done it unto one of the least of these my brethren, ye have done it unto me."

On March 16th I went to Axminster, and preached in several places in that neighbourhood, besides holding a meeting at Axminster. Whilst staying there I was requested to preach at Chard; but as I had never been away from Teignmouth on the Lord's day, I had to pray much, before I came to the conclusion to comply with the request. At last I had the fullest assurance that I ought to preach at Chard. I have since heard that the Lord used me in edifying the brethren, and through a general exhortation to all, to read the Scriptures with earnestness, a woman was stirred up to do so, and this was the means of her conversion. As to myself, I had a most refreshing season. I mention this circumstance to show how important it is to ascertain the will of God, before we undertake any thing, because we are then not only blessed in our own souls, but also the work of our hands will prosper.—One of the brethren at Chard forced a sovereign upon me, against the acceptance of which I strove much, lest it should appear as if I had preached for money. Another would give me a paper with money. I refused it for the same reason. At last he put it by force into my pocket, and ran away. The paper contained 11s. 6d.

April 16th. This morning I found that our money was reduced to 3s., and I said to myself, I must now go and ask the Lord earnestly for fresh supplies. But before I had prayed, there was sent from Exeter £2, as a proof that the Lord hears before we call.

I would observe here, by the way, that if any of the children of God should think that such a mode of living leads away from the Lord, and from caring about spiritual things, and has the effect of causing the mind to be taken up with the question, What shall I eat?

What shall I drink?—and Wherewithal shall I be clothed? and that on that account it would be much better to have a stated salary, particularly for one who labours in the word and doctrine, in order that he may be above these cares; I say, should any believer think so, I would request him, prayerfully to consider the following remarks:—1. I have had experience of both ways, and know that my present mode of living, as to temporal things, is connected with less care. 2. Confidence in the Lord, to whom alone I look for the supply of my temporal wants, keeps me, at least whilst faith is in exercise, when a case of distress comes before me, or when the Lord's work calls for my pecuniary aid, from anxious reckoning like this: Will my salary last out? Shall I have enough myself the next month? &c. In this my freedom, I am, by the grace of God, generally at least, able to say to myself something like this:—My Lord is not limited; He can again supply; He knows that this present case has been sent to me; and thus, this way of living, so far from leading to anxiety, as it regards possible future want, is rather the means of keeping from it. And truly it was once said to me by an individual,—You can do such and such things, and need not to lay by, for the church in the whole of Devonshire cares about your wants. My reply was: The Lord can use not merely any of the saints throughout Devonshire, but those throughout the world, as instruments to supply my temporal wants. 3. This way of living has often been the means of reviving the work of grace in my heart, when I have been getting cold; and it also has been the means of bringing me back again to the Lord, after I have been backsliding. For it will not do,—it is not possible, to live in sin, and, at the same time, by communion with God, to draw down from heaven every thing one needs for the life that now is. 4. Frequently, too, a fresh answer to prayer, obtained in this way, has been the means of quickening my soul, and filling me with much joy.

About April 20th I went to Chumleigh. Here and in the neighbourhood I preached repeatedly, and from thence I went to Barnstaple. Whilst we were at Barnstaple, there was found in my wife's bag a sovereign, put there anonymously. A sister also gave us £2. On our return to Teignmouth, May 2, when we emptied our travelling bag, there fell out a paper with money. It contained two sovereigns and threepence, the latter put in, no doubt, to make a noise in emptying the bag. May the Lord bless and reward the giver! In a similar way we found 4s. put anonymously into one of our drawers, a few days after.

June 6. Having prayed much on the previous days, that, when we wanted money, the Lord would be pleased to send some, today, after I had again asked for it, a poor sister brought half a sovereign, 5s. from herself, and 5s. from another very poor sister. This is not only a fresh proof that the Lord hears prayer, but also that He sends by whom He will. Our money had been reduced to 8s.

June 12. Lord's day. On Thursday last I went with brother Craik to Torquay, to preach there. I had only about 3s. with me and left my wife with about 6s. at home. The Lord provided beds for us through the hospitality of a brother. I asked the Lord repeatedly for money; but when I came home my wife had only about 3s. left, having received nothing. We waited still upon the Lord. Yesterday passed away, and no money came. We had 9d. left. This morning we were still waiting upon the Lord, and looking for deliverance. We had only a little butter left for breakfast, sufficient for brother E. and a relative living with us, to whom we did not mention our circumstances, that they might not be made uncomfortable. After the morning meeting, brother Y. most unexpectedly opened the box, and, in giving me quite as unexpectedly the money at such a time, he told me that he and his wife could not sleep last night on account of thinking that we might want money. The most striking point is, that, after I had repeatedly asked the Lord, but received nothing, I then prayed yesterday, that the Lord would be pleased to impress it on brother Y. that we wanted money, so that he might open the box. There was in it £1. 8s. 10 1/2d. Our joy on account of this fresh deliverance was great, and we praised the Lord heartily.

June 18. Brother Craik called on us today, and he then had only 1 1/2d. left. A few minutes after, he received: a sum of money, and in returning to us on his way home, he gave us 10s., when we had but 3s. left.

July 20. A shoulder of mutton and a loaf were sent to us anonymously.—I understood some time afterwards, that Satan had raised the false report that we were starving, in consequence of which a believer sent these provisions. I would mention by the way, that various reports have been circulated, on account of this our way of living. Sometimes it has been said that we had not enough to eat, and that surely such and such an infirmity of body we had brought on us, because we had not the necessaries of life. Now, the truth is, that, whilst we have been often brought low; yea, so low, that we have not had even as much as one single penny left; or so as to have the last bread on the table, and not as much money as was needed to buy another loaf;—yet never have we had to sit down to a meal, without our good Lord having provided nourishing food for us. I am bound to state this, and I do it with pleasure. My Master has been a kind Master to me, and if I had to choose this day again, as to the way of living, the Lord giving me grace, I would not choose differently. But even these very reports, false as they were, I doubt not the Lord has sometimes used as a means, to put it into the hearts of His children, to remember our temporal necessities.

About July 25th I preached several times at Collumpton, and in a neighbouring village, in the open air. My experience as it regards preaching in the open air has been very different from what I might have expected. I have often preached out of doors, and but once has it been blessed, as far as I know, and that was in the case of an officer in the army, who came to make sport of it; whilst almost in every place, if not in every place, where I have preached in rooms or chapels, the Lord has given testimony to the Word. Perhaps the Lord has not been pleased to let me see fruit from this part of my work, though I have been many times engaged in it; or it may be, that, because I did not pray so earnestly respecting my out-door preaching as respecting my in-door preaching, the former has not been so much blessed as the latter. But this testimony I cannot but bear, that, though I do not consider it at present my work, on account of want of bodily strength, yet it is a most important work, and I should delight in being so honoured now, as to be allowed to be engaged in it.

August 9. After extreme suffering, which lasted about seventeen hours, my wife was this day delivered of a still-born child.—Who of my readers would suppose, that whilst I was so abundantly blessed by God, and that in so many respects, my heart should have been again many times during several months previous to this day, cold, wretched, carnal? How long-suffering is the Lord! Repeatedly, during this time, I could let hours run on, after I had risen in the morning, before I prayed; at least, before I retired for prayer. And at that time when I appeared most zealous for God, perhaps more so than at any time before or since, I was often far from being in a spiritual state. I was not now, indeed, indulging in gross outward sins, which could be noticed by my brethren; but often—very often, the eye of my kind loving Father must have looked on me with much grief. On this account, I have no doubt, the Lord now, in great compassion, sent this heavy blow. I had not seriously thought of the great danger connected with childbearing, and therefore had never earnestly prayed about it. Now came this solemn time. The life of my dear wife was hanging, as it were, on a thread, and, in the midst of it, my conscience told me, that my state of heart made such a chastisement needful. Yet, at the same time, I was much supported.—When the child was still-born, I saw almost immediately afterwards, that this could not have been expected otherwise, for I had not looked on the prospect of having a child as on a blessing, which I was about to receive from God, but rather considered it as a burden and a hindrance in the Lord's work; for I did not know then, that, whilst a wife and children may be in certain respects, on the one hand, a hindrance to the servant of Christ, they also may fit him, on the other hand, for certain parts of his work, in teaching him things which are important to be known, especially for the pastoral work. The Lord now brought, in addition to this, very great sufferings upon my beloved wife, which lasted for six weeks, combined with a partial lameness of the left side.—Immediately after the eventful time of August 8th and 9th, the Lord brought me, in His tender mercy, again into a spiritual state of heart, so that I was enabled to look on this chastisement as a great blessing. May this my experience be a warning to believing readers, that the Lord may not need to chastise them, on account of their state of heart! May it also be a fresh proof to them, that the Lord, in His very love and faithfulness, will not, and cannot let us go on in backsliding, but that He will visit us with stripes, to bring us back to Himself!

There was one point, however, in which, by grace, I had continued to be faithful to God, i.e. in my mode of living, and, therefore, in as far as I had been faithfully sowing, I now reaped abundantly; for the Lord most graciously supplied, in rich abundance, all our temporal wants, though they were many. Another reason for this may have been, that the Lord never lays more on us, in the way of chastisement, than our state of heart makes needful; so that whilst He smites with the one hand, He supports with the other.—We saw it to be against the Lord's mind to put by any money for my wife's confinement, though we might have, humanly speaking, very easily saved £20. or £30. during the six months previous to August 7th. I say, humanly speaking, and judging from what we had received during all these months, we might have laid by as much as the above sums; but I have every reason to believe, that, had I begun to lay up, the Lord would have stopped the supplies, and thus, the ability of doing so was only apparent. Let no one profess to trust in God, and yet lay up for future wants, otherwise the Lord will first send him to the hoard he has amassed, before He can answer the prayer for more. We were persuaded, that, if we laid out our money in the Lord's service, He would send more when we needed it; and this our faith, His own gift, He graciously honoured, inasmuch as He not merely gave us what we needed, but much more.

On August 6th, just before this time of need, the Lord sent us £5. from a distance of about forty miles, and that from a sister, whom, up to this day, neither of us know personally. On August 7th I received £1. 0s. 9 1/2d. out of the box. August 15th, from a distance of twenty-five miles was sent £5., and from a distance of about seventy miles £1. August 18th, whilst preaching at Chudleigh, £1. was sent to me, and a brother sent from Exeter £2. August 21st was again sent from a distance of seventy miles £5., and August 23rd another £5. from the same place. Also, August 22nd, 16s. 9d. was given out of the box. August 24th, a brother, who is a day labourer, gave me 2s. 6d. August 31st, 5s. was given to me. September 3rd, whilst preaching at Chudleigh, £3. 10s. was given to me by a brother and three sisters. September 4th, a sister gave me a guinea, and also out of the box was given 9s. 8d. September 10th, £6. was given to me. Thus, within about one month, the Lord not only sent us nearly £40., but likewise all sorts of suitable provisions and refreshments, needful at such a time; and, in addition to this, the two medical gentlemen who attended my wife would not take any remuneration for their unwearied attention and kindness, during the space of six weeks. Thus the Lord gave us even more than we could have saved, if we had endeavoured to do so.

November 16th. This morning I proposed united prayer respecting our temporal wants. Just as we were about to pray, a parcel came from Exmouth. In prayer we asked the Lord for meat for dinner, having no money to buy any. After prayer, on opening the parcel, we found, among other things, a ham, sent by a brother at Exmouth, which served us for dinner. Thus not only our own family was provided for, but also a sister in the Lord then staying with us.

November 17th. Today we had not a single penny left. We had asked the Lord yesterday and today. We desired only enough money to be able to buy bread. We were reduced more than ever we had been before. But our gracious and faithful Lord, who never lays more upon His children than He enables them to bear, delivered us again this time, by sending us £1. 10s. 6d., about an hour before we wanted money to buy bread.

November 19th. We had not enough to pay our weekly rent; but the Lord graciously sent us again today 14s. 6d. I would just observe, that we never contract debts, which we believe to be unscriptural (according to Romans xiii. 8;) and therefore we have no bills with our tailor, shoemaker, grocer, butcher, baker, &c.; but all we buy we pay for in ready money. The Lord helping us, we would rather suffer privation, than contract debts. Thus we always know how much we have, and how much we have a right to give away. May I entreat the believing reader, prayerfully to consider this matter; for I am well aware that many trials come upon the children of God, on account of not acting according to Rom. xiii. 8.

November 27th, Lord's day. Our money had been reduced to 2 1/2d.; our bread was hardly enough for this day. I had several times brought our need before the Lord. After dinner, when I returned thanks, I asked Him to give us our daily bread, meaning literally that He would send us bread for the evening. Whilst I was praying, there was a knock at the door of the room. After I had concluded, a poor sister came in, and brought us some of her dinner, and from another poor sister, 5s. In the afternoon she also brought us a large loaf. Thus the Lord not only literally gave us bread, but also money.

In reading about all these answers to prayer, the believing reader may be led to think that I am spiritually minded above most of the children of God, and that, therefore, the Lord favours us thus. The true reason is this. Just in as many points as we are acting according to the mind of God, in so many are we blessed and made a blessing. Our manner of living is according to the mind of the Lord, for He delights in seeing His children thus come to Him (Matt. vi.); and therefore, though I am weak and erring in many points, yet He blesses me in this particular, and, I doubt not, will bless me, as long as He shall enable me to act according to His will in this matter.

After we had, on December 31st, 1831, looked over the Lord's gracious dealings with us during the past year, in providing for all our temporal wants, we had about 10s. left. A little while after, the providence of God called for that, so that not a single farthing remained. Thus we closed the old year, in which the Lord had been so gracious in giving to us, without our asking any one:—

1. Through the instrumentality of the box, £31. 14s.—

2. From brethren of the Church at Teignmouth, in presents of money, £6. 18s. 6d.

3. From brethren living at Teignmouth and elsewhere, not connected with the Church at Teignmouth, £93. 6s. 2d. Altogether, £131. 18s. 8d.

There had been likewise many articles of provision and some articles of clothing given to us, worth at least £20. I am so particular in mentioning these things, to show that we are never losers by acting according to the mind of the Lord. For had I had my regular salary, humanly speaking, I should not have had nearly as much; but whether this would have been the case or not, this is plain, that I have not served a hard Master, and that is what I delight to show. For, to speak well of His name, that thus my beloved fellow-pilgrims, who may read this, may be encouraged to trust in Him, is the chief purpose of my writing.

We had now in the new year to look up to our kind Father for new mercies, and during the year 1832 also we found Him as faithful and compassionate as before, not laying more on us than He enabled us to bear, though space will only permit me to mention a few particulars.

January 7, 1832. We had been again repeatedly asking the Lord today and yesterday to supply our temporal wants, having no means to pay our weekly rent; and this evening, as late as eleven o'clock, a brother gave us 19s. 6d., a proof that the Lord is not limited to time.

January 13. The Lord has again graciously fed us today. We have 5d. left, some bread, rice, meat, potatoes, and other good things, and, above all, the Lord Jesus. He who has provided will provide.

January 14. This morning we had nothing but dry bread with our tea; only the second time since we have been living by simple faith upon Jesus for temporal supplies. We have more than £40. of ready money in the house for two bills,2 which will not be payable for several weeks; but we do not consider this money to be our own, and would rather suffer great privation, God helping us, than take of it. I thank the Lord, who gives me grace to be more faithful in these matters than I used to be formerly, when I would have taken of it, and said, that by the time the money was actually due, I should be able to replace it. We were looking to our Father, and He has not suffered us to be disappointed. For when now we had but 3d. left, and only a small piece of bread, we received 2s. and 5s., the particulars concerning which would take up too much space.

February 18. This afternoon I broke a blood vessel in my stomach, and lost a considerable quantity of blood. I was very happy immediately afterwards. February 19. This morning, Lord's day, two brethren called on me, to ask me what arrangement there should be made today, as it regarded the four villages, where some of the brethren were in the habit of preaching, as, on account of my not being able to preach, one of the brethren would need to stay at home to take my place. I asked them, kindly to come again in about an hour, when I would give them an answer. After they were gone, the Lord gave me faith to rise. I dressed myself, and determined to go to the chapel. I was enabled to do so, though so weak when I went, that walking the short distance to the chapel was an exertion to me. I was enabled to preach this morning with as loud and strong a voice as usual, and for the usual length of time. After the morning meeting, a medical friend called on me, and entreated me not to preach again in the afternoon, as it might greatly injure me. I told him, that I should indeed consider it great presumption to do so, had the Lord not given me faith. I preached again in the afternoon, and this medical friend called again, and said the same concerning the evening meeting. Nevertheless, having faith, I preached again in the evening. After each meeting I became stronger, which was a plain proof that the hand of God was in the matter. After the third meeting I went immediately to bed, considering that it would be presumption to try my strength needlessly.

February 20. The Lord enabled me to rise early in the morning, and to go to our usual prayer-meeting, where I read, spoke, and prayed. Afterwards I wrote four letters, expounded the scriptures at home, and attended the meeting again in the evening. February 21. I attended the two meetings as usual, preached in the evening, and did my other work besides. February 22. Today I attended the meeting in the morning, walked afterwards six miles with two brethren to Newton Bushel, and rode from thence to Plymouth: February 23. I am now as well as I was before I broke the blood vessel. – In relating the particulars of this circumstance I would earnestly warn every one who may read this, not to imitate me in such a thing if he has no faith; but if he has, it will, as good coin, most assuredly be honoured by God. I could not say, that, if such a thing should happen again, I would act in the same way; for when I have been not nearly so weak as when I had broken the blood-vessel, having no faith, I did not preach; yet if it were to please the Lord to give me faith, I might be able to do the same, though even still weaker than at the time just spoken of.

About this time I repeatedly prayed with sick believers till they were restored. Unconditionally I asked the Lord for the blessing of bodily health, (a thing which I could not do now), and almost always had the petition granted. In some instances, however, the prayer was not answered. In the same way, whilst in London, Nov. 1829, in answer to my prayers, I was immediately restored from a bodily infirmity under which I had been labouring for a long time, and which has never returned since. The way in which I now account for these facts is as follows. It pleased the Lord, I think, to give me in such cases something like the gift (not grace) of faith, so that unconditionally I could ask and look for an answer. The difference between the gift and the grace of faith seems to me this. According to the gift of faith I am able to do a thing, or believe that a thing will come to pass, the not doing of which, or the not believing of which would not be sin; according to the grace of faith I am able to do a thing, or believe that a thing will come to pass, respecting which I have the word of God as the ground to rest upon, and, therefore, the not doing it, or the not believing it would be sin. For instance, the gift of faith would be needed, to believe that a sick person should be restored again though there is no human probability: for there is no promise to that effect; the grace of faith is needed to believe that the Lord will give me the necessaries of life, if I first seek the kingdom of God and His righteousness: for there is a promise to that effect." Matt. vi.

March 18. These two days we have not been able to purchase meat. The sister in whose house we lodge gave us today part of her dinner. We are still looking to Jesus for deliverance. We want money to pay the weekly rent and to buy provisions. March 19. Our landlady sent again of her meat for our dinner. We have but a half-penny left. I feel myself very cold in asking for money: still I hope for deliverance, though I do not see whence money is to come. We were not able to buy bread today as usual. March 20. This has been again a day of very great mercies. In the morning we met round our breakfast which the Lord had provided for us, though we had not a single penny left. The last half-penny was spent for milk. We were then still looking to Jesus for fresh supplies. We both had no doubt that the Lord would interfere. I felt it a trial that I had but little earnestness in asking the Lord, and had this not been the case, perhaps we might have had our wants sooner supplied. We have about £7. in the house; but considering it no longer our own, the Lord kept us from taking of it, with the view of replacing what we had taken, as formerly I might have done. The meat which was sent yesterday for our dinner, was enough also for today. Thus the Lord had provided another meal. Two sisters called upon us about noon, who gave us two pounds of sugar, one pound of coffee, and two cakes of chocolate. Whilst they were with us, a poor sister came and brought 1s. from herself, and 2s. 6d. from another poor sister. Our landlady also sent us again of her dinner, and also a loaf. Our bread would scarcely have been enough for tea, had the Lord not thus graciously provided. In the afternoon the same sister who brought the money, brought us also from another sister, one pound of butter and 2s., and from another sister 5s. Thus the Lord graciously has again answered our feeble and cold breathings. Lord, strengthen our faith.

March 29. I went to Shaldon this morning. Brother Craik has left for Bristol for four weeks. I think he will only return to take leave, and that the Lord will give him work there. [What a remarkable presentiment, which came to pass, concerning my beloved brother and fellow-labourer!]

April 4. Besides our own family, there are now four visitors staying with us, and we have but 2s. April 5. Four pounds of cheese, and one pound of butter were sent to us. April 7. Anonymously was sent to us, from Plymouth, a large ham, with two sovereigns tied in the corner of the cloth in which the ham was wrapped up. Thus the Lord, once more, in this our time of need, when our expenses are double, has graciously appeared for us.

April 8. I have again felt much this day that Teignmouth is no longer my place, and that I shall leave it.

I would observe that in August of the preceding year (1831), I began greatly to feel as if my work at Teignmouth were done, and that I should go somewhere else. On writing about this to a friend, I was led, from the answer I received, to consider the matter more maturely, and at last had it settled in this way, that it was not likely to be of God, because, for certain reasons, I should naturally have liked to leave Teignmouth. Afterwards I felt quite comfortable in remaining there. In the commencement of the year 1832 I began again much to doubt whether Teignmouth was my place, or whether my gift was not much more that of going about from place to place, seeking to bring believers back to the Scriptures, than to stay in one place and to labour as a pastor. I thought so particularly whilst at Plymouth, in February. On my return, however, I resolved to try whether it were not the will of God that I should still give myself to pastoral work among the brethren at Teignmouth; and, with more earnestness and faithfulness than ever, I was enabled to attend to this work, and was certainly much refreshed and blessed in it; and I saw immediately blessings result from it. This my experience seemed more than ever to settle me at Teignmouth. But notwithstanding this, the impression that my work was done there, came back after some time, as the remark in my journal of April 8th shows, and it became stronger and stronger. There was one point remarkable in connexion with this. Wherever I went, I preached with much more enjoyment and power than at Teignmouth, the very reverse of which had been the case on my first going there. Moreover, almost every where I had many more hearers than at Teignmouth, and found the people hungering after food, which, generally speaking, was no longer the case at Teignmouth.

April 10. I asked the Lord for a text, but obtained none. At last; after having again much felt that Teignmouth is not my place, I was directed to Isaiah li. 9-11. April 11. Felt again much that Teignmouth will not much longer be my residence. April 12. Still feel the impression that Teignmouth is no longer my place. April 13. Found a letter from Brother Craik, from Bristol, on my return from Torquay, where I had been to preach. He invites me to come and help him. It appears to me from what he writes, that such places as Bristol more suit my gifts. O Lord, teach me! I have felt this day more than ever, that I shall soon leave Teignmouth. I fear, however, there is much connected with it which savours of the flesh, and that makes me fearful. It seems to me as if I should shortly go to Bristol, if the Lord permit. April 14. Wrote a letter to Brother Craik, in which I said I should come, if I clearly saw it to be the Lord's will. Have felt again very much today, yea, far more than ever, that I shall soon leave Teignmouth. At last I was pressed in spirit to determine that tomorrow I would tell the brethren so, in order that by the result of this I might see more of the Lord's mind; and that, at all events, I might have their prayers, to be directed in this matter by the Lord.

April 15. Lord's day. This evening I preached again once more, as fully as time would permit, on the Lord's second coming. After having done so, I told the brethren what effect this doctrine had had upon me, on first receiving it, even to determine me to leave London, and to preach throughout the kingdom; but that the Lord had kept me chiefly at Teignmouth for these two years and three months, and that it seemed to me now that the time was near when I should leave them. I reminded them of what I told them when they requested me to take the oversight of them, that I could make no certain engagement, but stay only so long with them as I should see it to be the Lord's will to do so. There was much weeping afterwards. But I am now again in peace. [This would not have been the case, had the matter not been of God. I knew of no place to go to. My mind was much directed to Torquay, to preach there for a month or so, and then to go further. For though I had written that I would come to Bristol, I meant only to stay there for a few days, and to preach a few times.]

April 16. This morning I am still in peace. I am glad I have spoken to the brethren, that they may be prepared, in case the Lord should take me away.—Having again little money, and being about to leave Teignmouth for several days, I asked the Lord for a fresh supply, and within about four hours afterwards he sent me, from six different quarters, £3. 7s. 6d. I left today for Dartmouth, where I preached in the evening.—There was much weeping today among the saints at Teignmouth. This is already a trial to me, and it will be still more so should I actually leave.—It is a most important work to go about and stir up the churches; but it requires much grace, much self-denial, much saying over the same things, and the greatest watchfulness and faithfulness, in making use of one's time for prayer, meditation, and reading the Scriptures.—I had five answers to prayer today. 1. I awoke at five, for which I had asked the Lord last evening. 2. The Lord removed from my dear wife an indisposition, under which she had been suffering. It would have been trying to me to have had to leave her in that state. 3. The Lord sent us money. 4. There was a place vacant on the Dartmouth coach, which only passes through Teignmouth. 5. This evening I was assisted in preaching, and my own soul refreshed.

April 17. I preached again at Dartmouth. April 18. I am still at Dartmouth. I wrote to Brother Craik, that, the Lord willing, I should be with him at Bristol on the 21st. I preached again this evening, with especial assistance, before a large congregation. April 19. I awoke early, and had a good while to myself for prayer and reading the Word, and left happy in spirit for Torquay, where I preached in the evening with much help. The brethren are sorry, that, on account of my going to Bristol, my regular weekly preaching will be given up there for a while. I walked home after preaching, and arrived at Teignmouth at twelve o'clock.

April 20. I left this morning for Bristol. I preached with little power (as to my own feeling) in Exeter, from three till half-past four. At five I left for Taleford, where I preached in the evening, likewise with little power. I was very tired in body, and had had therefore little prayer. But still, in both places, the believers seemed refreshed. I went to bed at eleven, very, very tired.

April 21. This morning I rose a little before five, and attended a prayer meeting from a quarter past five, to a quarter past six. I spoke for some time at the meeting. Afterwards I prayed and read again with some believers, and likewise expounded the Scriptures. The Bristol coach took me up about ten. I was very faithless on the journey.

I did not speak a single word for Christ, and was therefore wretched in my soul. This has shown me again my weakness. Though the Lord had been so gracious to me yesterday, in this particular, both on my way from Teignmouth to Exeter, and from Exeter to Taleford, and had given me much encouragement, in that He made my fellow-travellers either thankfully to receive the word, or constrained them quietly to listen to the testimony; yet I did not confess Him today. Nor did I give away a single tract, though I had my pockets full on purpose. O wretched man that I am!

I would offer here a word of warning to my fellow-believers. Often the work of the Lord itself may be a temptation to keep us from that communion with Him which is so essential to the benefit of our own souls.—On the 19th I had left Dartmouth, conversed a good deal that day, preached in the evening, walked afterwards eight miles, had only about five hours sleep, traveled again the next day twenty-five miles, preached twice, and conversed very much besides, went to bed at eleven, and rose before five. All this shows that my body and spirit required rest, and, therefore, however careless about the Lord's work I might have appeared to my brethren, I ought to have had a great deal of quiet time for prayer and reading the Word, especially as I had a long journey before me that day, and as I was going to Bristol, which in itself required much prayer. Instead of this, I hurried to the prayer meeting after a few minutes' private prayer. But let none think that public prayer will make up for closet communion. Then again, afterwards, when I ought to have withdrawn myself, as it were, by force, from the company of beloved brethren and sisters, and given my testimony for the Lord (and, indeed, it would have been the best testimony I could have given them), by telling them that I needed secret communion with the Lord: I did not do so, but spent the time, till the coach came, in conversation with them. Now, however profitable in some respects it may have been to those with whom I was on that morning, yet my own soul needed food; and not having had it, I was lean, and felt the effects of it the whole day, and hence I believe it came that I was dumb on the coach.

April 22. This morning I preached at Gideon Chapel, Bristol. [Though this sermon gave rise to false reports, yet the Lord was pleased to bless it to several; and the false reports were likewise instrumental in bringing many individuals under the sound of the Word.] In the afternoon I preached at the Pithay Chapel. [This sermon was a blessing to many, many souls; and many were brought through it, to come afterwards to hear Brother Craik and me. Among others it was the means of converting a young man who was a notorious drunkard, and who was just again on his way to a public house, when an acquaintance of his met him, and asked him to go with him to hear a foreigner preach. He did so; and from that moment he was so completely altered, that he never again went to a public house, and was so happy in the Lord afterwards that he often neglected his supper, from eagerness to read the Scriptures, as his wife told me. He died about five months afterwards.] This evening I was much instructed in hearing Brother Craik preach. I am now fully persuaded that Bristol is the place where the Lord will have me to labour.

April 23. This evening I preached again with much assistance at Gideon. I was very happy. [The Lord made this testimony a blessing to several.] I feel that Bristol is my place for a while. The Lord mercifully teach me!

April 27. It seems to Brother Craik and myself the Lord's will that we should go home next week, in order that in quietness, without being influenced by what we see here, we may more inquire into the Lord's will concerning us. It especially appears to us much more likely that we should come to a right conclusion among the brethren and sisters in Devonshire, whose tears we shall have to witness, and whose entreaties to stay with them we shall have to hear, than here in Bristol, where we see only those who wish us to stay. Some asked me to stay with them while Brother Craik goes home. But it seems better that we should both go. [I observe here, it was evident that many preferred my beloved brother's gifts to my own; yet, as he would not come, except I came with him: and as I knew that I also had been called by the Lord for the ministry of the Word, I knew that I also should find my work in Bristol, and that though it might be a different one, yet I should fill up in some measure his lack, whilst he supplied my deficiencies; and that thus we might both be a benefit to the church and to the world in Bristol. The result has evidently confirmed this. I am, moreover, by the grace of God, strengthened to rejoice in my fellow-labourer's honour, instead of envying him; having, in some measure, been enabled to enter into the meaning of that word: "A man can receive nothing, except it be given him from above."]

April 28. It still seems to us the Lord's will that we should both leave soon, to have quiet time for prayer concerning Bristol. This afternoon I felt the want of retirement, finding afresh, that the society of brethren cannot make up for communion with the Lord. I spent about three hours over the Word and in prayer, this evening, which has been a great refreshment to my inner man.

April 29. I preached this morning with much outward power, but with little inward enjoyment, on Rev. iii. 14-22. [As it afterwards appeared, that testimony was blessed to many, though I lacked enjoyment in my own soul. May this be an encouragement to those who labour in word and doctrine!] This afternoon Brother Craik preached in a vessel called the Clifton Ark, fitted up for a chapel. In the evening I preached in the same vessel. [These testimonies also God greatly honoured, and made them the means of afterwards bringing several, who then heard us, to our meeting places. How did God bless us in everything we took into our hands! How was He with us, and how did He help us, thereby evidently showing that He Himself had sent us to this city!] Brother Craik preached this evening at Gideon for the last time previous to our going. The aisles, the pulpit stairs, and the vestry were filled, and multitudes went away on account of the want of room.

April 30. It was most affecting to take leave of the dear children of God, dozens pressing us to return soon, many with tears in their eyes. The blessing which the Lord has given to our ministry, seems to be very great.

We both see it fully the Lord's will to come here, though we do not see under what circumstances. A brother has promised to take Bethesda Chapel for us, and to be answerable for the payment of the rent: so that thus we should have two large chapels.-I saw, again, two instances today, in which my preaching has been blessed.

May 1. Brother Craik and I left this morning for Devonshire. May 2. I preached this evening at Bishopsteignton, and told the brethren, that, the Lord willing, I should soon leave them. May 3. I saw several of the brethren today, and felt so fully assured that it is the Lord's will that I should go to Bristol, that I told them so. This evening I had a meeting with the three deacons, when I told them plainly about it; asking them, if they see any thing wrong in me concerning this matter, to tell me of it. They had nothing to say against it; yea, though much wishing me to stay, they were convinced themselves that my going is of God.

May 4. I saw again several brethren today, and told them about my intention to go to Bristol. There is much sorrowing and sighing, but it does not move me in the least, though I desire to sympathize with them. I am still fully persuaded that the Lord will have us go to Bristol. May 5. One other striking proof to my mind, that my leaving Teignmouth is of God, is, that some truly spiritual believers, though they much wish me to stay, themselves see that I ought to go to Bristol.

May 7. Having received a letter from Bristol on May 5th, it was answered today in such a way that the Lord may have another opportunity, to prevent our going thither, if it be not of Him. Especially we will not move a single stone out of the way in our own strength, and much less still be guilty of a want of openness and plainness, nor would we wish by such means to obtain Bethesda chapel.

May 11. The Lord seems to try us about Bristol. There was reason to expect a letter the day before yesterday, but none came; also today there is no letter. Even this is very good for us. Yea, I do wish most heartily that we may not have Bethesda chapel, if it be not good for us.

May 15. Just when I was in prayer concerning Bristol, I was sent for to come to Brother Craik. Two letters had arrived from Bristol. The brethren assembling at Gideon accept our offer to come under the conditions we have made, i.e., for the present to consider us only as ministering among them, but not in any fixed pastoral relationship, so that we may preach as we consider it to be according to the mind of God, without reference to any rules among them; that the pew-rents should be done away with and that we should go on, respecting the supply of our temporal wants, as in Devonshire. We intend, the Lord willing, to leave in about a week, though there is nothing settled respecting Bethesda chapel.

May 16. I preached for the last time at Bishopsteignton, and took leave of the brethren. May 17. I went to Exmouth, and, after preaching, took leave of the brethren. May 21. I began today to take leave of the brethren at Teignmouth, calling on each of them. In the evening I went over to Shaldon to take leave of the brethren, of whom brother Craik has had the oversight. It has been a trying day. Much weeping on the part of the saints. Were I not so fully persuaded that it is the will of God we should go to Bristol, I should have been hardly able to bear it.

May 22. The brethren at Shaldon and Teignmouth say, that they expect us soon back again. As far as I understand the way in which God deals with his children, this seems very unlikely. In every respect we have seen the Lord's goodness, and all proves that it is His will that we should go to Bristol. This full persuasion has helped me to withstand all the tears of the saints. Towards the evening the Lord, after repeated prayer, gave me Col. i. 21-23, as a text, for the last word of exhortation. It seemed to me best to speak as little as possible about myself, and as much as possible about Christ. I scarcely alluded to our separation, and only commended myself and the brethren, in the concluding prayer, to the Lord. The parting scenes are very trying, but my full persuasion is, that the separation is of the Lord.

May 23. My beloved wife, Mr. Groves, my father-in-law, and I left this morning for Exeter. Dear brother Craik intends to follow us tomorrow.

Review of the time since I left London, up to my removal from Teignmouth.

I. All this time the Lord never allowed me to regret the step I had taken, in separating from the Society.

II. The results have most abundantly shown, that it was of God; for, by His help, 1, I have not lost in truth or grace since. 2, I have been in peace concerning the matter. 3, the Lord made it a blessing to many souls.

III. During this period it pleased the Lord, to convert, through my instrumentality, many souls at Teignmouth, Exmouth, Bishopsteignton, Exeter, Chudleigh, in the neighbourhood of Barnstaple, at Chard, and elsewhere. The church at Teignmouth increased from eighteen to fifty-one.

IV. The Lord most graciously supplied all my temporal wants during this period, so that I lacked no good thing.

V. We had unexpectedly received, just before we left Teignmouth, about £15., else we should not have been able to defray all the expenses connected with leaving, traveling, &c. By this also the Lord showed His mind concerning our going to Bristol.

VI. During these two years and five months, since I left London, I have sinned in many respects, though walking, it may be, in the eyes of the brethren, very near to God. Indeed, my confession concerning this time also is, that I have been an unprofitable servant.

The following record will now show to the believing reader how far, what I have said concerning my persuasion, that it was the will of God that we should go to Bristol, has been proved by facts.

May 25th, 1832. This evening we arrived in Bristol. May 27. This morning we received a sovereign, sent to us by a sister residing in Devonshire, which we take as an earnest that the Lord will provide for us here also. May 28. When we were going to speak to the brethren, who manage the temporal affairs of Gideon chapel, about giving up the pew-rents, having all the seats free, and receiving the free-will offerings through a box, a matter which was not quite settled on their part, as brother Craik and I had thought; we found that the Lord had so graciously ordered this matter for us, that there was not the least objection on the part of these brethren.

June 4. For several days we have been looking about for lodgings, but finding none plain and cheap enough, we were led to make this also a subject of earnest prayer; and now, immediately afterwards, the Lord has given us such as are suitable. They are the plainest and cheapest we can find, but still too good for servants of Jesus, as our Master had not where to lay His head. We pay only 18s. a week for two sitting-rooms and three bedrooms, coals and attendance. It was particularly difficult to find cheap furnished lodgings, having five rooms in the same house, which we need, as brother Craik and we live together. How good is the Lord to have thus appeared for us, in answer to prayer, and what an encouragement to commit every thing to Him in prayer!

June 5. Today we had already a testimony of a sinner having been converted by brother Craik's instrumentality, on the first Lord's day in April, simply through hearing the text read. [This aged sister lived eleven years afterwards, during which time her walk was according to the profession she made. She fell asleep in 1843.] June 7. We have daily fresh encouragements, and fresh proofs that our being here is of God. June 16. We saw another instance of conversion through brother Craik's instrumentality.

June 25. Today it was finally settled to take Bethesda chapel for a twelvemonth, on condition that a brother at once paid the rent, with the understanding, that, if the Lord shall bless our labours in that place, so that believers are gathered together in fellowship, he expects them to help him; but, if not, that he will pay all. This was the only way in which we could take the chapel; for we could not think it to be of God to have had this chapel, though there should have been every prospect of usefulness, if it had made us in any way debtors. We had tried to obtain a cheaper meeting-place, but could find none large enough to accommodate the hearers.

July 6. Today we commenced preaching at Bethesda Chapel. It was a good day. July 13. Today we heard of the first cases of cholera in Bristol. July 16. This evening, from six to nine o'clock, we had appointed for conversing at the vestry, one by one, with individuals, who wished to speak to us about their souls. There were so many, that we were engaged from six till twenty minutes past ten.

These meetings we have continued ever since twice a week, or once a week, or once a fortnight, or once a month, as our strength and time allowed it, or as they seemed needed. We have found them beneficial in the following respects:

1. Many persons, on account of timidity, would prefer coming at an appointed time to the vestry to converse with us, to calling on us in our own house. 2. The very fact of appointing a time for seeing people, to converse with them in private concerning the things of eternity, has brought some, who, humanly speaking, never would have called on us under other circumstances; yea, it has brought even those who, though they thought they were concerned about the things of God, yet were completely ignorant; and thus we have had an opportunity of speaking to them. 3. These meetings have also been a great encouragement to ourselves in the work, for often, when we thought that such and such expositions of the Word had done no good at all, it was, through these meetings, found to be the reverse; and likewise, when our hands were hanging down, we have been afresh encouraged to go forward in the work of the Lord, and to continue sowing the seed in hope, by seeing at these meetings fresh cases, in which the Lord had condescended to use us as instruments, particularly as in this way instances have sometimes occurred in which individuals have spoken to us about the benefit which they derived from our ministry, not only a few months before, but even as long as two, three, and four years before.

For the above reasons I would particularly recommend to other servants of Christ, especially to those who live in large towns, if they have not already introduced a similar plan, to consider whether it may not be well for them also to set apart such times for seeing inquirers. Those meetings, however, require much prayer, to be enabled to speak aright, to all those who come, according to their different need; and one is led continually to feel that one is not sufficient of one's self for these things, but that our sufficiency can be alone of God. These meetings also have been by far the most wearing out part of all our work, though at the same time the most refreshing.

July 18. Today I spent the whole morning in the vestry, to procure a quiet season. This has now for some time been the only way, on account of the multiplicity of engagements, to make sure of time for prayer, reading the Word and meditation. July 19. I spent from half-past nine till one in the vestry, and had real communion with the Lord. The Lord be praised, who has put it into my mind to use the vestry for a place of retirement!

August 5. When all our money was gone today, the Lord again graciously supplied our wants. August 6. This afternoon, from two till after six, brother Craik and I spent in the vestry, to see the inquirers. We have had again, in seeing several instances of blessing upon our labours, abundant reason brought before us to praise the Lord for having sent us to Bristol.

August 13, 1832. This evening one brother and four sisters united with brother Craik and me in church fellowship at Bethesda, without any rules, desiring only to act as the Lord shall be pleased to give us light through His word.

August 14. This day we set apart for prayer concerning the cholera, and had three meetings.

August 17. This morning, from six to eight, we had a prayer meeting at Gideon, on account of the cholera. Between two and three hundred people were present. [We continued these meetings every morning, as long as the cholera raged in Bristol, and afterwards changed them into prayer meetings for the church at large, so that we had them for about four months.]

August 24. This morning a sister in the Lord, within fifty yards of our lodging, was taken ill in the cholera, and died this afternoon. Her husband, also a believer, has been attacked, and may be near death. The ravages of this disease are becoming daily more and more fearful. We have reason to believe that great numbers die daily in this city. Who may be the next, God alone knows. I have never realised so much the nearness of death. Except the Lord keep us this night, we shall be no more in the land of the living tomorrow. Just now, ten in the evening, the funeral bell is ringing, and has been ringing the greater part of this evening. It rings almost all the day. Into Thine hands, O Lord, I commend myself! Here is Thy poor worthless child! If this night I should be taken in the cholera, my only hope and trust is in the blood of Jesus Christ, shed for the remission of all my many sins. I have been thoroughly washed in it, and the righteousness of God covers me.—As yet there have not been any of the saints, among whom brother Craik and I labour, taken in the cholera. [Only one of them fell asleep afterwards in consequence of this disease. I would observe, that though brother Craik and I visited many cholera cases, by day and by night, yet the Lord most graciously preserved us and our families from it.]

September 17. This morning the Lord, in addition to all His other mercies, has given us a little girl, who, with her mother, are doing well.

September 21. On account of the birth of our little one, and brother Craik's intended marriage, it is needful that we change our lodgings, as they will now be too small for us, because we shall want one room more. Just when we were thinking about this, the house belonging to Gideon chapel, which had been let for three years, was unexpectedly given up by the tenant, and it was now offered to us by the church. We said we could not think of going into it, as we had no furniture, and no money to buy any. The brother who proposed our going into that house, however, replied that the brethren would gladly furnish it for us, to which we objected, fearing it would burthen them. When, however, the matter was repeatedly mentioned, and when it was particularly expressed that it would be a pleasure to the brethren to furnish the house, we began to consider the subject in prayer, and we saw no scriptural objection to accept this kindness, provided the furniture was very plain. This was promised. The house was furnished, yet the love of the brethren had done it more expensively than we wished it.

September 23. Today an individual desired publicly to return thanks to the Lord, for having been supported under the loss of a child, mother, brother, and wife, in the cholera, within one month.

September 25. Last night brother Craik and I were called out of bed to a poor woman ill in the cholera. She was suffering intensely. We never saw a case so distressing. We could hardly say any thing to her on account of her loud cries. I felt as if the cholera was coming upon me. We commended ourselves into the hands of the Lord when we came home, and He mercifully preserved us. The poor woman died today.

Oct. 1. A meeting for inquirers this afternoon from two to five. Many more are convinced of sin through brother Craik's preaching than my own. This circumstance led me to inquire into the reasons, which are probably these:—1. That brother Craik is more spiritually minded than I am. 2. That he prays more earnestly for the conversion of sinners than I do. 3. That he more frequently addresses sinners, as such, in his public ministrations, than I do.—This led me to more frequent and earnest prayer for the conversion of sinners, and to address them more frequently as such. The latter had never been intentionally left undone, but it had not been so frequently brought to my mind as to that of brother Craik. Since then, the cases in which it has pleased the Lord to use me as an instrument of conversion have been quite as many as those in which brother Craik has been used. May the Lord be pleased to use this as a means to lead any of His servants, who may not have acted according to these two last points, to seek to do so, and may He graciously enable me to do so more abundantly!

October 3. This day we set apart as a day of thanksgiving, the cholera having decreased. Oct. 5. Prayer meeting this morning as usual. The cholera is very much decreasing, and the number at our morning prayer meetings likewise.—Hundreds of people were stirred up at that time, but many of them, when the judgment of God had passed away, cared no longer about their souls. Yet a goodly number, who were first led through the instrumentality of the cholera to seek the Lord, are now breaking bread with us, and are walking in the fear of the Lord. How merciful in its results has this heavy judgment been to many!

January 4, 1833. This morning we received letters from Bagdad. The missionary brethren there invite brother Craik and me to come and join them in their labours. The invitation was accompanied by drafts to the amount of £200., for our traveling expenses. What wilt Thou have me to do, gracious Lord? I do not know what may be the Lord's mind. There are points which ought to be much considered and prayed over: There are German villages not very far from Bagdad, where I might labour; upon our going, that of certain other individuals may depend; the brethren at Bagdad are of one mind respecting our going out; good may be done on the way; the going out without any visible support from a society, simply trusting in the Lord for the supply of our temporal wants, would be a testimony for Him; I have had for years a feeling as if one day I should go out as a missionary to the heathen or Mahomedans; and lastly, the hands of the brethren at Bagdad may be strengthened; these are the points, which must appear of no sufficient weight in comparison with the importance of our work here, before I can determine not to go.

January 5. I considered with brother Craik about going to Bagdad. We see nothing clearly. If the Lord will have me to go, here I am. January 7. I spent again some time in prayer, respecting our going to Bagdad, and examined more fully into it. January 8. I had from half-past five till eight this morning to myself in prayer and reading the Word. I prayed then, and repeatedly besides this day, respecting our going to Bagdad. I wrote also a letter to some believers at and near Barnstaple, to ask their prayers concerning this matter. I do not see more clearly than I did before. January 9. I again asked the Lord concerning Bagdad, but see nothing clearly respecting it. I told the Lord I should stay at my post, unless He Himself should most evidently take me away, and I did not feel afterwards my remaining here to be against His will. January 14. I feel more and more satisfied that it is not of the Lord that I should go to Bagdad. January 19. For some days past I have been reading brother Groves' journal of his residence at Bagdad, both for the sake of information respecting his position there, and also, if it please the Lord, that He may use this as a means to show me clearly wether I should go or stay. Blessed be His name that I have no desire of my own in this matter! [Forty-seven years have since passed away, and I think I may say this day still, according to the best of my knowledge, I had no desire of my own in this matter; but I never saw it to be the Lord's will to leave the work which He Himself had so evidently given me.]

February 9. I read a part of Franke's life. The Lord graciously help me to follow him, as far as he followed Christ. The greater part of the Lord's people whom we know in Bristol are poor, and if the Lord were to give us grace to live more as this dear man of God did, we might draw much more than we have as yet done out of our Heavenly Father's bank, for our poor brethren and sisters.

May 27. Today the two churches, assembling at Gideon and Bethesda, met together at tea.—These meetings we have often repeated, and found them profitable on several accounts. 1. They give a testimony to the world of the love of the brethren, by rich and poor meeting thus together to partake of a meal. 2. Such meetings may be instrumental in uniting the saints more and more together. 3. They give us a sweet foretaste of our meeting together at the marriage supper of the Lamb.—At these meetings we pray and sing together, and any brother has an opportunity to speak what may tend to the edification of the rest.

May 28. This morning, whilst sitting in my room, the distress of several brethren and sisters was brought to my mind, and I said to myself, "Oh that it might please the Lord to give me means to help them!" About an hour afterwards I received £60. from a brother, whom up to this day I never saw, and who then lived, as he does still, at a distance of several thousand miles. This shows how the Lord can provide in any way for His people, and that He is not confined to places. Oh that my heart might overflow with gratitude to the Lord! [Since the first edition was printed, I have become personally acquainted with the donor.]

May 29. Review of the last twelve months, since we have been in Bristol, as it regards the fruits of our labours. 1. It has pleased the Lord to gather a church, through our instrumentality, at Bethesda, which is increased to 60 in number, and there have been added to Gideon church 49; therefore the total number of those added to us within the year, has been 109. 2. There have been converted through our instrumentality, so far as we have heard and can judge respecting the individuals, 65. 3. Many backsliders have been reclaimed, and many of the children of God have been encouraged and strengthened in the way of truth. What clear proofs that we were not suffered to be mistaken, as it regards our coming to Bristol.

June 12. I felt, this morning, that we might do something for the souls of those poor boys and girls, and grown-up or aged people, to whom we have daily given bread for some time past, in establishing a school for them, reading the Scriptures to them, and speaking to them about the Lord. As far as I see at present, it appears well to me to take a place in the midst of those poor streets near us, to collect the children in the morning about eight, giving them each a piece of bread for breakfast, and then to teach them to read, or to read the Scriptures to them, for about an hour and a half. Afterwards the aged, or grown-up people, may have their appointed time, when bread may be given to them, and the Scriptures read and expounded to them, for, perhaps, half an hour. About similar things I have now and then thought these two years.—There was bread given to about 30 or 40 persons today; and though the number should increase, in the above way, to 200 or more, surely our gracious and rich Lord can give us bread for them also. No sooner had these thoughts arisen, and I communicated them to my dear brother Craik, than I was also directed to a place where the people may be assembled, holding comfortably 150 children. We went about it, and may have it at the rent of 10l., yearly. The Lord directed us, also, to an aged brother as a teacher, and he gladly accepted of our offer. Surely, this matter seems to be of God. Moreover, as I have just now a good deal of money left of the 60l., we have wherewith to begin; and if it be the Lord's will, and if He will accept it, I am willing to lay out at once 20l. of it in this way, yea, all that is left, if He will but speak; and, by the time that this is gone, He can send more. O Lord, if this matter be of Thee, then prosper it! [This desire was not carried out. As far as I remember, the chief obstacle in the way was a pressure of work coming upon brother Craik and me just about that time. Shortly after, the number of the poor who came for bread increased to between 60 and 80 a day, whereby our neighbours were molested, as the beggars were lying about in troops in the streets, on account of which we were obliged to tell them no longer to come for bread. But though, at this time, this matter was not carried out, the thought was, from time to time, revived and strengthened in my mind, and it ultimately issued in the formation of the Scriptural Knowledge Institution, and in the establishment of the Orphan-Houses.]

June 22. A brother sent a hat to brother Craik, and one to me, as a token of his love and gratitude, like a thank-offering, as he says.

This is now the fourth hat which the Lord has kindly sent me successively, whenever, or even before, I needed one. Between August 19th and 27th was sent to us, by several individuals, a considerable quantity of fruit. How very kind of the Lord, not merely to send us the necessaries of life, but even such things as, on account of the weakness of our bodies, or the want of appetite, we might have desired! Thus the Lord has sent wine or porter when we required it; or, when there was want of appetite, and, on account of the poverty of our brethren, we should not have considered it right to spend money upon such things, He has kindly sent fowls, game, &c., to suit our appetite. We have, indeed, not served a hard Master. I am quite ashamed when I still, sometimes, find my heart dissatisfied, or, at least, not grateful as it ought to be.

December 17. This evening brother Craik and I took tea with a family, of whom five have been brought to the knowledge of the Lord through our instrumentality. [When we took tea with them again, about a twelvemonth afterwards, the number had increased to seven.] As an encouragement to brethren who may desire to preach the Gospel in a language not their own, I would mention, that the first member of this family who was converted, came merely out of curiosity to hear my foreign accent, some words having been mentioned to her which I did not pronounce properly. Scarcely had she entered the chapel, when she was led to see herself a sinner. Her intention had been, to stay only a few minutes. But she felt herself as if bound to the seat whilst I was speaking, and remained to the close of the meeting. She then went hastily home, instead of pursuing her pleasures, washed the paint off her face, stayed at home that Lord's day, till the meeting began again, and from that day was truly converted. Having found the Lord, she entreated her brothers and sisters to go and hear the Gospel preached, who, in doing so, were likewise converted. May my dear missionary brethren always be mindful that the Lord can bless a few broken sentences, however badly the words are pronounced, as a means in the conversion of sinners!

December 31, 1833. In looking over my journal, I find:—I. That at least 260 persons (according to the number of names we have marked down, but there have been many more,) have come to converse with us about the concerns of their souls. Out of these, 153 have been added to us in fellowship these last eighteen months, 60 of whom have been brought to the knowledge of the Lord through our instrumentality. Besides these 60, five have fallen asleep before they were received into communion. In addition to these, there are many among the inquirers and candidates for fellowship, whom we have reason to believe God has given to us as seals to our ministry in this city. Some also were converted through our instrumentality who are in fellowship with other churches in this city.

II. In looking over the Lord's dealings with me as to temporal things, I find that He has sent me, during the past year,—

1. In freewill offerings through the boxes, as my part £152 14s. 5 1/4d.

2. Presents in money given to me £25 1s. 3d.

3. Presents in clothes and provisions worth at least £20 0s. 0d.

Altogether from the brethren in Bristol £197 15s. 8 1/4d.

4. A brother sent me, from a distance of several thousand miles £60 0s. 0d.

5. We live free of rent, which is worth for our part £10 0s. 0d.

Totaling £267 15s 8 1/4d.

It is just now four years since I first began to trust in the Lord alone for the supply of my temporal wants. My little all I then had, at most worth 100l. a year, I gave up to the Lord, having then nothing left but about 5l. The Lord greatly honoured this little sacrifice, and He gave me, in return, not only as much as I had given up, but considerably more. For during the first year, He sent me already, in one way or other, (including what came to me through family connexion) about 130l. During the second year, 151l. 18s. 8d. During the third year, 195l. 3s. During this year, 267l. 15s. 8 1/4d. The following points require particular notice:—1. During the last three years and three months I never have asked any one for any thing; but, by the help of the Lord, I have been enabled at all times to bring my wants to Him, and He graciously has supplied them all. And thus, the Lord helping me, I hope to be enabled to go on to the last moment of my life. 2. At the close of each of these four years, though my income has been comparatively great, I have had only a few shillings, or nothing at all left; and thus it is also today, by the help of God. 3. During the last year a considerable part of my income has come from a distance of several thousand miles, from a brother whom I never saw. 4. Since we have been obliged to discontinue the giving away bread to about 50 poor people every day, on account of our neighbours, our income has not been, during the second part of this year, nearly so great, scarcely one-half as much, as during the first part of it; as if the Lord would thereby show us that when the calls upon us are many, He is able to send in accordingly. Observe this!

January 1, 1834. It seemed well to brother Craik and me, to have an especial public meeting for thanksgiving to the Lord, for His many mercies towards us since we have been in Bristol, and for the great success which it has pleased Him to grant to our labours; and also for confession of our sinfulness and unworthiness, and to entreat Him to continue His goodness towards us. Accordingly we met last evening, and continued together from seven o'clock till half-past twelve. About four hundred individuals, or more, met with us on the occasion.

January 3. This evening, from six to a quarter past ten, we conversed with inquirers. After we had seen twelve, we had to send away six. There were several fresh cases of conversion among them. The work of the Lord is still going on among us. One of the individuals, who has lately been brought to the knowledge of the truth, used to say in his unconverted state, when he was tempted not to go to the chapel,—"I will go; the Lord may bless me one day, and soften my hard heart."—His expectation has not come to nothing.

January 9. Brother Craik and I have preached during these eighteen months, once a month, at Brislington, a village near Bristol, but have not seen any fruit of our labours there. This led me, today, very earnestly to pray to the Lord for the conversion of sinners in that place. I was also, in the chapel, especially led to pray again about this, and asked the Lord in particular that He would be pleased to convert, at least, one soul this evening, that we might have a little encouragement. I preached with much help, and I hope there has been good done this evening. [The Lord did according to my request. There was, that evening, a young man brought to the knowledge of the truth.]

January 13. The Lord verified in our experience the truths which I had preached last evening in speaking on "Hast thou not made an hedge about him, and about his house, and about all that he hath, on every side?" Job i. 10. Thieves attempted to break into Gideon Chapel. They had broken it open, but were either smitten with blindness, so as not to see a certain door which had been left unlocked, or were disturbed before accomplishing their design; for there was nothing missing.

January 14. I was greatly tried by the difficulty of fixing upon a text, from which to preach, on the morning of October 20, and at last preached without enjoyment. Today I heard of a NINTH instance in which this very sermon has been blessed. May my brethren in the ministry of the Word be encouraged by this to go quietly, yet prayerfully, forward in the work of the Lord!

January 31. This evening a Dorcas Society was formed among the sisters in communion with us, but not according to the manner in which we found one when we came to Bristol; for as we have dismissed all teachers from the Sunday School who were not believers, so now believing females only will meet together to make clothes for the poor. The being mixed up with unbelievers had not only proved a barrier to spiritual conversation among the sisters, but must have been also injurious to both parties in several respects. One sister, now united to us in fellowship, acknowledged that the being connected with the Dorcas Society, previous to her conversion, had been, in a measure, the means of keeping her in security; as she thought, that, by helping on such like things, she might gain heaven at last. Oh that the saints in faithful love, according to the word of God, (2 Cor. vi. 14-18) might be more separated, in all spiritual matters, from unbelievers, and not be unequally yoked together with them!

February 12. I prayed little, read little of the Word, and laboured little to day. On the whole an unprofitable day. May the Lord in mercy give me fervency of spirit!

February 19. Brother Craik preached this evening on Mark iv. 30-41, and was enabled to give out precious truths. Oh that I did feed more upon them! For several weeks I have had very little real communion with the Lord. I long for it. I am cold. I have little love to the Lord. But I am not, yea, I cannot be satisfied with such a state of heart. Oh that once more I might be brought to fervency of spirit, and that thus it might continue with me forever! I long to go home that I maybe with the Lord, and that I may love Him with all my heart. I fear that the Lord will chastise me at the time of my dear wife's confinement. Lord Jesus, take Thy miserable sinful servant soon to Thyself, that I may serve Thee better! Within the last week I have repeatedly set out, as it were, afresh; but soon, very soon, all has come again to nothing. The Lord alone can help me. Oh that it might please Him to bring me into a more spiritual state!

February 20. By the mercy of God I was today melted into tears on account of my state of heart. Oh that it might please the Lord to bring me into a more spiritual state! February 21. Through the help of the Lord I am rather in a better state of heart than for some time past.—I was led this morning to form a plan for establishing, upon scriptural principles, an Institution for the spread of the Gospel at home and abroad. I trust this matter is of God.—This evening we had again, from six to half-past ten, a meeting with inquirers. The work of the Lord is going on among us as much as ever. Oh that our hearts might overflow with gratitude! Even after we were worn out to the utmost, we could not see all, but had to send away several individuals.

February 25. The inquiries were so many yesterday, that though we conversed more than four hours with them, we had to appoint another meeting for today, and saw again several from two till five. I was led again this day to pray about the forming of a new Missionary Institution, and felt still more confirmed that we should do so.

[Some readers may ask why we formed a new Institution for the spread of the Gospel, and why we did not unite with some of the religious societies, already in existence, seeing that there are several Missionary-, Bible-, Tract-, and School Societies. I give, therefore, our reasons, in order to show, that nothing but the desire to maintain a good conscience led us to act as we did. For as, by the grace of God, we acknowledged the word of God as the only rule of action for the disciples of the Lord Jesus, we found, in comparing the then existing religious Societies with the word of God, that they departed so far from it, that we could not be united with them, and yet maintain a good conscience. I only mention here the following points.

1. The end which these religious societies propose to themselves, and which is constantly put before their members, is, that the world will gradually become better and better, and that at last the whole world will be converted. To this end there is constantly reference made to the passage in Habakkuk ii. 14. "For the earth shall be filled with the knowledge of the glory of the Lord, as the waters cover the sea," or the one in Isaiah xi. 9, "For the earth shall be full of the knowledge of the Lord, as the waters cover the sea." But that these passages can have no reference to the present dispensation, but to the one which will commence with the return of the Lord, that in the present dispensation things will not become spiritually better, but rather worse, and that in the present dispensation it is not the whole world that will be converted, but only a people gathered out from among the Gentiles for the Lord, is clear from many passages of the divine testimony, of which I only refer to the following: Matt. xiii. 24-30, and verse 36-43, 2 Tim. iii. 1-13, Acts. xv. 14.

A hearty desire for the conversion of sinners, and earnest prayer for it to the Lord, is quite scriptural; but it is unscriptural to expect the conversion of the whole world. Such an end we could not propose to ourselves in the service of the Lord.

2. But that which is worse, is the connexion of those religious societies with the world, which is completely contrary to the word of God (2 Cor. vi. 14-18). In temporal things the children of God need, whilst they remain here on earth, to make use of the world; but when the work to be done requires, that those who attend to it should be possessed of spiritual life (of which unbelievers are utterly destitute), the children of God are bound, by their loyalty to their Lord, entirely to refrain from association with the unregenerate. But alas! The connexion with the world is but too marked in these religious societies; for every one who pays a guinea, or, in some societies, half-a-guinea, is considered as a member. Although such an individual may live in sin; although he may manifest to every one that he does not know the Lord Jesus; if only the guinea or the half-guinea be paid, he is considered a member, and has a right as such

to vote. Moreover, whoever pays a larger sum, for instance, £10. or £20. can be, in many societies, a member for life, however openly sinful his life should be for the time, or should became afterwards. Surely, such things aught not to be!

3. The means which are made use of in these religious societies, to obtain money for the work of the Lord, are also, in other respects, unscriptural; for it is a most common case to ask the unconverted for money, which even Abraham would not have done (Genesis xiv. 21-24): and how much less should we do it, who are not only forbidden to have fellowship with unbelievers in all such matters (2 Cor. vi. 14-18), but who are also in fellowship with the Father and the Son, and can therefore obtain everything from the Lord which we possibly can need in His service, without being obliged to go to the unconverted world! How altogether differently the first disciples acted in this respect, we learn from 3 John 7.

4. Not merely, however, in these particulars is there a connexion with the world in these religious societies; but it is not a rare thing for even Committee Members (the individuals who manage the affairs of the societies) to be manifestly unconverted persons, if not open enemies to the truth; and this is suffered because they are rich, or of influence, as it is called.

5. It is a most common thing to endeavour to obtain for patrons and presidents of these societies, and for chairmen at the public meetings, persons of rank or wealth to attract the public. Never once have I known a case of a POOR, but very devoted, wise, and experienced servant of Christ being invited to fill the chair at such public meetings. Surely, the Galilean fishermen, who were apostles, or our Lord Himself, who was called the carpenter, would not have been called to this office, according to these principles. These things ought not so to be among the disciples of the Lord Jesus, who should not judge with reference to a person's fitness for service in the Church of Christ by the position he fills in the world, or by the wealth he possesses!

6. Almost all these societies contract debts, so that it is a comparatively rare case to read a Report of any of them, without finding that they have expended more than they have received, which, however,

is contrary both to the spirit and to the letter of the New Testament. (Rom. xiii. 8).

Now, although brother Craik and I were ready, by the grace of God, heartily to acknowledge that there are not only many true children of God connected with these religious societies, but that the Lord has also blessed their efforts in many respects, notwithstanding the existence of these and other principles and practices which we judged to be unscriptural, yet it appeared to us to be His will, that we should be entirely separate from these societies, (though we should be considered as singular persons, or though it should even appear that we despised other persons, or would elevate ourselves above them), in order that, by the blessing of God, we might direct the attention of the children of God in these societies to their unscriptural practices; and we would rather be entirely unconnected with these societies than act contrary to the Holy Scriptures. We therefore separated entirely from them, although we remained united in brotherly love with individual believers belonging to them; and would by no means judge them for remaining in connexion with them, if they do not see that such things are contrary to Scripture. But seeing them to be so ourselves, we could not with a clear conscience remain. After we had thus gone on for some time, we considered that it would have an injurious tendency upon the brethren among whom we laboured, and also be at variance with the spirit of the Gospel of Christ, if we did nothing at all for Missionary objects, the circulation of the Holy Scriptures, Tracts, etc.; and we were therefore led for these and other reasons to do something for the spread of the Gospel at home and abroad, however small the beginning might be. This was the origin of the Institution, of which the following part of my Narrative speaks.]

March 5. This evening, at a public meeting, brother Craik and I stated the principles on which we intend to carry on the institution which we propose to establish for the spread of the Gospel at home and abroad. There was nothing outwardly influential, either in the number of people present, or in our speeches. May the Lord graciously be pleased to grant His blessing upon the institution, which will be called "The Scriptural Knowledge Institutions for Home and Abroad."

I. THE PRINCIPLES OF THE INSTITUTION.

1. We consider every believer bound, in one way or other, to help the cause of Christ, and we have Scriptural warrant for expecting the Lord's blessing upon our work of faith and labour of love: and although, according to Matt. xiii. 24-43, 2 Tim. iii. 1-13, and many other passages, the world will not be converted before the coming of our Lord Jesus, still, while He tarries; all Scriptural means ought to be employed for the ingathering of the elect of God.

2. The Lord helping us, we do not mean to seek the patronage of the world; i.e., we never intend to ask unconverted persons of rank or wealth to countenance this Institution, because this, we consider, would be dishonourable to the Lord. In the name of our God we set up our banners, Ps. xx. 5; He alone shall be our Patron, and if He helps us we shall prosper, and if He is not on our side, we shall not succeed.

3. We do not mean, to ask unbelievers for money (2 Cor. vi. 14-18); though we do not feel ourselves warranted to refuse their contributions, if they, of their own accord should offer them. Acts xxviii. 2-10.

4. We reject altogether the help of unbelievers in managing or carrying on the affairs of the Institution. 2 Cor, vi. 14-18.

5. We intend never to enlarge the field of labour by contracting debts (Rom. xiii. 8), and afterwards appealing to the Church of Christ for help, because this we consider to be opposed both to the letter and the spirit of the New Testament; but in secret prayer, God helping us, we shall carry the wants of the Institution to the Lord, and act according to the means that God shall give.

6. We do not mean to reckon the success of the Institution by the amount of money given, or the number of Bibles distributed, &c, but by the Lord's blessing upon the work (Zech. iv. 6); and we expect this, in the proportion in which He shall help us to wait upon Him in prayer.

7. While we would avoid aiming after needless singularity, we desire to go on simply according to Scripture, without compromising the truth; at the same time thankfully receiving any instruction

which experienced Believers, after prayer, upon Scriptural ground, may have to give us concerning the Institution.

II. THE OBJECTS OF THE INSTITUTION ARE:

1. To assist Day-Schools, Sunday-Schools, and Adult-Schools, in which instruction is given upon Scriptural principles, and, as far as the Lord may give the means, and supply us with suitable teachers, and in other respects make our path plain, to establish Schools of this kind.

a. By Day-Schools upon Scriptural principles, we understand Day Schools in which the teachers are godly persons,—in which the way of salvation is scripturally pointed out,—and in which no instruction is given opposed to the principles of the gospel.

b. Sunday-Schools, in which all the teachers are believers, and in which the Holy Scriptures alone are the foundation of instruction,—are such only as the Institution assists with the supply of Bibles, Testaments, &c.; for we consider it unscriptural, that any persons, who do not profess to know the Lord themselves, should be allowed to give religious instruction.

c. The Institution does not assist any Adult-Schools with the supply of Bibles, Testaments, Spelling Books, &c., except the teachers are believers.

2. To circulate the Holy Scriptures.

We sell Bibles and Testaments to poor persons at a reduced price. But while we, in general, think it better that the Scriptures should be sold, and not given altogether gratis, still, in cases of extreme poverty, we think it right to give, without payment, a cheap edition.

3. The third object of this Institution is, to aid Missionary efforts.

We desire to assist those Missionaries whose proceedings appear to be most according to the Scriptures. It is proposed to give such a portion of the amount of the donations to each of the forementioned objects, as the Lord may direct; but if none of the objects should claim a more particular assistance, to lay out an equal portion upon each; yet so, that if any donor desires to give for one of the objects exclusively, the money shall be appropriated accordingly.

March 7. Today we have only one shilling left. Many times also in Bristol our purse has been either empty or nearly so, though we have not been brought quite so low as it regards provisions, as was sometimes the case at Teignmouth. This evening, when we came home from our work, we found a brother, our tailor, waiting for us, who brought a new suit of clothes both for brother Craik and me, which a brother, whose name was not to be mentioned, had ordered for us. March 8. Our brother brought us this evening also, from the same friend, a new hat for each of us.

March 10. Some time since, a brother who had been brought to the knowledge of the Lord through our instrumentality, having been previously guilty of habitual drunkenness and other open sins, requested with tears our prayers on behalf of his wife, who, like himself formerly, was still given to drinking, and who grew worse and worse. About ten days, after he had spoken to us, it pleased God to begin a work of grace in her heart, in answer to the many prayers of her husband, and this evening she was added to us in fellowship. There have come many instances before us, since we have been in Bristol, in which unbelieving partners have been given to believing ones, in answer to their prayers; yea, even such as had threatened to murder their wives, or leave them, they would still continue to go to our chapels.

March 19. This afternoon at five, my wife was in much pain, which she shortly afterwards considered as the token of her hour being near. I therefore set off to call in a sister, and then I went for the nurse, and my wife's sister, and our servant, who were at Clifton. The Lord having graciously speeded all this, I went to Bethesda Chapel, where I had to preach shortly after. I thought it better to spend the few minutes, which I had before preaching, in prayer for my wife, than to return home again, as I should have had to set off directly afterwards, believing that my mind would be thus more quiet and calm, and that I also might thus help my dearest wife much more effectually. The Lord most graciously kept me from excitement and anxiety, so that I went in peace, preached in peace, and walked home in peace, looking up to Jesus to prepare me for all that might await me, as I remembered but too well the two former times of my wife's confinement. I might have asked brother Craik to preach, and have gone home; but I thought it more honouring the

Lord to do His work. In walking home, the following words were a particular refreshment to me:—

Make you His service your delight,

Your wants shall be His care.

When I came home, I heard the joyful news, that all was over, and that my dear Mary had been delivered at twenty minutes past eight of a little boy. Observe! 1. The Lord graciously sent the medical attendant and the nurse (the latter nearly three miles off), in the right time. 2. The Lord put it into my heart to honour Him, by preferring the care of His house to that of my own, and thus He lovingly spared me three painful hours. May He be pleased to give me grace more than ever to love and serve Him!

March 31. Today the brethren and sisters in communion at Bethesda dined together, having been invited by a sister; and in the evening the churches of Gideon and Bethesda took tea together. Both times were refreshing seasons. At dinner we were together from one till half past three, at tea from five to nine. Both times we prayed repeatedly, sang hymns, read a little of the Word, and several brethren spoke of the Lord's dealings with them.

April 3. Today I have had again much reason to see how weak I am, and how prone to give way to every sin if I am not kept by God. May He have mercy upon me, and keep me from bringing an open disgrace upon His holy name! O wretched man that I am!!

April 14. Brother and sister Craik and ourselves have been living together hitherto; but now, as the Lord has given to them one child, and to us two, and there are but six rooms in our house, so that of late dear brother Craik and I have had repeatedly to go to another house to be uninterrupted: we came at last to the conclusion, that it would be better for our souls and the Lord's work that we should separate. April 15. Today I received from several sisters 25l. towards furnishing a house.

April 23. Yesterday and today I had asked the Lord to send us 20l., that we might be able to procure a larger stock of Bibles and Testaments than our small funds of the Scriptural Knowledge Institution would allow us to purchase; and this evening a sister, unasked, promised to give us that sum, adding that she felt a particular pleasure in circulating the Holy Scriptures, as the simple reading of them had been the means of bringing her to the knowledge of the Lord.

April 26. We have repeatedly conversed about the name which we should give to our babe; but, being unsettled about it, and considering that in all our ways we ought to acknowledge the Lord, I gave myself today to prayer concerning this matter, and the name Elijah, about which I never had thought, was particularly, whilst praying, impressed on my mind, and therefore we intend to name the child Elijah, i. e., my God is Jah, Jehovah. May the Lord in mercy grant Elijah's spirit and Elijah's blessing to our little one!

May 4. Today 15l. more was given to me towards furnishing a house. Thus the Lord has now graciously supplied our need in this particular also. May 13. Today 2l. more was given to us towards furnishing the house, and also some carpet. May 15. Today we moved into our house, having lived nearly two years with brother and sister Craik.

June 4. Today a sister called on me, and I felt irritated at her staying, after having given her to understand that I had but a few minutes time. I sinned thus against the Lord. Help Thou me, blessed Jesus, in future!

June 8. Lord's day. I obtained no text yesterday, notwithstanding repeated prayer and reading of the Word. This morning I awoke with these words:—"My grace is sufficient for thee." As soon as I had dressed myself, I turned to 2 Cor. xii. to consider this passage; but in doing so, after prayer, I was led to think that I had not been directed to this portion for the sake of speaking on it as I at first thought, and I therefore followed my usual practice in such cases, i. e., to read on in the Scriptures where I left off last evening. In doing so, when I came to Heb. xi. 13-16, I felt that this was the text. Having prayed, I was confirmed in it, and in a few minutes the Lord was pleased to open this passage to me. I preached on it with great enjoyment, both at Gideon and at Bethesda, particularly in the evening at Bethesda. This help was evidently from God. May He fill my heart with gratitude, and encourage me by this, to trust in Him for the future! I now understand why those words, "My grace is sufficient for thee," were brought to my mind when I awoke this morning.—[It pleased God, as I have heard since, greatly to bless what I said on that passage, and at least one soul was brought through it to the Lord.]

June 25. These last three days I have had very little real communion with God, and have therefore been very weak spiritually, and have several times felt irritability of temper. May God in mercy help me to have more secret prayer!—Let none expect to have the mastery over his inward corruption in any degree, without going in his weakness again and again to the Lord for strength. Nor will prayer with others, or conversing with the brethren, make up for secret prayer; for I had been engaged in both repeatedly, during the three previous days, as my journal shows.

June 26. I was enabled, by the grace of God, to rise early, and I had nearly two hours in prayer before breakfast. I feel now this morning more comfortable. May God in mercy help me to walk before Him this day, and to do His work; and may He keep me from all evil!

July 5. The Lord very mercifully kept us today from a great calamity, the apron of our Christian servant having caught fire; but the fire was extinguished, and she was kept from being burned!

July 11. I have prayed much about a master for a boys' school, to be established in connexion with our little Institution. Eight have applied for the situation, but none seemed to be suitable. Now at last the Lord has given us a brother, who will commence the work. The Lord allowed us to call upon Him many times before He answered, but at last He granted our request.

July 13. Today we finished reading through the Scriptures, at family prayer, the second time since we came to Bristol, which is little more than two years. I mention this circumstance to show how often we may read through the whole of the Scriptures, though we should read but little every day, if we go regularly onward.

August 18. Today brother Craik and I engaged a sister to be governess of another girls' school, which we intend to establish, in dependence upon the Lord for supplies. August 27. I had prayed repeatedly, and had read ten chapters of the Word to get a text, but obtained none, and had to go this evening to the chapel without knowing on what portion of His Holy Word the Lord would have me to speak. At the commencement of the meeting I was directed to Lament. iii. 22-26, on which I spoke with much assistance and enjoyment.

September 18. A brother, a tailor, was sent to measure me for new clothes. My clothes are again getting old, and it is therefore very kind of the Lord to provide thus. September 25. A brother sent me a new hat today.

October 9. Our little institution, established in dependence upon the Lord, and supplied by Him with means, has now been seven months in operation, and through it have been benefited with instruction,—1. In the Sunday-School, about 120 children. 2. In the Adult-School, about 40 Adults. 3. In the two Day-Schools for boys and, the two Day-Schools for girls, 209 children, of whom 54 have been entirely free; the others pay about one-third of the expense. There have been also circulated 482 Bibles, and 520 New Testaments. Lastly, 57l. has been spent to aid missionary exertions. The means which the Lord has sent us, as the fruit of many prayers, during these seven months, amount to 167l. 10s. 0 1/2d.

October 28. This afternoon brother Craik and I took tea with seven brethren and sisters, whom the Lord has brought to a knowledge of Himself through our instrumentality, within the last two years; all but one belonging to the same family. We heard there a most affecting account of a poor little orphan boy, who for some time attended one of our schools, and who seems there, as far as we can judge, to have been brought to a real concern about his soul, through what I said concerning the torments of hell, and who some time ago was taken to the poor-house some miles out of Bristol. He has expressed great sorrow that he can no longer attend our school and ministry. May this, if it be the Lord's will, lead me to do something also for the supply of the temporal wants of poor children, the pressure of which has occasioned this poor boy to be taken away from our school!

November 1. Today, our means being completely gone, we had them supplied in the following manner:—some time since some silver spoons were given to us, which we never used, from the consideration, that for servants of Christ it was better, for the sake of example, to use cheaper ones, and for that reason we had sold our plate at Teignmouth. Yet up to this day those spoons remained unsold. But now, as we wanted money, we disposed of them, considering that the kind giver would not be displeased at our doing so to supply our need.

November 4. I spent the greater part of the morning in reading the Word and in prayer, and asked also for our daily bread, for we have scarcely any money left.—We obtained today two large school-rooms, which we much needed. Thus the Lord graciously helps us concerning the Institution, and gives us faith to go forward in the work, enlarging the field more and more (though we have but little money), yet so that we do not contract debts.

November 5. I spent almost the whole of the day in prayer and reading the Word. I prayed also again for the supply of our own temporal wants, but the Lord has not as yet appeared. Still my eyes are up to Him. November 8. Saturday. The Lord has graciously again supplied our temporal wants during this week, though at the commencement of it we had but little left. I have prayed much this week for money, more than any other week, as far as I remember, since we have been in Bristol. The Lord has not answered our prayers by causing means to be sent in the way of a gift, but has supplied us through our selling what we did not need, or by our being paid what was awed to us.

December 10. Today we found that a departed brother had left both to brother Craik and me 12l. December 31, 1834.—I. Since brother Craik and I have been labouring in Bristol, 227 brethren and sisters have been added to us in fellowship. We found 68 believers in the church at Gideon, so that now the whole number would be 295, had there been no changes, but it is only 257; for twelve have fallen asleep; six have left Bristol; twelve have left the churches during the two years and six months, but are still in Bristol; eight are under church discipline, respecting some of whom, however, we hope that they maybe soon restored to communion. Of those 257, there belong 125 to Bethesda church, and 132 to Gideon church. Out of the 227 who have been added to us, 103 have been converted through our instrumentality, and many have been brought into the liberty of the Gospel, or reclaimed from backsliding. Forty-seven young converts are at Gideon, and fifty-six at Bethesda. Considering that some have fallen asleep who never were in communion with us, and yet converted through our instrumentality; and that some are united to other churches in and out of Bristol; and that many are now standing as candidates for fellowship, of those who have been given to us in this city, as seals to our ministry; the number added may be only one-half, or two-thirds of the real number. May the Lord fill our hearts with gratitude, for having thus condescended to use us! II. The income which the Lord has given me during this year is:—

1. My part of the freewill offerings through the boxes £135 13s. 2 1/4d.

2. Money given to me by saints in and out of Bristol £92 7s. 6d.

Altogether. . . £228 0s. 8 1/4d.

3. Besides this, many articles in provisions, clothing, and furniture, worth to us about £60 0s. 0d.

January 1, 1835. We had last evening an especial prayer-meeting of the two churches, and any other persons hat chose to attend, for the sake of praising the Lord for all His many mercies which we have received during the past year, and to ask Him to continue to us His favour during this year also. It was open to any of the brethren to pray, as they felt disposed, and eighteen did so, as I afterwards reckoned. We continued in prayer and praise, mixed with singing, reading the Word, and exhortation, from seven in the evening till one in the morning. January 13. From ten till one in the first part of the day, and from six to half-past eight this evening, I visited, from house to house, the people living in Orange Street, and saw in this way the families living in nine houses, to ascertain whether any individuals wanted Bibles, whether they could read, whether they wished their children to be put to our Day-Schools or Sunday-School, with the view of helping them accordingly. This afforded opportunities to converse with them about their souls. In this way I sold eight Bibles and two Testaments at reduced prices, and gave away one Testament; engaged one woman as an adult scholar, one boy as a day scholar; and spoke besides this to about thirty people about their souls.—January 15. This morning, from ten till one, I went again from house to house in Orange Street. I visited nine houses, sold a Bible and Testament at reduced prices, and engaged, a few children for the schools, and conversed with fifteen persons about their souls. I should greatly delight in being frequently engaged in such work, for it is a most important one; but our hands are so full with other work, that we can do but little in this way.—January 17. Today brother Groves arrived from the East Indies. One reason of his coming to England is, to go to Germany to obtain missionary brethren for the East Indies, having reason to believe that he will find them there; and he asked me, on account of my acquaintance with the language, to accompany him, that thus, through me, he may be enabled to judge about the state of the brethren, and to communicate to them what he thinks needful for them to know. This is a most important work. May the Lord direct me in this matter, and make me to act according to His will!—I received again today, after prayer respecting the funds, 10l. for the Scriptural Knowledge Institution.—January 21. Received, in answer to prayer, from an unexpected quarter, 5l. for the Scriptural Knowledge Institution. The Lord pours in, whilst we seek to pour out. For during the past week, merely among the poor, in going from house to house, fifty-eight copies of the Scriptures were sold at reduced prices, the going on with which is most important, but it will require much means.

January 28. I have, for these several days, again prayed much to ascertain whether the Lord will have me to go as a missionary to the East Indies, and I am most willing to go, if He will condescend to use me in this way. January 29. I have been greatly stirred up to pray about going to Calcutta as a missionary. May the Lord guide me in this matter! [After all my repeated and earnest prayer in the commencement of 1835, and willingness on my part to go, if it were the Lord's will, still He did not send me.]

February 4. I have been praying repeatedly and earnestly of late respecting my journey to the Continent. I desire to go, or not to go, just as the Lord will have it to be. May He graciously direct me! I feel the same about going to India. As a means to ascertain the Lord's will, I have been reading about the Hindoos, that I may know more clearly the state in which they are. May the Lord in mercy stir me up to care more about their state, whether it be His will that I should labour personally among them, or not!

February 16. I mentioned this evening, before the church at Bethesda, as also on the 13th before the church at Gideon, that I see it the Lord's will to go to the Continent, for the sake of assisting brother Groves by my knowledge of the German language, in conferring with those who may desire to go out as missionaries. There is not one believer amongst us who sees any objection to it, and several have expressed that it seems to be of the Lord, and that thus we could help, as churches, in the going forth of missionaries. This is very comforting to me, as the Lord confirms me still more, through this unanimity, in its being His will that I should go.

February 25. In the name of the Lord, and in dependence upon Him alone for support, we have established a fifth Day-School for poor children, which today has been opened. We have now two boys' schools, and three girls' schools. February 26. This afternoon I left Bristol for the Continent.

February 27. London. This morning I went to the Alien Office for my passport. On entering the office I saw a printed paper, in which it is stated that every alien neglecting to renew, every six months, his certificate of residence which he receives on depositing his passport, subjects himself to a penalty of £50, or imprisonment. This law I have ignorantly broken ever since I left London in 1829. It appeared to me much better to confess at once that I had ignorantly done so, than now willfully break it; trusting in the Lord as it regarded the consequences of the step. I did so, and the Lord inclined the heart of the officer with whom I had to do, to pass over my noncompliance with the law, on account of my having broken it ignorantly. Having obtained my passport, I found an unexpected difficulty in the Prussian ambassador refusing to sign it, as it did not contain a description of my person, and therefore I needed to prove that I was the individual spoken of in the passport. This difficulty was not removed for three days, when, after earnest prayer, through a paper signed by same citizens of London, to whom I am known, the ambassador was satisfied. This very difficulty, when once the Lord had removed it, afforded me cause for thanksgiving; for I now obtained a new passport, worded in such a way, that, should I ever need it again, will prevent similar difficulties.

March 3. This evening I preached comfortably in Johnstreet Chapel, for Brother Evans. I never preached in any place where I so much felt that he who statedly ministers was more worthy than myself. This feeling led me to earnest prayer, and the Lord heard and assisted me.

March 7. Dover. Last evening I left London, and arrived here this morning. The Lord enabled me to confess Him before my fellow-passengers. I have had a good deal of prayer and reading the Word in quietness, though staying in an hotel.—March 8. I preached this morning and evening comfortably in one of the chapels at Dover. March 9. All this day too we have been obliged to remain at Dover, the sea being so rough that no packet sails. I spent the day in writing letters, in reading the Word, and in prayer. We depend entirely upon the Lord as it regards our movements. This evening we asked the Lord twice, unitedly, that He would be pleased to calm the wind and the waves, and I now feel quite comfortable in leaving the matter with Him!

March 10. The Lord heard our prayer. We awake early in the morning, and found the wind comparatively calm. We left the hotel before break of day, to go to the packet. All being in great hurry, on our way towards the sea, I was separated from brothers G. and Y. I now lifted up my heart to the Lord, as He generally helps me to do on such occasions, to direct my steps towards the boat which went out to meet the packet, and I found it almost immediately. We had, in answer to prayer, a good passage. At Calais we obtained our passports, luggage out of the custom house, and places in the diligence without difficulty, and left a little after ten in the morning for Paris. What a blessed thing it is, in all such matters, to have a Father to go to for help! What a different thing, also, to travel in the service of the Lord Jesus, from what it is to travel in the service of the flesh!

March 11. Paris. We arrived here about ten this evening. March 12. Today we went about our passports, and I saw thus a good deal of the best part of Paris. Blessed be God, my heart is above these things! If ten years ago, when my poor foolish heart was full of Paris, I had come here, how should I have been taken up with these palaces, &c.; but now I look at these things, and my heart does not care about them, What a difference grace makes! There were few people, perhaps, more passionately fond of traveling, and seeing fresh places, and new scenes, than myself; but now, since, by the grace of God, I have seen beauty in the Lord Jesus, I have lost my taste for these things.

March 13. We again found difficulty in obtaining our passports, arising, probably, from a mistake of the police officers. May the Lord order this matter so, that it shall be for our real welfare!—March 14. By the help of the Lord we obtained our passports, and brother Groves and I took our places in the Malle Poste for Strasburg, to leave tomorrow evening. Brother Y. intends to remain here a few days, on account of his health.

March 15. This morning I preached in a little chapel in Palais Royal. We left Paris this evening at six.—March 17. From six o'clock in the evening of the 15th, till this afternoon at half-past one, when we arrived at Strasburg, We were continually shut up in the Malle Poste, with the exception of yesterday morning about seven, and last night about eleven, when we were allowed half an hour for our meals. I had refreshing communion with my beloved brother. This quickest of all conveyances in France carries only two passengers, and we were thus able freely to converse and to pray together, which was refreshing indeed. Though we had traveled forty-four hours, yet as we had soon finished our business at Strasburg, we left this evening for Basle, trusting in the Lord for strength for the third night's traveling. A little after we had started, we stuck fast in a new road. I lifted up my heart to the Lord, and we were soon delivered, otherwise the circumstance, in a cold night, and during a fall of snow, would have been trying, as we had to get out of the mail. I now found myself again, after six years, amidst fellow-passengers who spoke my native language; but alas! they spoke not for Christ.

March 18. This afternoon we arrived at Basle, where we were very kindly received by the brethren.—March 23. Basle. These six days we have received great kindness from the brethren. The Lord has given me an opportunity of bringing before several who are already engaged in the ministry of the Word, and before many who intend to give themselves to this work, many important truths, so that in these opportunities I have been richly repaid for the journey. This morning I conversed also with three brethren, journeymen, who have a desire to give themselves to missionary work; but nothing could be decided now. I awake very faint, but have been mercifully helped through the work. Brother Groves intends to go to Geneva, and I to Tubingen, in order to become acquainted with a brother, a student, who is likely to go out with Brother Groves as a tutor to his sons, and to combine with this, missionary service.

During my stay at Basle I attended one day a meeting at which a venerable pious clergyman expounded the Greek New Testament to several brethren, who purposed to give themselves to missionary service. The passage to which this dear aged brother had then come, in the original of the New Testament, was 1 Peter iii. 1, 2, which, in our English translation, reads thus: "Likewise, ye wives, be in subjection to your own husbands; that, if any obey not the word, they also may without the word be won by the conversation of the wives; while they behold your chaste conversation coupled with fear." After this aged brother had expounded the passage, he related a circumstance which had occurred in his own days, and under his own eyes, at Basle, which has appeared to me so encouraging for those children of God who have unbelieving relatives, and especially for sisters in the Lord who have unbelieving husbands; and which, at the same time, is such a beautiful illustration of 1 Peter iii, 1.; that I judge it desirable to insert the narrative of this fact here. I will do so as exactly as I remember it. There lived at Basle an opulent citizen, whose wife was a believer, but he himself feared not the Lord. His practice was, to spend his evenings in a wine-house, where he would often tarry till eleven, twelve, or even one o'clock. On such occasions his wife always used to send her servants to bed, and sat up herself; to await the return of her husband. When at last he came, she used to receive him most kindly, never reproach him in the least, either at the time or afterwards, nor complain at all on account of his late hours, by which she was kept from seasonable rest. Moreover, if it should be needful to assist him in undressing himself, when he had drunk to excess, she would do this also in a very kind and meek way. Thus it went on for a long time. One evening, this gentleman was again, as usual, in a wine-house, and having tarried there with his merry companions till midnight, he said to them: "I bet, that if we go to my house, we shall find my wife sitting up and waiting for me, and she herself will come to the door and receive us very kindly; and if I ask her to prepare us a supper, she will do it at once without the least murmur, or unkind expression, or look." His companions in sin did not believe his statement. At last, however, after some more conversation about this strange statement, (as it appeared to them,) it was agreed that they would all go, to see this kind wife. Accordingly they went, and, after they had knocked, found the door immediately opened by the lady herself, and they were all courteously and kindly received by her. The party having entered, the master of the house asked his wife to prepare supper for them, which she, in the meekest way, at once agreed to do; and, after awhile, supper was served by herself; without the least sign of dissatisfaction, or murmur, or complaint. Having now prepared all for the company, she retired from the party to her room. When she had left the party, one of the gentlemen said: "What a wicked and cruel man you are, thus to torment so kind a wife." He then took his hat and stick, and, without touching a morsel of the supper, went away. Another made a similar remark, and left, without touching the supper. Thus one after another left, till they were all gone, without tasting the supper. The master of the house was now left alone, and the Spirit of God brought before him all his dreadful wickedness, and especially his great sins towards his wife; and the party had not left the house half an hour, before he went to his wife's room, requesting her to pray for him, told her that he felt himself a great sinner, and asked her forgiveness for all his behaviour towards her. From that time he became a disciple of the Lord Jesus.

Observe here, dear reader, the following points in particular, which I affectionately commend to your consideration: 1, The wife acted in accordance with 1 Peter iii. 1. She kept her place as being in subjection, and the Lord owned it. 2, She reproached not her husband, but meekly and kindly served him when he used to come home. 3, She did not allow the servants to sit up for their master, but sat up herself; thus honouring him as her head and superior, and concealed also, as far as she was able, her husband's shame from the servants. 4, In all probability a part of those hours, during which she had to sit up, was spent in prayer for her husband, or in reading the word of God, to gather fresh strength for all the trials connected with her position. But whether this was the case or not, it is certain that thus, under similar circumstances, the time might be spent, and it would then indeed be spent profitably. 5, Be not discouraged if you have to suffer from unconverted relatives. Perhaps very shortly the Lord may give you the desire of your heart, and answer your prayer for them; but in the meantime seek to commend the truth, not by reproaching them on account of their behaviour towards you, but by manifesting towards them the meekness, gentleness, and kindness of the Lord Jesus Christ.

March 25. Tubingen in Wirtemberg. The day before yesterday I left Basle in the afternoon. The Lord enabled me to confess Him before a young man and his wife, who were going to Vienna to increase their riches. What a mercy that grace has made me to differ, and that I travel the service of another master! They listened very attentively, and were not at all opposed. They also esteem the people of God, and have been in the habit of meeting with them. Our parting was very affectionate and solemn, after I had charged them to care earnestly about the one thing needful.

I arrived, yesterday morning at six, at Schaffhausen. I found a brother waiting for me at the post office, a gentleman of title, who, having been informed by brethren at Basle of my arrival, kindly took me to his house for the two hours I had to stay in that town, to refresh my body with breakfast, and my soul with communion with the brethren whom he had invited to meet me. I was in this town about ten years ago. I was now again within a short distance of the fall of the Rhine, which was then most attractive to me. Now I considered that my time could be spent much more profitably than by going there. The little time that I was at Schaffhausen, I received much information concerning the state of the church in many parts of the Continent, from a believing physician and a clergyman; and I also communicated things which, with God's blessing, may be profitable. After this I continued my journey to Tubingen. It was with peculiar feelings; for all this way I had traversed nearly ten years ago, to gratify my natural desire for travelling, and now I went over the same ground in the service of the Lord Jesus.

I arrived here this morning at nine, having been strengthened to travel two nights and a day and a half, though I left Basle very weak. This morning I saw brother Gundert, the student of divinity, on whose account I am here, and spent about three hours in conversation with him. Afterwards I called on a Christian professor in the university, who received me kindly. This evening I had a meeting with the believing students, for whom the Lord gave me a word.

March 26. This morning I drove with brother Gundert to Stuttgart, both for the sake of seeing more of him, and also that we might unitedly talk over the matter with his father, who lives there. I am now staying at the house of brother Gundert senior, where I am kindly lodged. I think brother Gundert junior, will go to the East Indies. His father is not only willing to give him up for the Lord's sake, but seems to consider it an honour to have a son to give to the Lord in this way. This evening I again met several brethren, to whom I spoke about the things of God.

March 30. Halle. From the evening of the 27th till this afternoon, when I arrived here, I have traveled day and night, and have been strengthened by the Lord for it. The whole of this way, several hundred miles, I had gone step by step before. My thoughts were peculiarly affecting, as I retraced the mercies which I had experienced at the hands of God.—The Lord enabled me repeatedly to confess His name before my changing fellow-travelers. A student spoke to me about the peculiarly good and cheap wine of Weinheim, near Heidelberg. I told him that when, years ago, as a student like himself, I came through that place, I cared about such things, but that now I knew what was much better than wine.—Yesterday a Frenchman, having heard my testimony for Jesus once or twice, when the last merry companion had left the coach, quitted my society, it being too dull for him, and joined himself to an officer in the army, sitting in the forepart of the coach. (The coach was divided into the forepart and inside.) This gave me a blessed and most refreshing opportunity to pray for about an hour aloud in the coach, which strengthened and refreshed my soul. It was particularly kind of the Lord to give me an opportunity of praying aloud, as, on account of having then already traveled forty-eight hours uninterruptedly, my body was too tired to allow me to continue for any length of time in mental prayer.—Yesterday afternoon, at Eisenach (situated just under the hill on which stands the decayed castle called the Wartburg, where Luther translated the Holy Scriptures), I saw fearful scenes of profanity. How has the candlestick been removed!—

This afternoon I reached Halle, where it pleased the Lord to bring me to the knowledge of Himself, having been graciously preserved hitherto, though a spring was found broken when I got out of the mail. I greatly needed rest, but my heart was too full. I could not sleep. I went first to the house of the brother, where I was first impressed, and afterwards I called on my esteemed tutor, professor Dr. Tholuck, counsellor of the Consistory, who received me, after seven years' separation, with his former kindness and brotherly love. (He made me lodge with him, and gave thereby a testimony that differences of views, concerning certain parts of God's truth, ought not to separate the children of God; for I had written to him my mind from Bristol two years before.)

March 31. Today I rode with Dr. Tholuck and two young brethren to a believing clergyman, living in the neighbourhood of Halle, where we spent the day. Dr. Tholuck told me many encouraging things, particularly this, that several of my former fellow-students, who, at the time when I was at Halle, knew not the Lord, had been brought to know Him since, and are now labouring in His vineyard. And further, that certain brethren, formerly very weak in the faith, had been established, and are now going on well. May this encourage the heart of the believing reader still to pray for his unconverted friends, and may it strengthen him to hope for better days concerning those of his brethren in the Lord who are now weak in the faith!

April 1. Today I saw a clergyman, in whom I recognized an individual who studied at Halle, whilst I was there, living then in open sin, and who is now, by divine mercy, pointing sinners to the Lamb of God. In the evening I went to the large Orphan-house, built, in dependence on the Lord, by A. H. Franke, to see one of the classical teachers, who is the son of my father's neighbour, and whom I had not seen for about fifteen years. I found him, to the joy of my heart, to be a brother in the Lord. This evening I spent in the same room where it pleased the Lord to begin a work of grace in my heart, with several of the same brethren and sisters with whom I used to meet seven years ago, and told them of the Lord's faithfulness, gentleness, kindness, and forbearance towards me, since I had seen them last. Truly how good has the Lord been to me since!

April 2. This morning I again spent in calling on the brethren and sisters, being enabled, every where, before learned and unlearned, to testify about the blessedness of adhering to the Scriptures as our only guide in spiritual things. I left Halle this afternoon, having received much love from the brethren, and drove fifteen miles further, to a beloved brother and old friend, brother Stahlschmidt at Sandersleben, who has shown me much kindness even since I have been in England. I was received with much love by this brother and his dear wife, and his man servant, also a beloved brother. [This brother (the man servant) I met fifty-four years ago at Gnadau, a Moravian settlement, where I several times spent a few days for the refreshment of my soul, to which place he also came, a distance of about forty-five miles, for the same purpose. He was then living with a farmer, ploughing his fields, &c. At that time our hearts were knit together; for I wish it to be understood by any unconverted reader, that, whilst I should at one time have looked with scorn upon such a person, if he had attempted to be familiar with me, now the love of Jesus, in whom we were one, filled my heart with love to him, and these outward distinctions were broken down. In consequence of this acquaintance, he wrote me several letters to Halle, and I wrote to him. Those letters were particularly refreshing and spiritual, and therefore I read them to other brethren, and also to brother Stahlschmidt, a wine merchant. On account of this, he had a great desire to have brother Kroll living in his house. The Lord, after a time, brought it about, and this brother lived with him above forty years, and was a friend, a brother, and a most faithful servant to this merchant, so that his considerable business was in a great measure intrusted to him; and yet he treated his master with all due respect, and kept his place as a servant. This latter point is very important, and brings glory to God. For whilst a believing master should treat a believing servant with all kindness and brotherly love; yet the believing servant should with all obedience, with all faithfulness, and particularly with due respect, treat his believing master or mistress.]

April 3. Sandersleben. Today I saw several brethren and sisters, and among others a brother, who is in about the same state in which he was eight years ago. He has very little enjoyment, and makes no progress in the things of God. The reason is, that, against his conscience, he remains in a calling, which is opposed to the profession of a believer. We are exhorted in Scripture to abide in our calling; but only if we can abide in it "with God." 1 Cor. vii. 24.—This evening a believing clergyman, and the brethren and sisters of this small town and some neighbouring villages, were collected together in brother Stahlschmidt's house, and I spoke to them for two hours about the things of God, particularly about the way in which God has led me, since I saw them, and sought to strengthen their hands in God, and exhorted them to give themselves fully to the Lord. It was a time of refreshing. Indeed, the Lord has greatly refreshed my own soul, at Basle, Tubingen, Stuttgart, Halle, and elsewhere, whenever I have spoken well of His name. The child of God should make it his particular business to encourage sinners to seek after the Lord, and to increase the faith and love of the brethren, through speaking well of the name of the Lord.

April 4. I left Sandersleben this morning. My brother and host acted according to 3 John, 5 and 6; for he sent me on ten miles in his carriage.

When I arrived at Aschersleben, to which place brother Stahlschmidt had conveyed me, I had but one station more to my father's house. On the way I asked the driver about a certain individual, with whom I studied at Halle, once a companion with me in open sin. I found that he is still in the same state. What a difference has grace made between him and me! Nothing, nothing but grace has made this difference! I, guilty sinner, might now be still on the same road, and he, in my room, might have been plucked as a brand out of the fire. But it is not so. May the Lord help me to love him much, very much, for His distinguishing grace!—Such feelings I had in particular this afternoon, when I saw the town before me in which my father lives, as there are but two in the whole place, as far as I can find out, who love the Lord. How different is everything with me now from what it was when, as a wicked youth, I used to go to this town, at the time of my vacation. How truly happy am I now! How is my heart now raised above all those things in which I sought, and also fancied I found happiness! Truly all these things are like bubbles to me now! My heart is not here; yea, my heart is not even in England. My heart is, at least in a measure, in heaven, though I am still nothing but a poor weak worm. I felt the solemnity and importance of having once more the privilege of seeing my aged father. I also felt the importance of being at the place, where I had spent much of my time in my youth, and where I had been known as living in sin. My desire was, that I might be enabled to walk, the three days I intended to stay there, as it becomes a servant of Christ. For this I had been led to prayer before I left Bristol, and since I have been on the Continent. At last I arrived at my father's house. How affecting to meet him once more!

April 5. Heimersleben. This afternoon a friend of my father called-one who knows not the Lord. After a few minutes the Lord gave me an opportunity of setting before him the fundamental truths of the Gospel, and the joy and comfort they afford, and have afforded to me. Thus a way was opened to me of stating the truth more fully than ever I had been able to do before, by word of mouth, in the presence of my father and brother, without saying to them, "Thou art the man." I was assisted by the Lord. May He water the seed sown! This evening I went to the only two brethren in this little town, thus to own them as such. It has appeared well to me to call on none whom I know, else I should be expected to call on all; and as I see it right to spend but three days here, I consider that that little time should be wholly given to my father, as it may be the last time that I shall see him; yet, at the same time, I judged that it was well pleasing in the sight of the Lord, that I should call on these brethren to strengthen their hands.

When I saw these brethren last, in February, 1829, two or three more used to meet with them; but since then the reproach of the cross has driven the others back into the world. From that time, these brethren have scarcely seen a believer, and never hear the Gospel preached; it was therefore a great joy to them to see me. They told me that the Lord had blessed my last visit to them; and having been informed of my coming, they were prepared to ask me many questions. One of them, Knabe, about thirty years ago being possessed of property, was persuaded to lay it out in coal mines. He joined with two men who spent his property, and after some time they became bankrupts, so that there was not money enough to pay the workmen and some other creditors, even after all their goods had been sold. This evening brother Knabe asked me what he ought to do about the money which had been left unpaid three and twenty years; whether he was still under an obligation to pay it, if he could. My answer was at once that he was, being in the sight of the Lord still a debtor, though cleared by the laws of men. He then told me, that some years since some property was left to him, and that he also, in the years 1816, 1817, and 1818, when the corn prices were very high, had laid by some money, and that therefore he was fully able to pay the debt. He saw immediately that this was the right way, and said that he would act accordingly. He added that now he saw why he had made so little progress in divine things. I have learned that this brother has lately taken two destitute orphans into his house, whom he entirely supports by the labour of his hands (he earns his bread by thrashing corn), and that the people, though they consider him, on account of his love for the Lord, a weak and foolish person, yet look upon him with respect.

April 6. I spent this morning in answering questions which my father put to me about secular things in England. This I did for the following reasons:—1. I had scarcely ever spoken about these things in my letters, indeed so little, that my father told me, he had often intended to ask me whether it was forbidden in England to send letters abroad about such matters, as I never wrote about them. I had refrained from doing so, partly, on account of want of time; and, partly, because I had better things to write about, wishing to direct his mind to the things of God. 2. Now, however, I spoke on these subjects, because I particularly desired to be as kind, affectionate, and obliging as I conscientiously could, considering that this was the testimony I was especially called on to give. Formerly I had much pressed the things of God on him, and not with sufficient tenderness, knowing not then experimentally the helplessness of the creature. After it had pleased the Lord to show me the truth more clearly, in the summer of 1829, I wrote in a different way; but in the commencement of the year 1833 I felt pressed in spirit once more, most fully, not so much as a son, but as a servant of Christ, to write, and to point out to him minutely his state, showing him the danger of his soul, the grounds of which I fully laid before him. When this, as formerly, greatly displeased him, I ceased to speak any more in this way, and from that time I aimed and still aim more and more to show him love in action, as it becomes a believing son, telling him only how happy I am—how I am supported under such and such trials—how I am not caring about certain things as formerly I did—in what an awful state I was once living, and how God brought me out of it; and how any sinner, by forsaking his evil ways, and believing on the Lord Jesus, may be brought to the same joy and happiness, and what a delight it would be to me to meet my father at last in heaven, &c. Since I have corresponded with him in this way, things have been very comfortable, though I have brought as much truth before him as formerly, and though I have never sent a letter without speaking, comparatively, much about these things. On the same ground I have not on this visit spoken directly to my father about the state of his soul, though he has more than ever heard the truth from my lips. God has indeed been with me, and I believe that I have been led by Him to pursue this course. Different, however, has been the way in which I have dealt with my unconverted brother; for the relationship in which I stand to him is a different one. For this afternoon, I not only pointed out to him his danger, but spoke also respecting his sins, and have done so in my letters, and intend to do so still, if the Lord permit.

This afternoon brother Knabe called on me. He told me that he had already experienced a trial on account of his intention to pay the money, as his wife tried to keep him from it, by endeavouring to persuade him that God does not require him to do such a thing, as he has taken two orphan children into his house. He nevertheless is determined to do it. He saw, however, another difficulty, which was, that, when he looked over the papers containing the names of his creditors, it was found that all but three, out of about thirty, were dead, and he did not know what to do concerning them. I told him to go to those places where his creditors used to live, and he might find, perhaps, some needy widows and fatherless children, whom they had left behind; and, if not, he should inquire after the lawful heirs, and pay the money to them. He saw with me, and declared his full intention to do so, whatever it might cost, and seemed truly glad that God at last, through my advice, had delivered him from this burden; for from time to time the matter had pressed on his conscience that he ought to do it.—I spent this evening in relating to my father and brother some of the Lord's dealings with me in England, particularly how He has graciously provided for my temporal wants in answer to prayer, and they both seemed to feel, for the moment at least the blessedness of such a life.

April 7. I saw brother Knabe this morning, who is still determined to pay the money, though tried by his wife. I exhorted him to steadfastness. I also saw some persons who called on me to hear about England, for every one of whom the Lord gave me a word without any effort. It was especially so last night. A friend of my father, a Roman Catholic, called, and I was enabled to set the truths of the gospel before him, with their blessed effects, without entering upon the Roman Catholic controversy.—A part of this morning I spent in walking about with my father to see one of his gardens, and some of his fields, because I knew it would give him pleasure; and I felt that I ought in every way to show him kindness and attention, as far as I conscientiously could. Tomorrow, God willing, I intend to leave, and to return to England. The Lord, in His rich mercy, in answer to my prayer, has enabled me so to walk before my father, and has also impressed what I have said so far upon his heart, as to cause him to say today, "May God help me to follow your example, and to act according to what you have said to me."

April 9. Celle. Yesterday morning I drove with my father to Halberstadt, where, with many tears, he separated from me. I was alone in the mail, which was a great comfort to me. It was a solemn time. I found myself again on the road to Brunswick, which I had traversed twice in the service of the devil, and now I was traveling on it in the name of Jesus. I discerned, in passing, the inn at Wolfenbuttel, from whence I intended to run away, and where I was arrested. How peculiar were my feelings! In the evening we reached Brunswick, from whence we started the same night. During the night I heard a fearfully wicked, most profligate, infidel, and scoffing conversation between the conducteur and a student, and the only testimony I gave was, complete silence all the time. I arrived here this morning at eight, and have been here all the morning, as the mail will not start for Hamburg until four this afternoon. It has been far from well with me in my soul today. That awful conversation last night has been spiritual poison to me. How's very soon do we, even unconsciously, receive evil!

April 10. Hamburg. I arrived here at ten this morning.—April 11. I went on board last night, and at twelve we sailed. This morning at half-past eleven we arrived at Cuxhaven, where we cast anchor, on account of a strong contrary wind.—April 13. Though I desired as much, perhaps, as any of the passengers speedily to get to the end of our voyage, longing to get back again to my work in Bristol, and also to my wife and children, yet I was kept in peace; and whilst some murmured at the contrary wind, the Lord enabled me to lift up my heart in prayer that He would calm it, if it were His holy will, and, accordingly, after a delay of about nineteen hours, we plied again yesterday morning, at seven. At ten I was taken with sea sickness, from which I had been kept during my four previous short voyages in answer to prayer; but this time I on purpose refrained from praying about it, as I did not know whether it was better for my health to be seasick or not. The sickness continued the whole of yesterday. Today I am well. We have fine and calm weather. I consider it a mercy that the Lord has allowed me to be sea-sick.

April 15. Bristol. Yesterday at one we landed in London. In answer to prayer I soon obtained my things from the Custom-house, and reached my friends in Chancery Lane a little before two, where I found a letter from my wife, stating that brother Craik is ill, having an inflammation in the wind-pipe, and therefore, humanly speaking, will be unable to preach for some time. In consequence of this I started immediately for Bristol, where I arrived this morning. I found brother Craik better than I had expected, though completely unable to attend to the ministry of the Word.

April 16. Today brother Craik and I received 11l. 15s. 9d. each, being a legacy left to us some time since. We said once or twice to one another, that perhaps this money might be paid at a time when we much needed it. And so it is just now. May I and all my brethren leave the management of all our affairs entirely to the Lord, who best knows what is good for us; and may it be our concern to seek first the kingdom of God and His righteousness, and all temporal supplies shall be added to us!

May 1. I went to see brother Craik, and found him better, but heard from his medical attendant that he ought not to preach for several months. May 5. My father-in-law has been for several days very ill. May 15. Mr. Groves continues very ill. May 29. This morning brother Craik went into Devonshire for change of air.

June 3. Today we had a public meeting on account of the Scriptural Knowledge Institution for home and abroad. It is now fifteen months, since, in dependence upon the Lord for the supply of means, we have been enabled to provide poor children with schooling, circulate the Holy Scriptures, and aid missionary labours. During this time, though the field of labour has been continually enlarged, and though we have now and then been brought low in funds, the Lord has never allowed us to be obliged to stop the work. We have been enabled during this time to establish three day-schools, and to connect with the Institution two other charity day-schools, which, humanly speaking, otherwise would have been closed for want of means. In addition to this, the expenses connected with a Sunday-school and an adult school have been likewise defrayed, making seven schools altogether. The number of the children that have been thus provided with schooling, in the day-schools only, amounts to 439. The number of copies of the Holy Scriptures, which have been circulated, is 795 Bibles and 753 New Testaments. We have also sent, in aid of missionary labours in Canada, in the East Indies, and on the Continent of Europe, 117l. 11s. The whole amount of the free-will offerings put into our hands for carrying on this work, from March 5, 1834, to May 19, 1835, is 363l. 12s. 0 3/4d.

June 20. Our father is evidently today near his end. June 22. This morning at two our father died. June 23. Both our children are ill. June 24. Our little boy is very ill. June 25. The dear little boy is so ill, that I have no hope of his recovery. The disease is inflammation on the chest. I spoke this evening comfortably at Gideon, on Psalm cxlv. 1-4, thinking it right that neither the death of my father-in-law, nor my dying child should keep me from the Lord's work. The Lord's holy will be done concerning the dear little one. June 26. My prayer last evening was, that God would be pleased to support my dear wife under the trial, should He remove the little one; and to take him soon to Himself, thus sparing him from suffering. I did not pray for the child's recovery. It was but two hours after that the dear little one went home. The eldest and the youngest the Lord has thus removed from our family in the same week. My dear Mary feels her loss much, but yet is greatly supported. As to myself, I am so fully enabled to realize that the dear infant is so much better off with the Lord Jesus than with us, that I scarcely feel the loss at all, and when I weep, I weep for joy.

June 27. My dear wife is graciously supported. May the Lord grant that these afflictions may not be lost upon us! June 28. I preached today both times comfortably. June 29. This morning was the funeral. The remains of our father and infant were put into the same grave.

July 3. Our taxes are due, and may be called for any day, and for the first time we have no money to pay them, as we were obliged, on account of our late afflictions, to spend the money which we had put by for them. May the Lord in mercy provide! July 6. I was enabled today, by the free-will offerings through the boxes, and by what I had left, to pay the taxes before they were called for. How kind of the Lord to answer my prayer so soon! July 8. This evening I had 5l. sent from Weston-super-Mare. So the Lord has again appeared. May I praise His holy name for this seasonable help, which came when I had scarcely any money left! July 14. Today I had again a suit of new clothes given to me by a brother. My clothes were much worn and old, and our late funeral might have given a second reason for having new ones. But I did not order any, because I had no money to pay for them, and thought it wrong to contract debts.—A fresh paper was brought in today for taxes, which ought to have been asked for many months since. May the Lord give us the means to pay them!

July 15. We had again an especial prayer-meeting for the restoration of brother Craik, who, though well in his general health, is yet unable to preach, or even to converse for any length of time. July 18. I have felt for several days weak in my chest. This weakness has been increasing, and today I have felt it more than ever. I have thought it well to refrain next week from all public speaking. May the Lord grant that I may be brought nearer to Him through this, for I am not at all in the state in which I ought to be, and I think sometimes that our late afflictions have been lost upon me, and that the Lord will need to chastise me severely.

July 22. The last mentioned taxes were called for this morning, just after the Lord had sent us 5l., from a distance of about eighty miles. So the Lord has again of late, repeatedly, in answer to prayer, sent help. May this lead us to trust in Him for the future! July 28. Since the 14th I have felt unwell, and though sometimes a little better, on the whole I have been getting worse and worse. This morning I have seen our medical attendant, who thinks that all the disease arises from a disordered stomach.

July 31. Today brother C-r, formerly a minister in the establishment, who came to us a few days since, began, in connexion with the Scriptural Knowledge Institution, to go from house to house, to spread the truth as a city missionary. [This was a remarkable interposition of God. Brother Craik had before this, for some months, been unable on account of bodily infirmity, to labour in the work of the schools, the circulation of the Scriptures, &c., and my own weakness, shortly after brother C-r's arrival, increased so that I was obliged to give up the work entirely: How gracious, therefore, of the Lord, to send brother C-r, that thus the work might go on! Up to July, 1837, this brother was enabled to continue in his work, and thus this little Institution was in a most important way enlarged as it regards the field of labour.]

August 15. Today dear brother Craik returned from Devonshire, much better in his general health, but not better as it regards his voice.—August 24. I feel very weak, and suffer more than before from the disease. I am in doubt whether to leave Bristol entirely for a time. I have no money to go away for a change of air. I have had an invitation to stay for a week with a sister in the country, and I think of accepting the invitation, and going tomorrow. August 26. Today I had 5l. given to me for the express purpose of using change of air. Aug. 29. Today I received another 5l. for the same purpose.

August 30. Today, for the first Lord's day since our arrival in Bristol, I have been kept from preaching through illness. How mercifully has the Lord dealt in giving me so much strength for these years! I had another 5l. sent, to aid me in procuring change of air. How kind is the Lord in thus providing me with the means of leaving Bristol! September 2. Went with my family to Portishead. September 3 to 5. I read the lives of the English martyrs at the time of the reformation. My spirit has been greatly refreshed. May the Lord help me to follow these holy men as far as they followed Christ! Of all reading, besides that of the Holy Scriptures, which should be always THE book, THE CHIEF book to us, not merely in theory, but also in practice, such like books seem to me the most useful for the growth of the inner man. Yet one has to be cautious in the choice, and to guard against reading too much. At such a time as the present, when my mind and body are too weak for much exertion, as the study of the Word, conversation, writing letters, or walking, &c., I find it most refreshing to read a few pages of this kind, though these last six years I have not read the fifth part, perhaps not the tenth part as much of other books as of the Holy Scriptures.

September 14. We are still at Portishead. I am but little better. I am greatly bowed down today on account of my inward corruptions and carnality of heart. When will God deliver me from this state?! How I long to be more like Him! My present way of living is also a great trial to me. The caring so much about the body; the having for my chief employment eating and drinking, walking, bathing, and taking horse exercise; all this to which I have not been at all accustomed these six years, I find to be very trying. I would much rather be again in the midst of the work in Bristol, if my Lord will condescend to use His most unworthy servant.

September 15. As I clearly understood that the person, who lets me his horse, has no license, I saw, that being bound as a believer to act according to the laws of the country, I could use it no longer: and as horse exercise seems most important, humanly speaking, for my restoration, and as this is the only horse, which is to be had in the place, we came to the conclusion to leave Portishead tomorrow. Immediately after, I received a kind letter from a brother and two sisters in the Lord, who lived in the Isle of Wight, which contained a fourth invitation, more pressing than ever, to come and stay with them for some time. In addition to this, they wrote that they had repeatedly prayed about the matter, and were persuaded that I ought to come. This matter has been today a subject for prayer and consideration to us.

September 16. We came this morning to the conclusion to leave Portishead today, and that I should go to the Isle of Wight; but we saw not how my wife and child and our servant could accompany me, as we had not sufficient money for traveling expenses; and yet this seemed of importance, as otherwise my wife would be overburdened in my absence, and my mind would not be sufficiently free; and besides this, she also seems to need change of air. The Lord graciously removed the difficulty this evening; for we received most unexpectedly and unasked for 6l. 13s., which was owed to us, and, also, when we had already retired to rest, a letter was brought, containing a present of 2l. How very, very kind, and tender is the Lord!

September 19. This evening we arrived at our friends' in the Isle of Wight, by whom we were most kindly received.—September 21 to 26. Nothing remarkable has occurred. I feel very comfortable in this place, and find my stay here refreshing to my soul. My health is about the same. I am not fit for mental exercise, and am soon fatigued even by conversation. I have read during the last days, with great interest and admiration of the goodness of God, and to the refreshment of my soul, the life of John Newton, and the lives of some of the English martyrs at the time of the reformation.

Sept. 27. Today I am thirty years of age. I feel myself an unprofitable servant. How much more might I have lived for God than I have done! May the Lord grant, that, if I am allowed to stay a few days more in this world, they may be spent entirely for Him! September 29. Last evening, when I retired from the family, I had a desire to go to rest at once, for I had prayed a short while before; and feeling weak in body, the coldness of the night was a temptation for me to pray no further. However, the Lord did help me to fall upon my knees; and no sooner had I commenced praying, than He shone into my soul, and gave me such a spirit of prayer, as I had not enjoyed for many weeks. He graciously once more revived His work in my heart. I enjoyed that nearness to God and fervency in prayer, for more than an hour, for which my soul had been panting for many weeks past. For the first time, during this illness, I had now also a spirit of prayer as it regards my health. I could ask the Lord earnestly to restore me again, which had not been the case before. I now long to go back again to the work in Bristol, yet without impatience, and feel assured that the Lord will strengthen me to return to it. I went to bed especially happy and awoke this morning in great peace, rose sooner than usual, and had again, for more than an hour, real communion with the Lord before breakfast. May He in mercy continue this state of heart to His most unworthy child!

October 8. My strength has been during the last days increasing, but I feel still the symptoms of indigestion. I have been able to speak several times at family prayer, and to expound the Scriptures to the school children, without suffering in consequence of it.

October 9. I have many times had thoughts of giving in print some account of the Lord's goodness to me, for the instruction, comfort, and encouragement of the children of God; and I have been more than ever stirred up to do so since I read Newton's life a few days ago. I have considered, today, all the reasons for and against, and find that there are scarcely any against, and many for it.

October 15. Today we left our dear friends for Bristol. November 15. Brother C-r and I have been praying together, the last five days, that the Lord would be pleased to send us means for the carrying on of the work of the Scriptural Knowledge Institution. This evening a brother gave me 6s. 1d., being money which he formerly used to pay towards the support of a trade club, which he has lately given up for the Lord's sake.—November 18. This evening £30 was given to me; £25. for the Scriptural Knowledge Institution, and £5. for myself. This is a most remarkable answer to prayer. Brother C-r and I have prayed repeatedly together during the last week, concerning the work, and especially that the Lord would be pleased to give us the means to continue, and even to enlarge, the field. In addition to this, I have several times asked for a supply for myself, and He has kindly granted both these requests. Oh that I may have grace to trust Him more and more!—November 20. This evening I took tea at a sister's house, where I found Franke's life. I have frequently, for a long time, thought of labouring in a similar way, though it might be on a much smaller scale; not, to imitate Franke, but in reliance upon the Lord. May God make it plain! November 21. Today I have had it very much impressed on my heart, no longer merely to think about the establishment of an Orphan-House, but actually to set about it, and I have been very much in prayer respecting it, in order to ascertain the Lord's mind.—I received this day, from an unexpected quarter, £5. for the Scriptural Knowledge Institution, in answer to prayer; and I had also £1. 14s. 6d. sent from a distance of one hundred and twenty miles.-November 22. This evening I had sent for the Institution £1. 4s.—November 23. Today I had £10. sent from Ireland for our Institution. Thus the Lord, in answer to prayer, has given me, in a few days, about £50. I had asked only for £40. This has been a great encouragement to me, and has still more stirred me up to think and pray about the establishment of an Orphan-House.—November 25. I have been again much in prayer yesterday and today about the Orphan-House, and am more and more convinced that it is of God. May He in mercy guide me! The three chief reasons for establishing an Orphan-House are:—1. That God may be glorified, should He be pleased to furnish me with the means, in its being seen that it is not a vain thing to trust in Him; and that thus the faith of His children may be strengthened. 2. The spiritual welfare of fatherless and motherless children. 3. Their temporal welfare.

It may be well to enter somewhat more minutely, than my journal does, upon the reasons which led me to establish an Orphan-House. Through my pastoral labours among the saints in Bristol, through my considerable correspondence, and through brethren who visited Bristol; I had constantly cases brought before me, which proved, that one of the especial things which the children of God needed in our day, was, to have their faith strengthened. For instance: I might visit a brother, who worked fourteen or even sixteen hours a day at his trade, the necessary result of which was, that not only his body suffered, but his soul was lean, and he had no enjoyment in the things of God. Under such circumstances I might point out to him that he ought to work less, in order that his bodily health might not suffer, and that he might gather strength for his inner man, by reading the word of God, by meditation over it, and by prayer. The reply, however, I generally found to be something like this: "But if I work less, I do not earn enough for the support of my family. Even now, whilst I work so much, I have scarcely enough. The wages are so low, that I must work hard in order to obtain what I need. There was no trust in God. No real belief in the truth of that word: "Seek ye first the kingdom of God, and His righteousness: and all these things shall be added unto you." I might reply something like this: "My dear brother, it is not your work which supports your family, but the Lord; and He who has fed you and your family when you could not work at all, on account of illness, would surely provide for you and yours, if for the sake of obtaining food for your inner man, you were to work only for so many hours a day, as would allow you proper time for retirement. And is it not the case now, that you begin the work of the day after having had only a few hurried moments for prayer; and when you leave off your work in the evening, and mean then to read a little of the word of God, are you not too much worn out in body and mind, to enjoy it, and do you not often fall asleep whilst reading the Scriptures, or whilst on your knees in prayer?" The brother would allow it was so; he would allow that my advice was good; but still I read in his countenance, even if he should not have actually said so, "How should I get on, if I were to carry out your advice?" I longed, therefore, to have something to point the brother to, as a visible proof, that our God and Father is the same faithful God as ever He was; as willing as ever to PROVE Himself to be the LIVING GOD, in our day as formerly, to all who put their trust in Him.—Again, sometimes I found children of God tried in mind by the prospect of old age, when they might be unable to work any longer, and therefore were harassed by the fear of having to go into the poor-house. If in such a case I pointed out to them, how their Heavenly Father has always helped those who put their trust in Him, they might not, perhaps, always say, that times have changed; but yet it was evident enough, that God was not looked upon by them as the LIVING God. My spirit was ofttimes bowed down by this, and I longed to set something before the children of God, whereby they might see, that He does not forsake, even in our day, those who rely upon him.—Another class of persons were brethren in business, who suffered in their souls, and brought guilt on their consciences, by carrying on their business, almost in the same way, as unconverted persons do. The competition in trade, the bad times, the over-peopled country, were given as reasons why, If the business were carried on simply according to the word of God, it could not be expected to do well. Such a brother, perhaps, would express the wish, that he might be differently situated; but very rarely did I see, that there was a stand made for God, that there was the holy determination to trust in the living God, and to depend on Him, in order that a good conscience might be maintained. To this class likewise I desired to show, by a visible proof, that God is unchangeably the same.—Then there was another class of persons, individuals who were in professions in which they could not continue with a good conscience, or persons who were in an unscriptural position with reference to spiritual things; but both classes feared, on account of the consequences, to give up the profession in which they could not abide with God, or to leave their position, lest they should be thrown out of employment. My spirit longed to be instrumental in strengthening their faith, by giving them not only instances from the word of God, of His willingness and ability to help all those who rely upon Him, but to show them by proofs, that He is the same in our day. I well knew that the word of God ought to be enough, and it was, by grace, enough to me; but still, I considered that I aught to lend a helping hand to my brethren, if by any means, by this visible proof to the unchangeable faithfulness of the Lord I might strengthen their hands in God; for I remembered what a great blessing my own soul had received through the Lord's dealings with His servant A. H. Franke, who, in dependence upon the living God alone, established an immense Orphan-House, which I had seen many times with my own eyes. I, therefore, judged myself bound to be the servant of the Church of Christ, in the particular point on which I had obtained mercy: namely, in being able to take God by His word and to rely upon it. All these exercises of my soul, which resulted from the fact that so many believers, with whom I became acquainted, were harassed and distressed in mind, or brought guilt on their consciences, on account of not trusting in the Lord; were used by God to awaken in my heart the desire of setting before the church at large, and before the world, a proof that He has not in the least changed; and this seemed to me best done, by the establishing of an Orphan-House. It needed to be something which could be seen, even by the natural eye. Now, if I, a poor man, simply by prayer and faith, obtained, without asking any individual, the means for establishing and carrying on an Orphan-House: there would be something which with the Lord's blessing, might be instrumental in strengthening the faith of the children of God besides being a testimony to the consciences of the unconverted, of the reality of the things of God. This, then, was the primary reason, for establishing the Orphan-House. I certainly did from my heart desire to be used by God to benefit the bodies of poor children, bereaved of both parents, and seek, in other respects, with the help of God, to do them good for this life;—I also particularly longed to be used by

God in getting the dear orphans trained up in the fear of God;—but still, the first and primary object of the work was, (and still is:) that God might be magnified by the fact, that the orphans under my care are provided, with all they need, only by prayer and faith, without any one being asked by me or my fellow-labourers, whereby it may be seen, that God is FAITHFUL STILL, and HEARS PRAYER STILL. That I was not mistaken, has been abundantly proved singe November, 1835, both by the conversion of many sinners who have read the accounts, which have been published in connexion with this work, and also by the abundance of fruit that has followed in the hearts of the saints, for which, from my inmost soul, I desire to be grateful to God, and the honour and glory of which not only is due to Him alone, but which I, by His help, am enabled to ascribe to Him.

November 28. I have been, every day this week, very much in prayer concerning the Orphan-House, chiefly entreating the Lord to take away every thought concerning it out of my mind, if the matter be not of Him; and have also repeatedly examined my heart concerning my motives in the matter. But I have been more and more confirmed that it is of God.

December 2. I have again these last days prayed much about the Orphan-House, and have frequently examined my heart, that if it were at all my desire to establish it for the sake of gratifying myself I might find it out. To that end I have also conversed with brother Craik about it, that he might be instrumental in showing me any hidden corruption of my heart concerning the matter, or any other scriptural reason against my engaging in it. The one only reason which ever made me at all doubt as to its being of God, that I should engage in this work, is, the multiplicity of engagements which I have already. But that which has overbalanced this objection in my mind has been:—1. That the matter is of such great importance. 2. That if the matter be of God, He will in due time send suitable individuals, so that comparatively little of my time will be taken up in this service.

This morning I asked the Lord especially, that He would be pleased to teach me through the instrumentality of brother C.; and I went to him, that he might have an opportunity of probing my heart. For as I desire only the Lord's glory, I should be glad to be instructed through the instrumentality of any brother, if the matter be not of Him. But brother C., on the contrary, greatly encouraged me in it. Therefore I have this day taken the first actual step in the matter, in having ordered bills to be printed, announcing a public meeting on December 9th, at which I intend to lay before the brethren my thoughts concerning the Orphan-House, as a means of ascertaining more clearly the Lord's mind concerning the matter. December 4. Brother Craik told me this morning, that his voice is getting a little better. December 5. This evening I was struck, in reading the Scriptures, with these words: "Open thy mouth wide, and I will fill it." Ps. lxxxi. 10. Up to this day I had not prayed at all concerning the means or individuals needed for the Orphan-House. I was now led to apply this scripture to the Orphan-House, and asked the Lord for premises, 1000l., and suitable individuals to take care of the children. December 7. Today I received the first shilling for the Orphan-House. Afterwards I received another shilling from a German brother.

December 9. This afternoon the first piece of furniture was given—a large wardrobe. This afternoon and evening I was low in spirit as it regards the Orphan-House, but as soon as I began to speak at the meeting, I received peculiar assistance from God, felt great peace and joy, and the assurance that the work is of God. After the meeting, 10s. was given to me. There was purposely no collection, nor did any one speak besides myself; for it was not in the least intended to work upon the feelings, for I sought to be quite sure concerning the mind of God. After the meeting a sister offered herself for the work. I went home happy in the Lord, and full of confidence that the matter will come to pass, though but 10s. has been given. December 10. This morning I have sent to the press a statement which contains the substance of what I said at the meeting last evening. [For the sake of those who have not read it before, it is given here.]

Proposal for the Establishment of an Orphan-House in connexion with the
Scriptural Knowledge Institution for Home and Abroad.

Since the last Report of the operations of the Scriptural Knowledge Institution for home and abroad was published, the Lord has sent us, in answer to prayer, brother John C-r, formerly a minister of the establishment, as a city missionary, who goes from house to house, among the poor of this city, to converse with them about the things of God, to circulate the Scriptures among them, to get them to come to the adult school, if they cannot read, and to advise them to put their children to our schools, provided they go to no other. It was particularly gracious of the Lord to send this brother, nearly five months ago, as my brother and fellow labourer, Henry Craik, has been for these eight months laid aside from the ministry of the Word on account of bodily infirmity, and has therefore been unable to take an active part in this Institution. Thus I have not only found great help, but I have been greatly encouraged to enlarge the field. That to which my mind has been particularly directed, is, to establish an Orphan-House in which destitute fatherless and motherless children may be provided with food and raiment, and scriptural education. Concerning this intended Orphan-House I would say

1. It is intended to be in connexion with the Scriptural Knowledge Institution for home and abroad, in so far as it respects the Reports, accounts, superintendence, and the principles on which it is conducted, so that, in one sense, it may be considered as a new object of the Institution, yet with this difference, that only those funds shall be applied to the Orphan-House which are expressly given for it. If, therefore, any believer should prefer to support either those objects which have been hitherto assisted by the funds of this Institution, or the intended Orphan-House, it need only be mentioned, in order that the money may be applied accordingly.

2. It will only be established if the Lord should provide both the means for it, and suitable persons to conduct it.

As to the means, I would make the following remarks. The reason for proposing to enlarge the field, is not because we have of late particularly abounded in means; for we have been rather straitened. The many gracious answers, however, which the Lord had given us concerning this Institution, led brother C-r and me to give ourselves to prayer, asking him to supply us with the means to carry on the work, as we consider it unscriptural to contract debts. During five days, we prayed several times, both unitedly and separately. After that time, the Lord began to answer our prayers, so that, within a few days, about 50l. was given to us. I would further say, that the very gracious and tender dealings of God with me, in having supplied, in answer to prayer, for the last five years, my own temporal wants without any certain income, so that money, provisions and clothes have been sent to me at times when I was greatly straitened, and that not only in small but large quantities; and not merely from individuals living in the same place with me, but at a considerable distance; and that not merely from intimate friends, but from individuals whom I have never seen: all this, I say, has often led me to think, even as long as four years ago, that the Lord had not given me this simple reliance on Him merely for myself; but also for others. Often, when I saw poor neglected children running about the streets at Teignmouth, I said to myself: "May it not be the will of God, that I should establish schools for these children, asking Him to give me the means?" However, it remained only a thought in my mind for two or three years. About two years and six months since I was particularly stirred up afresh to do something for destitute children, by seeing so many of them begging in the streets of Bristol, and coming to our door. It was not, then, left undone on account of want of trust in the Lord, but through an abundance of other things calling for all the time and strength of my brother Craik and myself; for the Lord had both given faith, and had also shown by the following instance, in addition to very many others, both what He can and what He will do. One morning, whilst sitting in my room, I thought about the distress of certain brethren, and said thus to myself:—"O that it might please the Lord to give me the means to help these poor brethren!" About an hour afterwards I had 60l. sent as a present for myself, from a brother, whom up to this day I have never seen, and who was then, and is still, residing several thousand miles from this. Should not such an experience, together with promises like that one in John xiv. 13, 14, encourage us to ask with all boldness, for ourselves and others, both temporal and spiritual blessings? The Lord, for I cannot but think it was He, again and again, brought the thought about these poor children to my mind, till at last it ended in the establishment of "The Scriptural Knowledge Institution, for Home and Abroad;" since the establishment of which, I have had it in a similar way brought to my mind, first about fourteen months ago, and repeatedly since, but especially during these last weeks, to establish an Orphan-House. My frequent prayer of late has been, that if it be of God, He would let it come to pass; if not, that He would take from me all thoughts about it. The latter has not been the case, but I have been led more and more to think that the matter may be of Him. Now, if so, He can influence His people in any part of the world, (for I do not look to Bristol, nor even to England, but to the living God, whose is the gold and the silver,) to intrust me and brother C-r, whom the Lord has made willing to help me in this work, with the means. Till we have them, we can do nothing in the way of renting a house, furnishing it, &c. Yet, when once as much as is needed for this has been sent us, as also proper persons to engage in the work, we do not think it needful to wait till we have the Orphan-House endowed, or a number of yearly subscribers for it; but we trust to be enabled by the Lord, who has taught us to ask for our daily bread, to look to Him for the supply of the daily wants of those children whom He may be pleased to put under our care. Any donations will be received at my house. Should any believers have tables, chairs, bedsteads, bedding, earthenware, or any kind of household furniture to spare, for the furnishing of the house; or remnants or pieces of calico, linen, flannel, cloth, or any materials useful for wearing apparel; or clothes already worn; they will be thankfully received.

Respecting the persons who are needed for carrying on the work, a matter of no less importance than the procuring of funds, I would observe, that we look for them to God Himself, as well as for the funds; and that all who may be engaged as masters, matrons, and assistants, according to the smallness or largeness of the Institution, must be known to us as true believers; and moreover, as far as we may be able to judge, must likewise be qualified for the work.

3. At present nothing can be said as to the time when the operations are likely to commence; nor whether the Institution will embrace children of both sexes, or be restricted either to boys or girls exclusively; nor of what age they will be received, and how long they may continue in it; for though we have thought about these things, yet we would rather be guided in these particulars by the amount of the means which the Lord may put into our hands, and by the number of the individuals whom he may provide for conduc-

ting the Institution. Should the Lord condescend to use us as instruments, a short printed statement will be issued as soon as something more definite can be said.

4. It has appeared well to us to receive only such destitute children as have been bereaved of both parents.

5. The children are intended, if girls, to be brought up for service; if boys, for a trade; and therefore they will be employed, according to their ability and bodily strength, in useful occupations, and thus help to maintain themselves; besides this they are intended to receive a plain education; but the chief and especial end of the Institution will be to seek, with God's blessing, to bring them to the knowledge of Jesus Christ, by instructing them in the Scriptures.

GEORGE MULLER.

Bristol, Dec. 10th, 1835.

December 11. I have been enabled to pray all this week with increased confidence concerning the Orphan-House, as it regards means, a house, suitable individuals to take care of the children, furniture, &c. December 16. Brother C-n, whom the Lord has kindly allowed to stay above two months among us, to supply brother Craik's lack of service, left us today. How very gracious has the Lord been to us in this affliction! Many brethren have been sent to us as helpers for a little while—brother C-t for the greater part of the time, and brother C-n for more than two months. And, in addition to this, when brother Craik and I were both ill, the brethren were kept in peace, and there was a spirit of prayer among them. December 31. This evening we had an especial meeting for prayer and praise. We continued together from seven till after twelve.

There have been received into the church at Gideon during the past year—29

Ditto, Bethesda—30

Altogether—59

Of these 59, 30 have been brought to the knowledge of the Lord through the instrumentality of brother Craik and me. There are now, of those who have been begotten again through us, since we have been in Bristol, at Gideon 63, and at Bethesda 71—altogether 134. Besides this, several have fallen asleep in the faith, who never were in communion with us, and several of our spiritual children have joined other churches, in and out of Bristol, and many are now standing as hopeful characters on the list of candidates for communion. There have been added to the church at Gideon, since we came, 125; to Bethesda, 163—altogether 288; so that the number of both churches would have been 356 (68 believers we found at Gideon), had there been no changes; but

Of Gideon are at present

under church discipline 6, of Bethesda, 7, altogether, 13

Do. have fallen asleep 12 do. 5 do. 17

Do. have left Bristol 10 do. 4 do. 14

Do. have left us, but are

still in Bristol 11 do. 4 do. 15

39 20 59

So that there are at present in communion with us 297:—143 at Bethesda, and 154 at Gideon.

As it regards the way in which the Lord, in His faithful love, supplied my temporal wants, during the past year, I mention that I received—

1. In free-will offerings, given through the boxes, as my part £130 3s. 7 1/4d.

2. In free-will offerings given by believers in and out of Bristol, not through the boxes £120 7s. 6d.

3. Towards the house rent I received from brother Craik, in consideration that he has no rent to pay, for nine months £7 10s. 0d.

4. The presents sent to us in clothes and provisions, &c., were worth to us at least £27 0s. 0d.

Altogether £285 1s. 1 1/4d.

January 3, 1836. This morning brother Craik spoke a little in public for the first time after about nine months.

January 6. Today we had three especial prayer meetings, for the full restoration of brother Craik's voice. We had also, on January 7, 8, 9, and 10, especial prayer meetings for brother Craik's full restoration. January 16. Today I put into the press another statement, containing a further account respecting the Orphan-House. [It is here reprinted.]

Further account respecting the Orphan-House, intended to be established in Bristol, in connection with the Scriptural Knowledge Institution for Home and Abroad.

When, of late, the thoughts of establishing an Orphan-House, in dependence upon the Lord, revived in my mind, during the first two weeks I only prayed, that, if it were of the Lord, He would bring it about; but, if not, that He graciously would be pleased to take all thoughts about it out of my mind. My uncertainty about knowing the Lord's mind did not arise from questioning whether it would be pleasing in His sight, that there should be an abode and scriptural education provided for destitute fatherless and motherless children; but whether it were His will that I should be the instrument of setting such an object on foot, as my hands were already more than filled. My comfort, however, was, that, if it were His will, He would provide not merely the means, but also suitable individuals to take care of the children, so that my part of the work would take only such a portion of my time, as, considering the importance of the matter, I might give, notwithstanding my many other engagements. The whole of those two weeks I never asked the Lord for money, or for persons to engage in the work. On December 5th, however, the subject of my prayer all at once became different. I was reading Psalm lxxxi, and was particularly struck, more than at any time before, with ver. 10: "Open thy mouth wide, and I will fill it." I thought a few moments about these words, and then was led to apply them to the case of the Orphan-house. It struck me that I had never asked the Lord for any thing concerning it, except to know His will respecting its being established or not; and I then fell on my knees, and opened my mouth wide, asking Him for much. I asked in submission to His will, and without fixing a time when He should answer my petition. I prayed that He would give me a house, i.e. either as a loan, or that some one might be led to pay the rent for one, or that one might be given permanently for this object;

further, I asked Him for £1000; and likewise for suitable individuals to take care of the children. Besides this, I have been since led to ask the Lord, to put into the hearts of His people to send me articles of furniture for the house, and some clothes for the children. When I was asking the petition, I was fully aware what I was doing, i.e., that I was asking for something which I had no natural prospect of obtaining from the brethren whom I know, but which was not too much for the Lord to grant. As I have stated, that I desire to see clearly the Lord's will concerning the Orphan-House, by His providing both the means and suitable individuals for it, I will now mention how He has been dealing with me in these respects.

December 7, 1835.—Anonymously was given 2s. In the paper in which they were enclosed was written "1s. for the Orphan-House, and 1s. for the Scriptural Knowledge Institution. In the name of the Lord alone lift up your banners, so shall you prosper." 1s. besides was given. December 9. I found 3s. in the box, which I had put up two days before in my room for the Orphan-House, and a large wardrobe given just before the meeting in the evening, when I stated publicly my desire concerning this object before the brethren. After the meeting 10s. was given. Also a sister offered herself at the same time for the work. December 10. This morning I received a letter, in which a brother and sister wrote thus:—"We propose ourselves for the service of the intended Orphan-House, if you think us qualified for it; also to give up all the furniture, &c., which the Lord has given us, for its use; and to do this without receiving any salary whatever; believing, that if it be the will of the Lord to employ us, He will supply all our need, &c." In the evening a brother brought from several individuals three dishes, 28 plates, three basins, one jug, four mugs, three salt stands, one grater, four knives, and five forks.

December 12. While I was praying this morning that the Lord would give us a fresh token of His favour concerning the Orphan-House, a brother brought three dishes, 12 plates, one basin, and one blanket. After this had been given, I thanked God, and asked Him to give even this day another encouragement. Shortly after, £50. was given, and that by an individual from whom, for several reasons, I could not have expected this sum. Thus the hand of God appeared so much the more clearly. Even then I was led to pray, that this day the Lord would give still more. In the evening, accordingly, there were sent 29 yards of print. Also a sister offered herself for the work. Dec. 13. A brother was influenced this day to give 4s. per week, or 10l. 8s. yearly, as long as the Lord gives the means; 8s. was given by him as two weeks' subscriptions. Today a brother and sister offered themselves, with all their furniture, and all the provisions which they have in the house, if they can be usefully employed in the concerns of the Orphan-House.

December 14. Today a sister offered her services for the work. In the evening another sister offered herself for the Institution. December 15. A sister brought from several friends, ten basins, eight mugs, one plate, five dessert spoons, six tea spoons, one skimmer, one toasting fork, one flour dredge, three knives and forks, one sheet, one pillow case, one table cloth; also 1l. In the afternoon were sent 55 yards of sheeting, and 12 yards of calico. December 16. I took out of the box in my room 1s. December 17. I was rather cast down last evening and this morning about the matter, questioning whether I ought to be engaged in this way, and was led to ask the Lord to give me some further encouragement. Soon after were sent by a brother two pieces of print, the one seven and the other 23 3/4 yards, 6 3/4 yards of calico, four pieces of lining, about four yards altogether, a sheet, and a yard measure. This evening another brother brought a clothes' horse, three frocks, four pinafores, six handkerchiefs, three counterpanes, one blanket, two pewter salt cellars, six tin cups, and six metal tea spoons; he also brought 3s. 6d. given to him by three different individuals. At the same time he told me that it had been put into the heart of an individual to send tomorrow 100l.

December 18. This afternoon the same brother brought from a sister, a counterpane, a flat iron stand, eight cups, and saucers, a sugar basin, a milk jug, a tea cup, 16 thimbles, five knives and forks, six dessert spoons, 12 tea spoons, four combs, and two little graters; from another friend a flat iron and a cup and saucer. At the same time he brought the 100l. above referred to. [Since the publication of the second edition it has pleased the Lord to take to Himself the donor of this 100l., and I therefore give in this present edition some further account of the donation and the donor, as the particulars respecting both, with God's blessing, may tend to edification. Indeed I confess that I am delighted to be at liberty, in consequence of the death of the donor, to give the following short narrative, which, during her lifetime, I should not have considered it wise to publish. A. L., the donor, was known to me almost from the beginning of my coming to Bristol in 1832. She earned her bread by needlework, by which she gained from 2s. to 5s. per week; the average, I suppose, was not more than about 3s. 6d., as she was weak in body. But this dear, humble sister was content with her small earnings, and I do not remember ever to have heard her utter a word of complaint on account of earning so little. Some time, before I had been led to establish an Orphan-House, her father had died, through which event she had come into the possession of 480l., which sum had been left to her (and the same amount to her brother and two sisters) by her grandmother, but of which her father had had the interest during his lifetime. The father, who had been much given to drinking, died in debt, which debts the children wished to pay; but the rest, besides A. L., did not like to pay the full amount, and offered to the creditors 5s. in the pound, which they gladly accepted, as they had not the least legal claim upon the children. After the debts had been paid according to this agreement, A. L. said to herself; "However sinful my father may have been, yet he was my father, and as I have the means of paying his debts to the full amount, I ought, as a believing child, to do so, seeing that my brothers and sisters will not do it." She then went to all the creditors secretly, and paid the full amount of the debts, which took 40l. more of her money, besides her share which she had given before. Her brother and two sisters now gave 50l. each of their property to their mother; but A. L. said to herself: "I am a child of God, surely I ought to give my mother twice as much as my brother and sisters." She, therefore, gave her mother 100l. Shortly after this she sent me the 100l. towards the Orphan-House. I was not a little surprised when I received this money from her, for I had always known her as a poor girl, and I had never heard any thing about her having come into the possession of this money, and her dress had never given me the least indication of an alteration in her circumstances. Before, however, accepting this money from her, I had a long conversation with her, in which I sought to probe her as to her motives, and in which I sought to ascertain whether, as I had feared, she might have given this money in the feeling of the moment, without having counted the cost. I was the more particular, because, if the money were given, without its being given from Scriptural motives, and there should be regret afterwards, the name of the Lord would be dishonoured. But I had not conversed long with this beloved sister, before I found that she was, in this particular, a quiet, calm, considerate follower of the Lord Jesus, and one who desired, in spite of what human reason might say, to act according to the words of our Lord: "Lay not up for yourselves treasures upon earth." Matthew vi. 19. "Sell that ye have, and give alms." Luke xii. 33. When I remonstrated with her, in order that I might see, whether she had counted the cost, she said to me: "The Lord Jesus has given His last drop of blood for me, and should I not give Him this 100l.?" She likewise said: "Rather than the Orphan-House should not be established, I will give all the money I have." When I saw that she had weighed the matter according to the word of God, and that she had counted the cost, I could not but take the money, and admire the way which the Lord took, to use this poor, sickly sister as an instrument, in so considerable a measure, for helping, at its very commencement, this work, which I had set about solely in dependence upon the living God. At that time she would also have me take 5l. for the poor saints in communion with us. I mention here particularly, that this dear sister kept all these things to herself; and did them as much as possible in secret; and during her life-time, I suppose, not six brethren and sisters among us knew that she had ever possessed 480l., or that she had given 100l. towards the Orphan-House. But this is not all. Some time after this 100l. had been given by her, brother C-r, (who was then labouring as a City Missionary in connexion with the Scriptural Knowledge Institution, and who about that very time happened to visit from house to house in that part of the city where A. L. lived), told me that he had met with many cases, in which A. L. had given to one poor woman a bedstead, to another some bedding, to another some clothes, to another food; and thus instance upon instance of acts of love, on the part of our dear sister A. L., had come before him. I relate one instance more. August 4, 1836, seven months and a half after she had given the 100l., she came one morning to me and said: "Last evening I felt myself particularly stirred up to pray about the funds of the Scriptural Knowledge Institution; but whilst praying I thought, what good is it for me to pray for means, if I do not give, when I have the means, and I have therefore brought you this 5l." As I had reason to believe that by this time by far the greater part of her money was gone, I again had a good deal of conversation with her, to see whether she really did count the cost, and whether this donation also was given unto the Lord, or from momentary excitement, in which case it was better not to give the money. However, she was at this time also steadfast, grounded upon the word of God, and evidently constrained by the love of Christ; and all the effect my conversation had upon her was, that she said: "You must take five shillings in addition to the 5l., as a proof that I give the 5l. cheerfully." And thus she constrained me to take the 5l. 5s. Four things are especially to be noticed about this beloved sister, with reference to all this period of her earthly pilgrimage: 1, She did all these things in secret, avoiding to the utmost all show about them, and thus proved, that she did not desire the praise of man. 2, She remained, as before, of an humble and lowly mind, and she proved thus, that she had done what she did unto the Lord, and not unto man. 3, Her dress remained, during all the time that she had this comparative abundance, the same as before. It was clean, yet as simple and inexpensive as it was at the time when all her income had consisted of 3s. 6d., or at most 5s., per week. There was not the least difference as to her lodging, dress, manner of life, etc. She remained in every way the poor hand-maid of the Lord, as to all outward appearance. 4, But that which is as lovely as the rest, she continued working at her needle all this time. She earned her 2s. 6d., or 3s., or a little more, a week, by her work, as before: whilst she gave away the money in Sovereigns or Five Pound Notes.—At last all her money was gone, and that some years before she fell sleep, and as her bodily health never had been good, as long as I had known her, and was now much worse, she found herself peculiarly dependent upon the Lord, who never forsook her up to the last moment of her earthly course. The very commencement of her life of simple dependence upon the Lord, was such as greatly to encourage her. She related the facts to me as I give them here. When she was completely without money, and when her little stock of tea and butter was also gone, two sisters in the Lord called on her. After they had been a little while with her, they told her that they had come to take tea with her. She said to herself; I should not at all mind to go without my tea, but this is a great trial, that I have nothing to set before these sisters; and she gave them therefore to understand, that their staying to tea would not be convenient at that time. The sisters, however, I suppose, not understanding the hint, remained, and presently brought out of a basket tea, sugar, butter and bread, and thus there was all that was requisite for the tea, and the remainder of the provisions was left with her. She told me, that at that time she was not accustomed to trials of faith, as she afterwards was.

Her body became weaker and weaker, in consequence of which she was able to work very little, for many months before she died; but the Lord supplied her with all she needed, though she never asked for anything. For instance, a sister in communion with us sent her for many months all the bread she used.—Her mouth was full of thanksgiving, even in the midst of the greatest bodily sufferings. She fell asleep in Jesus in January 1844.—I have related these facts, because they tend to the praise of the Lord, and may be instrumental in stirring up other children of God, to follow this dear departed sister in so far as she followed the Lord Jesus; but,in particular, that I may show in what remarkable ways the Lord proved, from the very beginning, that the Orphan-House was His and not mine. I now go on to narrate further how the Lord provided me with means for it.] This evening a sister sent five small forms. December 20. A sister gave me 5l. December 21. A friend sent 1l. Weekly subscription of 4s. December 22. A sister gave me 1l. and a friend sent 2s. 6d. December 23. A brother gave this evening a piece of blind line and a dozen of blind tassels. About ten in the evening, a gentleman brought me from an individual, whose name he was not to mention, 4l., of which I was allowed to take 2l. for the Orphan-House, and to give the other 2l. to poor believers. December 28. During the last four days I had received no offerings, and was rather cast down about it, not knowing why the Lord dealt thus. Yet, in the midst of it, I had a hope, that He was in the mean time working for the Orphan-House, though nothing had been given. I was again stirred up to pray, that the Lord would appear today. A little after, I saw a brother who told me, that ever since he had received the printed proposal for the establishment of an Orphan-House, he had considered the matter, and that he was willing to give for the use of it certain premises, which he built some years since, and which cost him 2,600l., provided there could be raised about 500l., to add to the buildings what may be needed, to fit them for the purpose. There is a piece of ground belonging to the premises, sufficiently large to build thereon what may be required. The buildings are very suitable for an Orphan-House, containing some very large rooms. If, therefore, the Lord should put it into the hearts of His people, who have the means, to give this sum of money, the premises will be given. The reason why they are offered under the above-mentioned condition is, that in the state in which they are now, on account of the peculiar purpose for which they were built, they could accommodate only about 15 children, but, by the proposed addition, would be large enough for 50 or 60. For the present, however, the premises are let, and a notice of six months must be given. If this matter should be brought about by the Lord, my prayer concerning a house, which has been repeatedly brought before Him since December 5th, will have been answered. Yet I leave the matter in the hands of Him, who has the power to give us a place, of which we may take immediate possession, or who can put it into the hearts of His children to pay the rent for a house, or to give us the 500l. necessary to complete the building.—Weekly subscription of 4s. December 29. A clergyman gave 10s. December 30. A brother at Sidmouth sent 5l.

January 1, 1836. Through a sister was given 6s., being six different donations; also from herself 1l. as a donation, besides 1s. as a monthly subscription. Also a lady sent through her 1l. 1s. as a yearly subscription. Jan. 2. 4 sister sent 5l. Jan. 3. A gentleman sent 5s, Jan. 4. Weekly subscription of 4s. Through a brother from two friends, 1s. The same brother brought also one dish, three plates, two basins, two cups and saucers, and two knives and forks. Jan. 5. 10s., and 12s. 9d., and 2l. were given. This evening some one rang our house bell. When the door was opened, no one was there, but a kitchen fender and a dish were found at the door, which, no doubt, were given for the Orphan-House.

Jan. 7. 10s. was sent. Jan. 8. 2l. was given, also 10s. A sister offered herself for the work. Jan. 9. From E. G. 1l. 5s., and from a brother 6d. Jan. 10. 2s. 6d. was given. In the paper was written, "Two widows mites for the Orphan-school. In the name of the Lord establish it." Jan. 11. Weekly subscription 4s. Jan. 12. 6d., 6d., 4d., 4d., and 1d. were given. Jan. 14. An old great coat was given; 1l. by a brother. A sister in Dublin offered 2l. 12s. yearly. There was sent a deal box, a small looking-glass, a candlestick, a jug, a basin, two plates, two knives and forks, and a tin dish.

All this money, and all these articles have been given, and all these above-mentioned offers have been made, without my asking any individual for anything; moreover, almost all has been sent from individuals concerning whom I had naturally no reason to expect any thing, and some of whom I never saw. Upon the ground of these facts, therefore, I am clearly persuaded, that it is the will of the Lord that I should proceed in the work, and I shall therefore now state something more definite than I could in the former paper.

1. If the Lord should not provide previous to the middle of February a house in the way of gift, which in a few weeks may be occupied for an Orphan-House, or put it into the heart of some one who loves Him to pay the rent for one, or to lend us one for this purpose, I intend, God willing, to rent certain suitable premises, which are to be had for about 50l. yearly. I purpose to take them for a twelvemonth, for that time would be required, before the building could be finished, should the Lord provide the above-mentioned 500l.

2. It is intended, God willing, to open the institution about April 1.

3. It is purposed to confine the Orphan-house, for the present, to female children. My desire is to help both male and female orphans, and that from their earliest youth; but hitherto the Lord has pointed out only a small commencement. Should it, however, please Him to give me the means, and to increase my faith and light, I shall gladly serve Him more extensively in this way. It has appeared well to me to commence with female children, because they are the more helpless sex, and they need more particularly to be taken care of, that they may not fall a prey to vice. The house which is to had will accommodate about 30 children, which number I intend to receive at once, should the Lord give me the means to clothe that number, and to furnish the house for so many; but, if not, I purpose, at all events, the Lord willing, to commence the work, though with a smaller number.

4. It is intended to receive the children from the seventh to the twelfth year, and to let them stay in the house, till they are able to go to service.

5. As the children will be brought up for service, they will be employed in useful household work.

GEORGE MÜLLER.

Bristol, Jan. 16, 1836.

Jan. 24. Today brother Craik preached once for the first time. Jan. 30. Today I went to meet two sisters, who were expected from London. I sat down in the coach office, took out my Bible, and began to read; and though in the midst of the noise of the city, the Lord most especially refreshed my soul, so much so, that I remember scarcely ever to have had more real communion with Him, which lasted for more than an hour. It was the love of Christ which led me there. I would gladly have remained at home, to have had time for prayer and reading the Word, especially as I had to leave the house early in the morning. Yet I went for the Lord's sake, and He gave me a blessing: so that, though I had to wait more than two hours, and after all the sisters did not arrive, I was richly repaid. May I but leave myself more and more in His hands! He orders all things well!

February 3. I have been very weak for some days. This evening brother Craik was able to preach instead of me, for the first time at the week meetings. How good is the Lord in restoring him thus far! Feb. 16. Today was a day of thanksgiving on account of brother Craik's restoration. We had three public meetings. Feb. 17. I had been repeatedly praying today far a text, but obtained none. About five minutes before the time of preaching, I was directed to Rev. ii. 19, on which I preached with much assistance and enjoyment to my own soul, without any previous preparation; and the word was felt by many to be a word in season. Feb. 26. This evening both churches met at tea together, with the brethren and sisters who intend to leave us in a few days for missionary work. Feb. 29. This evening we had a meeting on behalf of the missionary brethren and sisters. They were by seven brethren commended to the Lord in prayer.

March 1. This afternoon brother and sister Groves, and the brethren and sisters going with them for missionary purposes, twelve in number, left us for the East Indies. In consequence of the journey to the Continent, at the commencement of last year, four brethren and two sisters have gone out, two brethren in October last, and two brethren and two sisters today. This evening we had again a prayer meeting for the dear missionary party. May the Lord soon give us the privilege of seeing some one of our own number go forth. April 21. This day was set apart for prayer and thanksgiving concerning the Orphan-House, as it is now opened. In the morning several brethren prayed, and brother Craik spoke on the last verses of Psalm xx. In the afternoon I addressed our Day and Sunday-School children, the orphans and other children present. In the evening we had another prayer-meeting. There are now 17 children in the Orphan-House.

May 3. I have now been for many days praying for the supply of our own temporal wants, and for the funds of the Scriptural Knowledge Institution; but, as yet, I have had not only no answers to my prayer, but our income has been less than usual, and we have had also but very little coming in for the funds of the Institution. We have not been able to put by our taxes, and expect them daily to be called for. My clothes also are now worse than any I ever wore, and I have also but one suit. May 6. I have now been for some years, and especially these last few months, more or less thinking and praying respecting publishing a short account of the Lord's dealings with me. Today I have at last settled to do so, and have begun to write.

May 16. For these several weeks our income has been little; and though I had prayed many times that the Lord would enable us to put by the taxes, yet the prayer remained unanswered. In the midst of it all, my comfort was that the Lord would send help by the time it would be needed. One thing particularly has been a trial to us of late, far more than our own temporal circumstances, which is, that we have scarcely in any measure been able to relieve the distress among the poor saints. Today, the Lord at last, after I had many times prayed to Him for these weeks past, answered my prayers, there being 7l. 12s. 0 1/4d. given to me as my part of the free-will offerings through the boxes, two 5l. notes having been put in yesterday, one for brother Craik and one for me. Thus the Lord has again delivered us, and answered our prayers, and that not one single hour too late; for the taxes have not as yet been called for.

May He fill my heart with gratitude for this fresh deliverance, and may He be pleased to enable me more and more to trust in Him, and to wait patiently for His help! May He also be pleased to teach me more and more the meaning of that word, with reference to my own circumstances: — "Mine hour is not yet came."

A third statement, containing the announcement of the opening of the Orphan-House for destitute female children, and a proposal for the establishment of an Infant Orphan-House, was on May 18th, 1836, sent to the press, and is here reprinted.

Opening of the Orphan-House for Destitute Female Children, established in Bristol, in connexion with the Scriptural Knowledge Institution for Home and Abroad; and Proposal for the Establishment of an Infant-Orphan-House.

In a previous printed account, a statement has been given of the success with which the Lord has been pleased to crown the prayers of His servant, respecting the establishment of an Orphan-House in this city. The subject of my prayer was, that He would graciously provide a house, either as a loan, or as a gift, or that some one might be led to pay the rent for one; further, that He would give me 1000l. for the object, and likewise suitable individuals to take care of the children. A day or two after, I was led to ask, in addition to the above, that he would put it into the hearts of His people to send me articles of furniture, and some clothes for the children. In answer to these petitions, 184l. 2s. 6d. and many articles of furniture and clothing were sent, a conditional offer of a house, as a gift, was made, and individuals proposed themselves to take care of the children, the particulars of which have been given in the statement already referred to, dated Jan. 16, 1836. I shall now proceed to show how, since that time, the Lord has continued to answer my prayers.

January 16, 1836, there was given 6d., six yards of calico, three plates, a cup and saucer, and a jug. January 18, 4s. Jan. 19, a saucepan and steamer, a tin dish, a teapot, some drugget; also 4d., and 1s. Jan. 21. 1l., also 5s. Jan. 22. 2s. 6d. Jan. 23. A brother gave 5s., the first fruits of the increase of his salary. Jan. 24. 5s.; also 1l., and 1l. Jan. 25. A brother promised to give 50l. within a twelvemonth, with the particular object of thus securing the payment of the rent of a house. Thus the Lord has answered the prayer respecting this point.

There were also given 1l., 6d. and 4s. Jan. 27. A form was sent. Jan. 28. A deal table was given, also, anonymously, were sent a coal box and 4s., also a bedstead. Jan. 29. Two little waiters, two candlesticks, two chandeliers, two night shades, a tin kettle, a warmer, a bread basket, a fire guard; also one dozen tin cups, six plates, and 1s. 6d.; also 1s., a water jug, six plates, a sugar basin, a teapot, a tea canister, and a knife. Jan. 30. A frying pan, a tea canister, a metal teapot, a tin dish, a pepper box, a flour scoop, a skimmer, a grater, two tin saucepans, a tin warmer, 55 thimbles, five parcels of hooks and eyes; also 1l. Jan. 31. 5l. 5s.; an old white dress and a fur tippet.

February 1. 4s., 2s. 6d., also a sister in the Lord offered today to make the bonnets for the children gratuitously, if any one would buy the straw, and that her husband would make a bedstead, if any one would buy the wood; she also mentioned that they would gladly give both the straw and the wood, if they had the means. Feb. 2. 6d., 2d and out of the box in my room was taken 3s. Feb. 4. 2s. 6d.,6d.; also a desk and a kitchen table; there was also promised a subscription of 8s. annually. Feb. 5. 1s. 6d. Feb. 6. A brother sent 100l., being induced to do so an having had the former paper read to him. Feb. 7. 1l. 2s., 1s., 6d., 2s. 6d., 5s., 2s. 6d., 5s., 2s. 6d., 3l. 10s. Feb. 8. A table and two chairs, 4s., 5l., also 30l. was sent from Ireland; 10s., 10s., 1l. Feb. 9. 1l., 4s. 1d., 10s., 1s. 1d., 1s. 1d., 1s., 1s., 1s., 1s., 1d., 5s., 2s. 6d., 2s. 6d., 2s. 6d., 2s. 6d., 2s. 6d., 6d., 6d., 6d., 4d., 4d., 1d., 1s. Feb. 11. Three yards of print, 2s. 6d., 5s.; 5s., 10s. Feb. 12. A clothes' horse, a coffee pot, and 1s.; also a washing tub, a coffee mill, a pepper mill, two dozen pieced of bobbin, three dozen stay laces, two dozen thimbles, two dozen bodkins, 300 needles, a gridiron, six pots of blacking paste, a pound of thread, and a large deal table. Feb. 14. 10s., 1l., put anonymously into Bethesda boxes, for the Orphan-House. Feb. 15. Two glass salt cellars, a mustard pot, a vinegar cruet, and a pepper box, also 4s., 4d., 4d., 4d., 4d., 2s. 6d. Feb. 16. 4d. 1s., 4d., Feb. 17. 5s. Feb. 18. A bedstead, and by two poor persons, 2d. Feb. 19. There were sent from London 34 yards of print, six yards of calico, one dozen pocket handkerchiefs, four pairs of stockings, and two New Testaments. Feb. 20. Two salt cellars, two mugs, two plates, also two pocket handkerchiefs. Feb. 21. 1l. Feb. 22. 4s., 1s. Feb. 23. Twelve yards of gingham from two Swiss sisters. Feb. 25. 2s. 6d., 2s. 6d. Feb. 28. 1l. Feb. 29. 1l., 5s., 4s.

March 2. 1l., 1s., 1s. 6d., 1s., 1s., 1s., 1/2d., 2s., 1s., 1s., 2s. 6d.; also out of the box in my room, 1l. 2s. 6d.; two large iron pots were sent anonymously. March 4. 10l., 10s., 3s., 7d., 10s., 2s. 6d., 10s., 10s., 3s.; all these offerings were sent from Clapham; also a desk. March 5. Some fancy worsted and 1s., the produce of the sale of some old map rollers. March 7. 4s., 10s., 5s., 5s., 2s. 6d., 2s. 6d., 2s., 2s. 6d., 5s.; all these offerings were sent from Cleve, also 5s.; also, from a distance of about 100 miles, was sent the valuable and useful present of five pewter dishes, three dozen pewter plates, three dozen metal spoons, two coral necklaces, a pair of coral earrings, and a large gold brooch—the trinkets to be sold for the benefit of the Orphan-House. Also from the same place was sent 10s. "which had been laid up for a time of need, but which were sent because the donor thought that the time of trust in the Lord in Bristol was her time of need to give."

March 10. 8s., 1s. 6d., 2s. 6d., 6d., 6d., 6d., 1d., 4d., 4d., 4d., 5s., 2s. March 11. 1l., 5s. March 13. A little girl sent, from a distance of more than 200 miles, 2s. 6d. March 14. A brother at Plymouth promised to send 20l., also 4s. were given. March 15. 7d., 10s., 6d., 1s., 1s., 1d., 6d. March 16. 1s.; anonymously was sent from London 1l., also 2s. 6d. March 18. 10 s. March 19. 3s., 1s., 4d., 4d., 4d., 4d. March 21. 4s. March 22. 1l. March 23. A large deal box, also anonymously six dishes. March 24. 5s. March 25. A ton of coals. March 27. 1l., 1l., 1l., 10s.; these offerings were sent from Trowbridge, also 10s. From the Isle of Wight, 2l., 2l., 1l., 10s., a large piece of green baize, and two metal spoons. March 28. 1l., 4s., 3d., 3l., 10 s., 6s., 10 s., 2s. 6d., 5s., 5s., also an iron kettle and some drugget. March 29. 1s. 3d., 1s. 3d., 1s., 1s. 6d. March 31. 2s.

April 2. 1s., 2s. 6d., 6d., 6d., also six blankets, two counterpanes, four sheets, eight bonnets, five frocks, six pinafores, with the promise to send also six chemises (sent since). April 4. 4s., 1s., 1s., 8d., 1s., 1d., 1s., 3d., 6s., 2s. 6d., 1l., 1l., 3s., also 14 tippets, three pinafores, one frock, three chemises (two more promised), six flannel petticoats; also six stuff petticoats; also six flannel petticoats (and six chemises promised), also a sheet. April 5. 2l., 7s., 6d., 6d., 4d., 4d., 1d., 4d., 6d. April 6. One dozen of washing basins and one jug. April 7. 2s. 2d., 3s., 1s., 2s. 2d., 1s. 1d. April 8. 10s., 10s., 6d., 1s., 2s., also a bench. April 9. 4d., 4d., 4d., 4d., 2s., also three knives and forks, also some marking ink. April 10. Two patent locks. April 11. 4s. April 12. 1s., 8d., 2s., a jug, also twelve bonnets and six tippets. April 13. A set of fire irons, a tea kettle, a coal box, a tin saucepan, a tripod, a tea pot, three cups and saucers, a wash-hand basin, three small basins, and two plates. April 15. 10s., 10s. April 16. 5l., also 1l. and 22 Hymn Books. Also anonymously were sent two dozen pocket handkerchiefs, also a hymn, "The Orphan's Hope," in a frame. April 17. A cask, also a hundred weight of treacle, and 36 pounds of moist sugar.

April 18, 4s. April 19. 2s. 6d., 1s. April 20. A new bedstead. From Clapham were sent 21l. and 11l., likewise three flannel petticoats, some print, six frocks, four pinafores, seven tippets, 12 caps, 14 chemises, 24 furnished work bags, 12 pocket handkerchiefs, 16 pairs of stockings, one pair of sleeves; besides this, with an orphan child, was sent from Clapham, a complete new outfit.

April 21. 2l., 2s., 1s., 6d., 6d., 6d., 5s., 2s., also two candlesticks, a pepper box, and a handkerchief. April 22. 1s., 10s., 2s. 6d., 2s. 2 3/4d., also a long handled brush and 6d., also an ironing blanket, and 32 yards of flannel. April 23. 2l., 5s., 10s., a cheese, and 18 pounds of beef. April 25. 1s. and eight plates. April 26. 6d., 6d., 5s. April 27. 10d. April 28. 1s., also two tons of coal, also two patchwork quilts, 15 work bags and pin-cushions, 12 needle cases, three little bags, one tippet, two pairs of stockings, one kettle holder, also six pairs of worsted stockings.

May 2. 8s., 1l., 10 s. May 3. 8d., 2s. 6d., and a pair of shoes. May 4. A gentleman and lady, who saw the Institution, left six chemises, seven pocket handkerchiefs, two flannel petticoats, four pairs of stockings, and four pairs of gloves; there were also sent 18 thimbles, a gross of buttons, a gross of hooks and eyes. May 5. 2s. 6d., 1s. May 6. 15 pairs of worsted stockings. May 7. 5s., 2s. 6d. May 8. 5s., 6d., 2s. 6d. May 9. 4s., 10s., 6d., 4d., 4d., 4d. May 10. 6d., 4d., 6d., 6d., 4d., 1d., 4d., 2s. May 11. 1l., 2s. 6d., 1s. May 13. A bonnet, also a dish, sent by a poor person in an almshouse; a well-wisher sent, for little orphan boys, six frock pinafores, six little shirts, six frocks and trousers. May 14. 9 pounds of soap. May 15. S. S. 2s. 6d. May 16. 4s. May 17. Out of the box in the Orphan-House, 3s. 0 1/2d., also 1s.

1. It may be well to state, that the above results have followed in answer to prayer, without any one having been asked by me for one single thing, from which I have refrained, not on account of want of confidence in the brethren, or because I doubted their love to the Lord, but that I might see the hand of God so much the more clearly. For as the work has been begun without any visible support, in dependence only upon the living God, it was of the utmost importance to be sure of His approbation at the very commencement.

2. From this statement, and from that contained in the last printed account, it will be seen how the Lord, in a great measure, has already answered the petition of December 5, 1835; for a house has been given, suitable individuals have offered themselves to take care of the children, and much more furniture, and many more articles of clothing have been sent than I ever had expected. The only part of the prayer, which has not been as yet quite fulfilled, is, that which respects the 1000l., which, however, the Lord, I doubt not, will likewise send in His own time. In the meantime, let my brethren help me to praise Him, that He has sent already more than one half of that sum, and therefore more than for the present has been needed.

3. So far as I remember, I brought even the most minute circumstances concerning the Orphan-House before the Lord in my petitions, being conscious of my own weakness and ignorance. There was, however, one point I never had prayed about, namely, that the Lord would send children; for I naturally took it for granted that there would be plenty of applications. The nearer, however, the day came, which had been appointed for receiving applications, the more I had a secret consciousness, that the Lord might disappoint my natural expectations, and show me that I could not prosper in one single thing without Him. The appointed time came, and not even one application was made. I had before this been repeatedly tried, whether I might not, after all, against the Lord's mind, have engaged in the work. This circumstance now led me to lie low before my God in prayer the whole of the evening, February 3, and to examine my heart once more as to all the motives concerning it; and being able, as formerly, to say, that His glory was my chief aim, i.e., that it might be seen that it is not a vain thing to trust in the living

God,—and that my second aim was the spiritual welfare of the orphan-children,—and the third their bodily welfare; and still continuing in prayer, I was at last brought to this state, that I could say from my heart, that I should rejoice in God being glorified in this matter, though it were by bringing the whole to nothing. But as still, after all, it seemed to me more tending to the glory of God, to establish and prosper the Orphan-House, I could then ask Him heartily, to send applications. I enjoyed now a peaceful state of heart concerning the subject, and was also more assured than ever that God would establish it. The very next day, February 4, the first application was made, and since then 42 more have been made.

4. The house mentioned in the last printed account, which we had intended to rent, having been let before any applications had been made, and nothing more having been done about the premises offered as a gift, on account of the want of money needed to complete the building, I rented, at least for one year, the house No. 6, Wilson Street, as being, on account of its cheapness and largeness, very suitable, and in which, up to March 25th, I had been living myself. Having furnished it for 30 children, we began an April 11th, 1836, to take them in, and on April 21st the Institution was opened by a day being set apart for prayer and thanksgiving. There are now 26 children in the house, and a few more are expected daily. They are under the care of a matron and governess.

5. In the last printed account it was mentioned that we intended to take in the children from the seventh to the twelfth year. But after six applications had been made for children between four and six years of age, it became a subject of solemn and prayerful consideration, whether, as long as there were vacancies, such children should not be received, though so young. For it appeared to me, that if it becomes the saints to care in this way, according to their ability, for those whom God has bereaved of both parents, when they become seven years of age, that it becomes them equally so, to take care of them whilst they are under seven years, and therefore completely unable to help themselves. Further, orphan children are often left to themselves, and thus, at the age of 11 or 12 years, have already made much progress in wickedness. Therefore I came at last to the conclusion to take in the little girls under seven years of age, for whom application had been made. Further, there are exceedingly

few institutions in the kingdom, in which infant orphans are received, and provided with scriptural education. Further, it has been repeatedly brought before me, how desirable it would be to establish also in this city an orphan-house for male children, and there were even the above-mentioned articles sent for little orphan boys. Partly, then, on account of these reasons; and partly, because the Institution already opened will be quite filled in a few days, and applications continue to be made; and partly, because the Lord has done hitherto far above what I could have expected: I have at last, after repeated prayer, come to the conclusion, in the name of the Lord, and in dependence upon Him alone for support, to propose the establishment of an Infant-Orphan-House. It is intended to open this Institution, as soon as suitable premises and individuals, to take care of the children, &c., have been obtained.

a. It is intended to receive into this Infant-Orphan-House destitute male and female infants bereaved of both parents, from their earliest days up to the seventh year, and to provide them with food, clothing, needful attendance, and Scriptural education.

b. It is intended to let the female children stay up to the seventh year in the Infant-Orphan-House, and then to remove them to the Institution already opened, till they are able to go to service.

c. It is also intended, as far as the Lord may help, to provide for the boys, when they are above seven years, though we cannot at present say in what manner.

In proposing the establishment of this second Orphan-House, I do it in the same simple dependence upon God alone, as in the case of the former. And feeling my own weakness, and knowing that it is not in my power to give faith to myself, I ask the brethren to help me with their prayers, that my faith may not fail.

6. To avoid misunderstandings, I would expressly state, that both the last mentioned Institution, and the one already opened, are for orphan children living in any part of the United. Kingdom.

GEORGE MÜLLER.

Bristol, May 18, 1836.

June 3. From May 16 up to this day I have been confined to the house, and a part of the time to my bed, on account of a local inflammation, which keeps me from walking. Almost every day during this time I have been able to continue writing a narrative of the Lord's dealings with me, which had been again laid aside after May 7, on account of a number of pressing engagements. It is very remarkable, that the greatest objection against writing it for the press was want of time. Now, through this affliction, which leaves my mind free, and gives me time, on account of confinement to the house, I have been able to write about 100 quarto pages. May the Lord in mercy teach me about this matter!

June 8. I am still getting better. The abscess is now open. This affliction has been, by the mercy of the Lord, an exceedingly light one. Not one day have I had severe pain, and not one day have I been kept altogether from working. June 9. I was able to go again today to the Orphan-House, and to read the Scriptures with the children. This day came three more children, who have made up our number, so that there are now thirty in the house.

June 11. I am, by the mercy of God, still getting better, but, as yet, unable to walk about. All this week I have been again enabled to go on writing for the press. June 12. Today the Lord very kindly allowed me to preach again, and that most undeservedly, and much sooner than I could have expected. June 14. This morning, brother C-r and I prayed unitedly, chiefly about the schools and the circulation of the Scriptures. Besides asking for blessings upon the work, we have also asked the Lord for the means which are needed; for on July 1, 17l. 10s. will be due for the rent of school-rooms, and, besides this, we want at least 40l. more to go on with the circulation of the Scriptures, to pay the salaries of the masters, &c. Towards all this we have only about 7l. I also prayed for the remainder of the 1000l. for the Orphan-House.

June 18. We have had, for many weeks past, generally little money for our personal expenses, which has been a trial to us, not on our own account, but because we have thus been able to do but very little for the poor brethren. Today, Saturday, we have 3s. left, just enough to pay for a fly to take me to and bring me back from Bethesda tomorrow, as I am unable to walk. This money we should not have had, but for our baker, a brother, who refused today to take money for the usual quantity of bread, which we daily take.

June 21. This evening brother C-r and I found, that the Lord has not only been pleased to send us, through the offerings which have come in during the last week, in answer to our prayers, the 17l. 10s. which will be due for the rent of two school-rooms on July 1st, but that we have 5l. more than is needed. Thus the Lord once more has answered our prayers.

June 25. Saturday. We have been again helped through this week, as it regards our personal need, and have 3s. left, though we had many shillings to pay for driving about. Now the Lord has put it into the hearts of some of His children, to provide me with a fly every Lord's-day, as long as I may need it.

July 1. Today a suit of new clothes was given to me, which came very seasonably. May this fresh instance of the Lord's loving-kindness lead me to love Him more; and may He also be pleased richly to reward those brethren, who have thus ministered to my need! July 16. Today a brother sent me a new hat, the seventh which in succession has been given to me.

July 28. For some weeks past we have not been able to pay the salary of the masters and governesses a month in advance, but have been obliged to pay it weekly. Brother C-r and I have lately prayed repeatedly together respecting the funds, but we were now brought so low, that we should not have been able to pay even this weekly salary of the teachers, had not the Lord most remarkably helped us again today. For besides 1l. which was given to us, this evening a brother gave 8l., which sum had been made up by a number of his workmen paying weekly one penny each, of their own accord, towards our funds. The money had been collecting for many months, and, in this our necessity, it had been put into the heart of this brother to bring it. My faith has been greatly strengthened through this circumstance. For before today, though I have never been in the least allowed to doubt the Lord's faithfulness, I did not understand His purpose in His dealings with us of late, in not sending us more than we have needed just to be kept from stopping; and I have sometimes thought, whether it might not be His will, on account of my want of faithfulness in His work, to decrease the field; but now I see, that notwithstanding my unworthiness, His allowing us to pray so frequently, was only that the deliverance might be felt so much the more when it came.

July 29. This evening from six to half-past nine we had again a meeting for inquirers. There came twelve fresh cases before us, and there were six more than we could see. Thus we saw, that the work of the Lord, even as it regards conversion, is still going on among us.

October 1. Today, in dependence upon the Lord alone for means, we engaged a brother as a master for a sixth day school. Last Saturday, for the first time, we were so low in funds, that we needed 1l. more than we had, to pay the salaries a week in advance; but one sister, on account of the death of her father, as we afterwards learned, was kept from calling for her money, and on the next day we received more than was needed to pay her. On account, therefore, of the many deliverances which we have had of late, we have not hesitated to enlarge the field, as another boys' school was greatly needed, there having been many applications for admission standing these several months past.

October 5. This evening 25l. was given to me for the Scriptural Knowledge Institution. Thus the Lord has already given the means of defraying the expenses of the new boys' school for some months to come.

October 19. Today, after having many times prayed respecting this matter, I have at last engaged a sister as matron for the Infant-Orphan-House, never having been able, up to this day, to meet with an individual who seemed suitable: though there has been money enough in hand for some time past for commencing this work, and there have been also applications made for several infant orphans.

October 25. Today we obtained without, any trouble, through the kind hand of God, very suitable premises for the Infant-Orphan-House. If we had laid out many hundred pounds in building a house, we could scarcely have built one more suitable for the purpose. How evident is the hand of God in all these matters! How important to leave our concerns, great and small, with Him; for He arranges all things well! If our work be His work, we shall prosper in it.

November 30. On account, as I suppose, of many pressing engagements, I had not been led for some time past to pray respecting the funds. But being in great need, I was led yesterday morning, earnestly to ask the Lord, and in answer to this petition a brother gave me last evening 10l. He had had it in his heart for several months past, to give this sum, but had been hitherto kept from it, not having the means. Just now, in this our great necessity, the Lord furnished him with the means, and we were helped in this way. In addition to this 10l., I received last evening a letter with 5l., from a sister whom I never saw, and who has been several times used by God as an instrument to supply our wants. She writes thus: "It has been so much on my mind lately to send you some money, that I feel as if there must be some need, which the Lord purposes to honour me by making me the instrument of supplying. I therefore enclose you 5l., all I have in the house at this moment; but if you have occasion for it, and will let me know, I will send you as much more." Besides these two donations, I received today 3l. 3s.

December 15. This day was set apart for prayer and thanksgiving respecting the Infant-Orphan-House, which was opened on November 28. In the morning we had a prayer-meeting. In the afternoon, besides prayer and thanksgiving, I addressed the children of our day-schools and the orphans, about 350, on Ecclesiastes xii. 1. In the evening I gave a further account of the Orphan-Houses, commencing from the time when the last printed account had been issued, dated May 18, 1836. The substance of this account was printed, and is reprinted here for the sake of those who are as yet unacquainted with it.

Further account of the Orphan-House for Female Orphans above Seven Years of Age; and Opening of the Infant-Orphan-House, for destitute Male and Female Orphans under Seven Years of Age.

It is now a twelve-month since the proposal for the establishment of an Orphan-House was first made. Since then the Lord has given me almost all I requested of Him, and in some respects even more. This was in part stated in the last two papers which were printed on this subject dated January 16, and May 18, 1836. Of the 1,000l. which I had asked of God on December 5, 1835, I had actually received on May 18, 1836, 450l. 13s. 6 3/4d.; and besides this, 70l. had been promised by two brethren. As it regards premises, articles of clothing, furniture, &c., I had received even beyond my petition. I have now the pleasure of detailing, still further, how God has continued to answer my prayer since May 18, 1836.

May 19th was given 1l. 23rd 1l. and 4s. There were also sent two buckets and 1s. 24th., 10 s. 6d., 2d., 1s. 6d. 25th, one pound of butter, 2s., 1s., 1s. There was also sent 14s., and in the paper was written: "The history of this money is: A lady was going to purchase a dress. The enclosed sum was the difference between the fashionable one, which took her fancy, and one less fashionable. So she thought, the orphans should profit by this sacrifice of her fancy." May 27th, there was left at my house a sovereign, and in the paper was written: 1 Thess. v. 25." [Pause with me a few moments, dear reader, before going on with the account. In preparing the third edition for the press, I have been struck with the very many cases in which individuals, who are spoken of in this narrative, are no more in the land of the living. So it is with the two donors of the last mentioned sums. The dear sister who would not indulge her fancy in having a more fashionable dress, but who would rather give the fourteen shillings, which thus could be saved, to the orphans, has been with her Lord for more than two years. Will she regret not having indulged her fancy in that instance? Will she now suffer loss on account of it? Surely not!—The dear brother who gave the sovereign, was a gracious devoted clergyman of the City of Bristol. He had written in the paper in which the sovereign was enclosed, "1 Thess. v. 25." ("Brethren, pray for us.") This dear man of God does now no longer need our prayers. He entered into his rest several years ago. Yet a little while, dear believing reader, and, if the coming of the Lord prevent not, we too shall fall asleep in Jesus. Therefore, let us work, "while it is day: the night cometh, when no man can work." And, "Whatsoever thy hand findeth to do, do it with thy might: for there is no work, nor device, nor knowledge, nor wisdom in the grave, whither thou goest."—But how would it be with you, dear reader, if you are unprepared, and should be taken out of the world? Let me beseech you to seek the Lord while He may be found. Jesus died to save sinners. He shed His blood. He fulfilled the law of God, and died the JUST for the UNJUST: and whosoever depends for salvation upon His perfect obedience, and upon His sufferings and death, shall be saved; for God has said it.] May 28th, A fender and two coal scuttles. 29th, 5l. 30th, 4s. Also 2s. 6d., with two gowns and a tippet. The brother who left a sovereign with "1 Thess. v. 25," gave today 10s. more; 2s. 4d. June 1st, from a few sisters in Dublin, nine pocket handkerchiefs, 19 1/2 yards of stuff, and forty-two yards of print. 4th, 5s. 6d., eighteen little books. 5th, 6d., 4d., 4d., 4d. 6th, 4s. 7th, 5s. 1d., 2l. 2s. 6d. 8th, 4d., 1s., 1s., 3s. 9th, six pairs of gentlemen's trousers, two coats, one waistcoat, five pairs of socks, two gowns—all worn. 10th, 1l., also from a friend in Ireland 1l. 12th, S. S. 2s. 6d. 13th, 4s., 5l. 14th, 1s. 1d., 1s., 2s. 6d., 6d., 1s., 2s. 6d., 2s. 6d., 3s. 3d., 1s. 1d., 1s. 1d. 15th, a brother at Plymouth sent 25l., 20l. of which had been previously promised. 18th, 1l., 1d., 6 1/4 pounds of bacon, a form, a chopping knife. 19th, 1l. 1s., 10s.; 12s. by sale of ornaments. 20th, 4s. Also from Teignmouth, 5s., 5s., 2s. 6d., 2s. 6d., 2s. 6d., 2s. 6d., 3l., 10s., 2s. 6d., 1s. 1d., 5s., together with a gown, a boy's pinafore, a pair of socks, coloured cotton for three children's frocks, two babies' bed gowns, and five babies' night caps. 21st, 5l. 10s., 6d., 4d., 2d., 4d., 2d., 6d., 6d., twenty pounds of bacon and ten pounds of cheese. 22d, box in the Orphan-House, 2s. 4d. 24th, 2s. 6d., 3s. 8 1/2d. 27th, 4s. 28th, 2s. 6d., 4s., 4d., 6d., 10s., 6s. 6d. 29th, six straw bonnets. 30th, 5s., 2l. July 4th, 6d., 4d., 4d., 4d., 4s. There was also sent from "two orphans" 48l., 1s. 1d., 10s., 8s. 6d., 2s. 6d., 1s. 1d., 1s. 1d., 1s. 1d., 1s. 4d. 5th, 1s., 1s. 2d., 3d., 4s., 4d., 1s. 6th, six new cane chairs. 7th, 2l., 12s., 10s., 2s. 8th, 1s., 2s. 6d., 3s. 10th, 10s., 10s., 1l., 1l. 11th, 8s., 13s. 12th, 13s. 2d. 13th, 12s. 14th, there were sent six chemises, which had been promised on April 14th. Also fourteen pin cushions. 15th, six night caps and 2 petticoats. 20th, 10s., 5s., 1l., 6d., 2d., 6d., 6d., 4d., 6d., 4d., 2d., 4d. 24th, 1l. 25th, 8s., S. S. 5s. Also 25 3/4 yards of print, 12 little shawls and 16 yards of flannel. 26th, box in the Orphan-House 5s. 9d., 4d. 27th, two pairs of shoes. 28th, 3s. 8 1/2d. 29th, 2s. 6d., 6d., 4d., 4d., 4d. August 1st, 4s., 1l. 10., two chemises, three night caps, and ten pocket handkerchiefs; two chemises, three night caps, and six pocket handkerchiefs. 2nd, 8d., 1s., 1s. 3d., 1s. 3d., 1s., 1s., 6d.., 5s., 2s. 6d., 1s., 1d., 1d., one patch work quilt. 5th, 6s. 8th, 4s. 10th, a box, six canisters, and an inkstand, 13th, 5s. 15th, 1l., S. S. 2s. 6d., 4s. 16th, 6d., 6d., 4d., 4d., 4d., 6d., 1s., 1s. 6d. 19th, 1s. 2 1/2d. 23rd, 1s., 10s., 1l., 2s. 6d. September 1st, 1s. 6d., 2s. 6d., 2s., 1s., 4d., 6d., 4d., 6d., 2s. 6d., 2s. 6d., 1s. 6d., 6d., 6d., 2d., 1l., 1l., twelve chemises, one worn stuff frock, 4d., 4d., a basket of apples, and three pounds of sugar. 3rd, 1l., 5l. 5th, 12s. 7th, 5s., 2s. 6d. 8th, 5s. 13th, 1s., 1s., 1s., 2s. 6d., 2s. 6d., 2s. 6d., 2s. 6d., 2s. 3d., 1s., 1s. 1d., 1s. 1d., 2d., 6d., 6d., 2s. 6d., 6d. 14th, 1l., 10s., 10s., 14 pinafores, a basket of apples. 19th, 8s., 2s. 6d. Box in the Orphan-House 1l. 6s. 1 1/4d., 10s. 20th, 6d., 6d., 4d., 4d., 1d, 4d. 27th, several numbers of the "Record" were sent to be sold for the benefit of the Orphan-House, 4d., 4d., 2s., 2s. 6d. 30th, 1l. was given as "A Thank-offering for spiritual mercies vouchsafed to a child." Also Mr. B-sen., Surgeon, kindly offered, today, to give his attendance and medicine gratuitously to the orphans. October 1st, 6d., 4d., 4d., 4d. A worn cloak. 3rd, 5s., 3s. 3d., 1s. A gallon of dried peas. 4th, 1l. 3s. 6d. 10th, 4s., 1s. 1d., 1s. 1d., 1s. 1d., 1s. 11th, 10s., 2d., 6d., 3s. 3d. 14th, 4 1/2 gallons of beer. 16th, three tippets, 8d., 4d., 5s., 5s., 5s., 2s. 6d., 2s. 6d., 10s., 10s., 2s., 1s., 1s., 2s. 6d., 5s. 17th, 4s. 18th, 10s., 6d., 6d., 4d., 4d., 6d., 1d., 4d., 1s. 19th, 1l. 24th, 4s. 25th, three frocks, two pinafores, two tippets, three pairs of sleeves, 10s., 10s., 4d., 1s. 27th, three tippets. Anonymously was sent by post, 10s., with the request that prayer should be made for the donor, for divine guidance under circumstances of much doubt and anxiety. 29th, 12 cloth tippets. 31st, 4s. November 2nd, 1s. 3d., 1s. 3d., 1s. 4th, two little cloaks, four quarterns of bread. 5th, two turkeys, 6d., 4d., 4d., 4d. There was also given by a brother £100.—£50. of which was previously promised, to ensure the rent for premises. It is a remarkable fact concerning this donation, that I had, in December of last year, repeatedly asked the Lord to incline the heart of this brother to give one hundred pounds, and I made a memorandum of this prayer in my journal of December 12, 1835. On January 25th, 1836, fifty pounds was promised by him, and on November 5, fifty pounds besides that sum was given; but it was not till some days after, that I remembered, that the very sum, for which I had asked the Lord, had been given. Thus we often may receive an answer to prayer, and scarcely remember that it is an answer. When it came to my mind that this prayer had been noted down in my journal, and I showed it to the donor, we rejoiced together; he, to have been the instrument in giving, and I to have had, the request granted. November 6th, S. S. 7s. 6d. 7th, anonymously was sent a ton of coals, 4s., one petticoat, two pairs of gloves, two ruffs. 8th, 5l., 2s. 2d., 3s., 2s. 2d., 2s. 2d., 1s. 6d., 2d., 6d., 1s. 6d., 2s. 6d., 2s. 6d. 14th, there was given 20l. for the Orphan-house, and 20l. for the Infant-Orphan-House. Both papers, in which the money was enclosed, contained these words: "If the Lord prolongs the life of the unworthy giver of the enclosed, the same sum will be given at Christmas."—It has been more than once observed to me that I could not expect to continue to receive large sums; for that persons, when first such an institution is established, might be stirred up to give liberally, but that afterwards one had to look to a number of regular subscribers, and that, if those were lacking, it was not likely that such a work could go on. On such occasions, I have said but little; but I have had the fullest assurance, that it is a small matter for the Lord to incline donors to give liberally, a second or third time, if it were for our real welfare. And accordingly the donor, above referred to, added to the first 50l. another 50l., and the last mentioned benefactor, to the 50l., given on a former occasion, added the just mentioned 40l., with the promise to give another 40l. at Christmas. I would only add on this subject, that there are some subscribers, and even some who give considerably; yet I would state, for the Lord's glory, that if they were twenty times as many, I should desire that my eyes might not be directed to them, but to the Lord alone, and that I might be enabled to take the payment of every subscription as a donation from HIM. On the other hand, if there were no subscribers at all, yet the Lord, who heareth prayer, is rich to give according to our need.—There was given also today, "A widow's mite," 10s.—also 4d. November 14th, 4s., also four ducks. For the Infant-Orphan-House, five frocks, four shirts, four chemises, a bed gown, two petticoats; three quarterns bread. 15th 6d., 6d., 4d., 6d., 4d. 16th, by sale of trinkets, 1l. 5s., 4s. 18th, anonymously were sent a boy's cap, a bonnet, a small piece of print. 19th, four quarterns of bread. 21st, 4s., 2s. 6d. 22nd, 4d., 6d., 6d. 23rd, three frocks, a tippet, six pairs of sheets, three pairs of blankets. 25th, 12 hymn books, a worn cloak, a new tent bedstead. 27th, anonymously put into Bethesda boxes 5s. 28th, 4s. 29th, two turkeys. 30th, 10s., five yards of blanketing, a worn shawl. December 1st, a patch-work quilt and five yards of print, 3d., 10s. 4th, 5l. 5s. 5th, 4s., 1l. 5s. 6th, 6d., 2d., a worn cloak, a petticoat, a piece of linen for window curtains. 8th, box in the Orphan-House 2l. 4s. 1 1/2d. 9th, 1l. Also 1l. with "Mark ix. 36, 37," written on the paper. A most encouraging passage for this work, the force of which I had never felt before.—About a hundred weight of treacle.

I. From this statement it appears, that 770l. 0s. 9 1/2d. has been actually given, and that 40l. is promised. All the money, and all the articles of furniture, clothing, provision, &c., have been given, without one individual having been asked by me for anything, from which I have still refrained, that the Lord's own hand might be clearly seen in the matter, and that the whole might clearly appear as an answer to prayer.

II. After frequent prayer, that, if it were the will of God, He would be pleased to send us a Matron and Governess for the Infant-Orphan-House, this petition also has been answered. In addition to this we obtained a convenient house for the purpose, No. 1, Wilson Street, together with a piece of ground for a play-ground; and we therefore began to furnish it on November 21st, and on November 28th we took in the first children.

III. Of late it has appeared well to us to employ some of the strongest and eldest girls of the Orphan-House in the work of the Infant-Orphan-House, under the direction of the Matron and Governess. From this plan it appeared the following advantages would result. 1st. Thus the wages which we should have to pay to assistants would be saved. 2nd. Without any further expense to the Institution, we should in this way be able to support five or six orphans more. 3rd. If thus the bigger girls of the Orphan-House pass through the Infant-Orphan-House, before they are sent into service, they will be accustomed to nursery work, which is so important for young servants. 4th. This plan would allow us to have the bigger girls longer under our care, as we should have full employment for them.

[In the original paper follow eight other paragraphs, containing the audited account and various other points of information respecting the two Orphan-Houses, which, at the time when this Report was issued, were of importance to the donors, but are left out now, as it seems desirable to make this edition of the Narrative as concise as may be. This plan has also been adopted concerning the three previous papers, and will be further adhered to.]

GEORGE MÜLLER.

Bristol, Dec. 20, 1836.

December 31. We had this evening a prayer-meeting to praise the Lord for His goodness during the past year, and to ask Him for a continuance of His favours during the coming year. We continued together till half-past eleven. During the past year there have been received into the church of Gideon, 23 brethren and sisters, and into that of Bethesda, 29—altogether 52. Of these 52, 31 have been brought to the knowledge of the Lord through the instrumentality of brother Craik and me. There have now been admitted into Gideon Church, 79 brethren and sisters who have been converted through our instrumentality, and 86 into the Church of Bethesda: 165 seals to our ministry in Bristol. Besides this, several have fallen asleep in the faith who never were in communion with us; several of our spiritual children are connected with other churches in and out of Bristol; and many are now standing as hopeful characters on the list of candidates for fellowship. There have been added to the church of Gideon, since we came to Bristol, 154; to the church at Bethesda, 193—altogether 347; so that the number of both churches would be 415 (68 believers we found at Gideon), had there been no changes; but:

Of Gideon church are under church discipline 5; of Bethesda 8; altogether 13

Do. have fallen asleep 15 do. 7 do. 22

Do. have left Bristol 12 do. 6 do. 18

Do. have left us, but are still in Bristol . . 9 do. 4 do. 13

41 25 66

There are, therefore, at present, in fellowship with us at Gideon 181, and at Bethesda 168—altogether 349.

The Lord has been pleased to give me during the past year, as it regards my temporal supplies:—

1. In offerings through the boxes £133 8s. 9d.

2. In presents of money, from brethren in and out of Bristol £56 13s. 0d.

3. Through family connexion £5 0s. 0d.

4. Besides this have been sent to us clothes, provisions, &c., which were worth to us at least £30 0s. 0d.

5. We have been living half free of rent during the last nine months, whereby we have saved at least £7 10s. 0d.

Altogether £232 11s. 9d.

January 2, 1837. This evening the two churches had again an especial prayer-meeting, which was continued till half-past ten.

January 5. Today a sister called and told me about the conversion of her father, who, in his eightieth year, after having for many years lived openly in sin, is at last brought to the knowledge of the Lord. May this encourage the children of God to continue to pray for their aged parents and other persons; for this sister had long prayed for the conversion of her father, and at last, though only after twenty years, the Lord gave her the desire of her heart. It was an especial refreshment to my spirit to hear the particulars of this case, as I had known so much of the sinful life of this aged sinner.

January 31, and February 2. These two days we have had especial meetings for prayer and humiliation, on account of the influenza, to acknowledge the hand of God in this chastisement, as the disease is so prevalent in Bristol.

April 8. There are now 60 Children in the two Orphan-Houses, 30 in each.

April 22. The Lord has mercifully stayed the typhus fever in the Orphan-House, in answer to prayer. There were only two cases, and the children are recovering.

April 24. This evening we had a comfortable meeting with 30 brethren and sisters over the Word. (Of late brother Craik and I have frequently set apart an evening, generally once a week, to meet with ten, twenty or thirty brethren and sisters, to take tea with them, and to spend the rest of the evening in prayer and meditation over the Scriptures. We began these meetings chiefly on account of having thus an opportunity of seeing more of the saints, as the greatness of the number of those in communion with us makes it impossible to see them as often in their houses, as it might be profitable, or as often as we desire. We commenced these meetings in our own houses, choosing those in particular, of whom we had seen little. After we had had several meetings in our own houses, we were invited by the brethren and sisters, and they have asked others to meet us. Sometimes also we have proposed those for invitation whom we see but seldom. These meetings we have found both for ourselves and others very useful, and they will, no doubt, continue to be a blessing, as long as the Lord shall enable us to precede and follow them with prayer. They are also particularly important as a means of the brethren becoming acquainted with each other, and of uniting their hearts.)

May 13. Today I have had again much reason to mourn over my corrupt nature, particularly on account of want of gratitude for the many temporal mercies by which I am surrounded. I was so sinful as to be dissatisfied on account of the dinner, because I thought it would not agree with me, instead of thanking God for the rich provision, and asking heartily the Lord's blessing upon it, and remembering the many dear children of God who would have been glad of such a meal. I rejoice in the prospect of that day when, in seeing Jesus as He is, I shall be like Him. May 14. Lord's-day. The Lord, instead of chastising me today for the ingratitude and discontent, of yesterday, by leaving me to my own strength in preaching, and bringing temporal want upon me, has given me a good day. I have preached with much assistance and comfort, and the Lord has given me rich temporal supplies: for besides the freewill offerings of 2l. 8s. 10d., a 5l. note was put into my hand for the supply of any want I may have. Thus the Lord melted the heart by love, and made me still more see the baseness of my conduct yesterday. Thanks be to God, the day is coming, when Satan will triumph no more!

May 18. There are now 64 children in the two Orphan-Houses, and two more are expected, which will fill the two houses.

May 28. The narrative of some of the Lord's dealings with me is now near being published, which has led me again most earnestly this day week, and repeatedly since, to ask the Lord that He would be pleased to give me what is wanting of the 1000l., for which sum I have asked Him on behalf of the orphans; for though, in my own mind, the thing is as good as done, so much so, that I have repeatedly been able to thank God, that He will surely give me every shilling of that sum, yet to others this would not be enough. As the whole matter, then, about the Orphan-House had been commenced for the glory of God, that in this way before the world and the church there might be another visible proof, that the Lord delights in answering prayer; and as there was yet a part of the 1000l. wanting; and, as I earnestly desired, the book might not leave the press, before every shilling of that sum had been given, in answer to prayer, without one single individual having been asked by me for any thing, that thus I might have the sweet privilege of bearing my testimony for God in this book:—for these reasons, I say, I have given myself earnestly to prayer about this matter since May 21. On May 22 came in 7l. 10s., and on May 23, 3l. On May 24 a lady, whom I never saw before, called on me and gave me 40l. This circumstance has greatly encouraged me; for the Lord showed me thereby afresh His willingness to continue to send us large sums, and that they can even come from individuals whom we have never seen before. On May 26th 3l. 6s. was sent, from two unexpected quarters. On May 27 was sent anonymously, a parcel of worn clothes from London and a sovereign. Today (May 28) I received again 4l. 3s. 6d.; and also a parcel was sent from a considerable distance, containing seven pairs of socks, and the following trinkets, to be sold for the support of the orphans: 1 gold pin with an Irish pearl, 15 Irish pearls, 2 pine, 2 brooches, 2 lockets, 1 seal, 2 studs, 11 rings, 1 chain, and 1 bracelet, all of gold.

June 15. Today I gave myself once more earnestly to prayer respecting the remainder of the 1000l. This evening 5l. was given, so that now the whole sum is made up. To the glory of the Lord, whose I am, and whom I serve, I would state again, that every shilling of this money, and all the articles of clothing and furniture, which have been mentioned in the foregoing pages, have been given to me, without one single individual having been asked by me for any thing. The reason why I have refrained altogether from soliciting any one for help is, that the hand of God evidently might be seen in the matter, that thus my fellow-believers might be encouraged more and more to trust in Him, and that also those who know not the Lord, may have a fresh proof that, indeed, it is not a vain thing to pray to God. As the Lord then has con-descended most fully, and even above my expectations, to answer my prayers, arid to Fill my mouth (Psalm lxxxi. 10,) will you help me, brethren and sisters beloved in the Lord, to praise Him for His condescension. It is a wonderful thing that such a worthless, faithless servant as I am, should have power with God. Take courage from this for yourselves, brethren. Surely, if such a one as I am, so little conformed to the mind of Jesus, has his prayers answered, may not you also, at last, have your requests granted to you. During eighteen months and ten days this petition has been brought before God almost daily. From the moment I asked it, till the Lord granted it fully, I had never been allowed to doubt that He would give every shilling of that sum. Often have I praised Him beforehand in the assurance, that he would grant my request. The thing after which we have especially to seek in prayer is, that we believe that we receive, according to Mark xi. 24. "What things soever ye desire, when ye pray, believe that ye receive them, and ye shall have them." But this I often find lacking in my prayers. Whenever, however, I have been enabled to believe that I receive, the Lord has dealt with me according to my faith. This moment while I am writing (June 28, 1837), I am waiting on the Lord for 17l. 10s., the rent for two school-rooms, which will be due in three days, and I have but 3l. towards that sum. I believe God can give; I believe God is willing to give it, if it be for our real welfare; I also have repeatedly asked God for it; but as yet I cannot in the triumph of faith praise Him beforehand, that He will assuredly give me this small sum. I am waiting at every delivery of letters, at every ring at the bell, for help; I am truly waiting on God, and God alone for it; but as yet I do not feel as sure of being able to pay the rent of those school rooms, as I should, if I had the money already in my pocket.

As the Lord has so greatly condescended to listen to my prayers, and as I consider it one of the particular talents which He has intrusted to me, to exercise faith upon His promises regarding my own temporal wants and those of others; and as an Orphan-House for boys above seven years of age seems greatly needed in this city; and as also, without it, we know not how to provide for the little boys, in the Infant-Orphan-House when they are above seven years of age; I purpose to establish an Orphan-House for about forty boys above seven years of age. But there are three difficulties in the way, which must first be removed, before I could take any further step in this work. 1. My hands are more than filled already through the work arising from the ministry of the Word, the attending to the ordering of church affairs, and the oversight of 370 brethren and sisters. And yet, in addition to this, I have also the work which comes upon me in connexion with the six day-schools, a Sunday-school, an adult-school, the two Orphan-Houses, and the circulation of the Scriptures. (This latter part of the work is more and more increasing; for merely within the last seven months 836 copies of the Scriptures have been circulated). For these reasons, then, I could not in any degree enlarge the field of labour, except the Lord should be pleased to send us a brother, who, as steward, could take from me the work which arises from keeping the accounts, obtaining and circulating the Scriptures, giving advice in ordinary matters respecting the Orphan-Houses, attending to the applications for admission of children in the Orphan-Houses, &c. But whether there is an Orphan-House for boys established or not, such a brother is greatly needed, even as the extent of the work is now, and I therefore lay it on the hearts of the believers who may read this, to help me with their prayers, that such a brother may be found. 2. In addition to this, it would be needful, before I could take any further step, to obtain a truly pious master for the boys, add other suitable individuals who may be needed to take care of the children. 3. The third thing by which I desire to be assured, that it is the will of God that I should go forward in the Orphan-House is, that He provide the means for such an enlargement of the work. Whilst, on the one hand I would confess to the praise of God, that He has been pleased to give me faith to trust in Him; yet, on the other hand, I desire to be kept from presumption and enthusiasm. I do not intend to wait till thousands are raised, or till the Institution is endowed; but I must have such a sum given to me as is needed to furnish a house for forty boys, and to clothe that number, and to have a little to begin with: without such a sum I should not consider it to be the will of God to enlarge the field. What I ask then from the brethren who may feel interested in seeing an Orphan-House for boys established in Bristol is, that they would help me with their prayers, that if it be the will of God, He Himself would be pleased to remove these three difficulties out of the way.

[Whilst the preceding pages of the first edition of this Narrative were in the press, and before the reception of the last proof sheet for correction, the same friend who gave me on May 24, 1837, Forty Pounds for the orphans, and whom up to that time I had never seen, gave on July 12, 1837, Four Hundred and Sixty Pounds more, being altogether Five Hundred Pounds.]

REVIEW OF THE LAST FIVE YEARS, THE TIME THAT I HAVE LABOURED IN BRISTOL WITH BROTHER CRAIK.

JULY, 1837.

I. Some of the mercies which the Lord has granted to us during this period.

Concerning all this time I have most especially to say, that goodness and mercy have followed me every day. My blessings have been many and great, my trials few and small. To the praise of God I will mention a few of the many mercies which He has bestowed on me.

1. I consider it one of the especial mercies that, amidst so many engagements I have been kept in the ways of God, and that this day I have as much desire as ever, yea more than ever, to live alone for Him, who has done so much for me. My greatest grief is that I love Him so little. I desire many things concerning myself; but I desire nothing so much, as to have a heart filled with love to the Lord. I long for a warm personal attachment to Him.

2. I consider it likewise a great mercy, for which I can never sufficiently praise God, that, whilst during these last five years so many of His children have fallen into great errors, and even those who once ran well, I, who am so faithless to Him, should have been kept from them. There is scarcely one point of importance, comparatively speaking, respecting which I have had scriptural reason to alter my views, since I have come to Bristol. My views concerning the fundamental truths of the gospel are the same as they were at the end of the year 1829 though I have been more and more established in them during these last five years, and have seen more minutely the

mind of God concerning many truths. My relish for the study of the word of God has not decreased.

3. I consider it further an exceeding great mercy, that I have been kept in uninterrupted love and union with my brother, friend, and fellow-labourer, Henry Craik. Very few of the blessings that the Lord has bestowed on him, on me, and on the two churches, whose servants we are, are of greater importance. There is not one point of importance, as it regards the truth, on which we differ. In judgment, as to matters connected with the welfare of the saints among whom we labour, we have been almost invariably at once of one mind. (Lord, to Thee is the praise due for this!!!) We are as much, or more than ever united in spirit; and if the Lord permit, we desire to labour together till He come. Who that knows the proneness in man to seek his own, and to get glory to himself; who that knows that the heart naturally is full of envy; who that is acquainted with the position which we both hold in the church, and the occasions thereby occurring for the flesh to feel offended:—who that considers these things will not ascribe our union, our uninterrupted union and love, entirely to the Lord? Let the brethren among whom we labour praise God much for it! Let the brethren everywhere, who may read this, praise God for it! This union has glorified God! This union has sprung from God! But, for this union we depend now as much as ever upon God, and therefore let the brethren pray, that God in mercy would give us grace, to put aside every thing that might hinder it.

4. We have had much joy on account of the scriptural conduct of many of the children of God among whom we labour. The two churches have on the whole shown, in some measure, that even in our day there can be love among the brethren. I do not mean that we have been without trials on account of the behaviour of the saints under our care; nor do I mean to say, that either we or they have followed Christ as we might or ought to have done; but only, that we have been mercifully kept hitherto from great divisions; that the cases in which acts of discipline were needed (as the list at the end of the last two years shows) were so few; that we have had much more joy than sorrow on account of the brethren and sisters:—these are matters, worthy to be noticed among the special blessings which God has bestowed on us during the last five years.

5. Another mercy I mention is, that it has pleased God to keep us from some most awful characters, who either actually had proposed themselves for fellowship, or desired to do so, and who, so far as the testimony by word of mouth went, could fully satisfy us. From several such individuals who lived in open sin, we have been kept, by the Spirit constraining them to confess, and that, perhaps, even against their own will, their wicked deeds, which they were practicing; in other instances we suspected them, and, on making inquiry, found out their sins.

6. Another mercy which the Lord has kindly bestowed on us is, that though neither Brother Craik nor I am strong in body, yet we have been helped through much work; and, at the time when we were laid aside, the Lord made up our lack of service, either by sending help from without, or by putting into exercise the gifts of the brethren among us. At those seasons disunion might so easily have sprung up among the brethren; but the good shepherd of the sheep watched so graciously over the flock, that they were kept together in much love and union, whereby also a testimony was given for God, that their faith stood not in the power of man.

7. Sometimes, when particular trials were laid on us, and things appeared very dark, the Lord most mercifully not only supported us under those trials, but also unexpectedly delivered us much sooner out of them, than we could have at all anticipated. May this especially encourage brethren who labour in word and doctrine, or who rule in the church, to trust in the Lord in Seasons of peculiar trial!

8. My temporal wants have all these five years been most richly supplied, so that not once have I lacked the necessaries of life, and generally I have abounded; and all this without having one shilling of regular income. I am not tired of this way of living, nor have I even for once been allowed to regret having begun to live in this way.

II. The work of the Lord in our hands.

1. It has pleased the Lord to continue to bless the word preached by us to the conversion of many sinners, and there seems to have been no period during these five years, in which this work has been stopped by Him. There have come again several cases before us

lately, in which individuals have been recently brought to apprehend their lost state by nature, and to see that Jesus of Nazareth alone can save them. The whole number of those who have been converted through our instrumentality in Bristol, and who have been received into fellowship with us is 178; besides this, the Lord has given us many seals to our ministry in this city, but the individuals are now either only standing on the list of candidates for fellowship, or are united to other churches in and out of Bristol, or have fallen asleep before they were united to us.

2. The whole number of the brethren and sisters, now in fellowship with us, is 370: 189 at Gideon, 181 at Bethesda.

3. It is now three years and four months since brother Craik and I began, in dependence upon the Lord for funds, to seek to help the spread of the Gospel through the instrumentality of schools, the circulation of the Holy Scriptures, and by aiding Missionary exertions. Since then there have been circulated through our instrumentality 4030 copies of the Scriptures; four Day-Schools for poor children have been established by us; 1119 children have been instructed in the six Day-Schools, and 353 children are now in those six Day-Schools. Besides this, a Sunday-School, and an Adult-School have been supplied with all they needed, and Missionary exertions in the East Indies, in Upper Canada, and on the Continent of Europe, have been aided. In addition to this the word of God has been preached from house to house among the poor, in connexion with the Scriptural Knowledge Institution, by brother C-r, within the last two years.

4. There have been received into the Orphan-Houses 74 orphans, and there are now 64 in them.

And now, in conclusion, I would say that the reason, why I have spoken so plainly about the sins of my unconverted days, is, that I may magnify the riches of the grace of God, which has been bestowed on me, a guilty wretch. I have weighed much whether I should do so or not, knowing well what contempt it may bring on me; but it appeared to me, after much prayer, that as the object of this little work is to speak well of the Lord, I should say in a few words what I once was, in order that it might be seen so much the more clearly, what He has done for me. I also judged that, in doing so, some, who live at present in sin, might see through my example the misery into which sin leads, even as it regards the present life, and the happiness which is connected with the ways of God; and that they also might be encouraged through what God has done for me, to turn to Him. I have made myself therefore a fool, and degraded myself in the eyes of the inhabitants of Bristol, that you, my dear unconverted fellow sinners, who may read this, may, with God's blessing, be made wise. The love of Christ has constrained me to speak about my former lies, thefts, fraud, &c., that you might be benefited. Do not think that I am a fool, and therefore I have told out my heart in my folly; but I have made myself a fool for the benefit of your souls. May God in mercy, for His dear Son's sake, grant that these pages may be a savour of life unto life to you!

The reason why I have spoken so plainly about some of the sins and errors into which I have fallen since my conversion, and about my answers to prayer, and the supplies of my temporal wants, and some of my family concerns, and the success which God has given to our labours,—is not, because I do not know that it is contrary to worldly custom, and against the interests of my worldly reputation; nor is it, as if I made light of my falls; nor as if I would boast in having had my prayers so often answered, and having been in such a variety of ways used as an instrument in doing the Lord's work; but, I have written what I have written for the benefit of my brethren. I have mentioned some of my sins and errors, that through my loss the brethren who may read this may gain. I have mentioned the answers of prayer, that through them they may be encouraged to make known their requests unto God. I have spoken about my temporal supplies, that through seeing how richly God has supplied my temporal wants, since the commencement of 1830, when I left London, they may be stirred up "to seek first the kingdom of God and His righteousness," resting assured, that, in doing so, He will give them what is needful for the life that now is. I have alluded to some family circumstances, that children of God may be encouraged to cast their family burdens upon the Lord, in order that, in doing so, they may find Him carrying the burdens for them. And lastly, I have written about the success which God has been pleased to grant us in His work, that it may be seen, that, in acting on scriptural principles, we have the Lord on our side, and that our mode of preaching is honoured by Him. If in anything which I have written I have been mistaken (and what human work is there which is free from error), I have been mistaken after much prayer. Whilst writing I have often asked help of God. Whilst revising the work, I have still again and again bowed my knees. I have also frequently entreated the Lord to bless this feeble effort of mine to speak to His praise, and I have not the slightest hesitation in saying, that, from the earnestness and comfort which I have enjoyed in prayer, and from the sincere self-examination of my heart, I know that God will bless this little work. May I ask you then, my brethren and sisters, who have been benefited in reading this book, to help me with your prayers, that it may be blessed to others. May I also ask you, my brethren and sisters, who think I ought not to have published it, to ask God to bless that which you yourselves consider good and scriptural in it.

And, now last of all, brethren beloved in the Lord, remember me in your prayers.

END OF THE FIRST PART